Her Husba

'This terrific book will force a re-thinking of certain widespread assumptions concerning the history of relations between women. It deserves – and needs – a wide readership.'

Lucy Bland, *London Metropolitan University*

'Alison Oram has changed the history of when British people became aware of lesbians. In her entertaining book, she demonstrates that the early twentieth-century popular press described women who passed as men as amazing, strange and marvelous rather than perverted or deviant. This is an important theoretical and historical contribution, but it is also fun to read.'

Anna Clark, *University of Minnesota*

'Astonishing' reports of women masquerading as men frequently appear in the mass media from the turn of the twentieth century to the 1960s.

Alison Oram's pioneering study of women's gender-crossing explores the popular press to analyse how women's cross-gender behaviour and same-sex desires were presented to ordinary working-class and lower middle-class people. It breaks new ground in focusing on the representation of female sexualities within the broad sweep of popular culture rather than in fiction and professional literature.

Her Husband was a Woman! surveys these engaging stories of cross-dressing in mass-circulation newspapers and places them in the wider context of variety theatre, fairgrounds and other popular entertainment. Oram catalogues the changing perception of female cross-dressing and its relationship to contemporary ways of writing about gender and desire in the popular press. In the early twentieth century cross-dressing women were not condemned by the press for being socially transgressive, but celebrated for their trickster joking and success in performing masculinity. While there may have been earlier 'knowingness', it was not until after the Second World War that cross-dressing was explicitly linked to lesbianism or transsexuality in popular culture.

Illustrated with newspaper cuttings and postcards, *Her Husband was a Woman!* is an essential resource for students and researchers, revising assumptions about the history of modern gender and sexual identities, especially lesbianism and transgender.

Alison Oram is Professor in Social and Cultural History at Leeds Metropolitan University. She is one of the foremost British scholars in the history of gender and sexuality. Her publications include *The Lesbian History Sourcebook: Love and Sex between Women in Britain from 1780 to 1970* (Routledge, 2001), co-authored with Annmarie Turnbull.

Women's and Gender History

Edited by June Purvis

The Women's Suffrage Movement in Britain and Ireland
A regional survey
Elizabeth Crawford

Students
A gendered history
Carol Dyhouse

Women in the British Army
War and the gentle sex, 1907–48
Lucy Noakes

Quaker Women – The Emotional Life, Memory and Radicalism in the Lives of Women Friends, 1800–1920
Sandra Stanley Holton

Her Husband was a Woman!

Women's gender-crossing in
modern British popular culture

Alison Oram

Routledge
Taylor & Francis Group

LONDON AND NEW YORK

First published 2007
by Routledge
2 Park Square, Milton Park, Abingdon, Oxon OX14 4RN

Simultaneously published in the USA and Canada
by Routledge
270 Madison Ave, New York, NY 10016

Routledge is an imprint of the Taylor & Francis Group, an informa business

Typeset in Baskerville by
Book Now Ltd, London
Printed and bound in Great Britain by
T J International Ltd, Padstow, Cornwall

British Library Cataloguing in Publication Data
A catalogue record for this book is available from the British Library

Library of Congress Cataloging in Publication Data
Oram, Alison.
Her husband was a woman!: women's gender-crossing in modern British
popular culture / Alison Oram.
   p. cm.—(Women's and gender history)
Includes bibliographical references and index.
1. Transvestism—Great Britain—History. 2. Male impersonators—Great
Britain—History. 3. Female-to-male transsexuals—Great Britain—History.
4. Lesbianism—Great Britain—History. I. Title.
HQ77.2.G7O73 2007
306.77'809410904—dc22   2007022516

ISBN10: 0–415–40006–6 (hbk)
ISBN10: 0–415–40007–4 (pbk)

ISBN13: 978–0–415–40006–0 (hbk)
ISBN13: 978–0–415–40007–7 (pbk)

Contents

Illustrations

Acknowledgements

The ideas in this book have been discussed in a number of conference and seminar papers over the past few years and I have benefited from helpful responses, comments and additional information from many people in the wider academic community. My thanks in relation to specific queries and discussions of particular issues go to: Paula Bartley, Joe Bristow, H. G. Cocks, Lesley Hall and Lizzie Thynne, and for assistance in the final stages of the research to Jenny Collieson. I am enormously grateful to the friends and colleagues who read all or some of the chapters at various stages and gave me very valuable feedback and encouragement: Lucy Bland, Anna Clark, Laura Doan, Lesley Hall, Reina Lewis and Sarah Waters. The process of writing was also aided by the "History Girls" writing group at the Institute of Historical Research which has been a supportive and inspiring forum. I have learned a great deal from: Lucy Bland, Clare Midgley, Krisztina Robert, Katharina Rowold and Cornelie Usborne.

The research for this book began with a Small Grant from the British Academy (award no. SG/29750). This enabled me to employ two research assistants, Marie-Clare Balaam and the late Chris Willis to scan the newspapers at Colindale for cross-dressing stories. Both were brilliant researchers, and I owe a lot to their discoveries and insightful comments. This book was researched and written while I was working at the University of Northampton and I would like to acknowledge the contribution of the School of the Arts in the form of study leave in the first semester of 2005–06, the assistance of the campus librarians and the help given by colleagues there. The book was completed with support from the AHRC Research Leave Scheme (award no. RL/119922) in 2006. I would also like to thank my editors at Routledge, Eve Setch and Annamarie Kino.

An earlier version of one section of Chapter 2 appeared as "'A Sudden Orgy of Decadence': Writing about Sex between Women in the Interwar Popular Press" in L. Doan and J. Garrity (eds), *Sapphic Modernities: Sexuality, Women and National Culture*, 2006, Palgrave Macmillan and is reproduced with permission of Palgrave Macmillan.

Finishing this book (and remembering there was a life outside it) would not have been possible without the tangible support and warm friendship of many of the people named above, and especially of Margaret Kitching, Monika Bobinska,

Cathy Smith, Clare Midgley, Sarah Waters and Julia Shelley. My love and thanks to you all.

Disclaimer

While every effort has been made to trace and acknowledge ownership of copyright material used in this volume, the Publishers will be glad to make suitable arrangements with any copyright holders whom it has not been possible to contact.

Introduction: sex, scandal and the popular press

In May 1929, the *News of the World*, along with most of the British popular press, reported the story of William Holton, a woman discovered to be passing as a man on admission to the Evesham Poor Law Hospital. Forty-two-year-old Holton had been living for some years with another woman who had two children, one of whom she believed to be Holton's. The *News of the World* drew the attention of readers with the headlines: 'Another Man-Woman: Amazing Fortitude of Masquerader'. It published two photographs of Holton, her wife and child, and devoted two lengthy columns to detailed discussion of the 'perplexing' features of this 'remarkable instance of sex impersonation'.

> So completely did the latest man–woman adopt masculine guise that she worked as a timber haulier, a coal heaver, a cow-man, a road mender, and a navvy, drank heavily and smoked black twist, and, most astonishingly of all, claimed paternity of a child born to a woman with whom she had lived for over four years.
>
> Exposure came when, stricken with a grievous illness, she was admitted to a Poor Law infirmary in a Midland town.
>
> Only this sudden affliction could have betrayed the secret of her sex, for until physical breakdown came she had cheerfully undertaken heavy manual labour of a kind which would have taxed the endurance of the strongest of men . . .
>
> Meanwhile the woman whose life was linked to hers in a strange association is bewildered by the startling turn of events. 'I believed him to be a man,' she declares, 'and our life together was perfectly normal.'[1]

Similar reports of cross-dressing women appeared regularly and repeatedly in the twentieth-century British popular press through to the 1950s. Like William Holton, these women successfully passed as men in everyday life, some briefly, some for months or years. They worked in masculine employment, and were often reported to have courted or married other women. Nowadays, readers might understand such women through modern categories of sexual identity. Holton was a woman with a woman partner, and the question of a marital sexual relationship is tantalisingly raised through the interview with the unsuspecting wife and the astonishing existence of a baby. So was this story about lesbian desire? Or was Holton's primary motivation for the masquerade the feeling that she was really a man? Perhaps today we would see her as transgender-identified. Yet in the 1920s – and, significantly, later too – such stories carried quite different meanings, far from the scientific categories of modern sexual identity.

I started this research because I was fascinated by the cross-dressing woman and her place in lesbian and transgender histories. The case of Colonel Barker, who claimed to have served in the First World War and was prosecuted in 1929 for marrying another woman, was extensively reported at the time and consequently has been much analysed by twentieth-century historians.[2] I was keen to discover whether the practice of cross-dressing by women was more widespread. The quest was fuelled by my frustration with the lack of scholarly attention paid to changing ideas and knowledge about women's same-sex love or female-to-male gender-crossing at the level of British popular culture. The history of lesbianism and 'female masculinity' has concentrated on elite cultures, creating an extremely rich and nuanced body of work on the period between the turn of the century and the 1920s in particular, but neglecting working-class and lower middle-class women. This research on educated and bohemian women focuses especially on their creation of a sense of sexual identity in their relationships with other women or in their cross-gender fantasy.[3] But until we know more about the wider representation of same-sex desire and gender-crossing, the exploration of sexual subjectivity, among other questions in the history of sexuality, will be constrained.

We know little enough about the circulation of knowledge concerning heterosexual sex and reproduction, despite Roy Porter and Lesley Hall's valuable survey of 'the facts of life' and their careful discussion of the methodological issues. Oral histories of sexual knowledge before the Second World War suggest widespread ignorance among young women (and also young men) about menstruation, sexual intercourse, birth control and childbirth, only remedied to some extent by marital experience and the continuing importance of 'folk' beliefs.[4] But other studies argue that birth control literature and pornography were fairly easily obtained in urban areas.[5] Mass culture remains under-researched in relation to changing understandings of sexuality generally and ideas about women's same-sex desire and cross-gender identification in particular.[6]

The history of sexuality has been dominated by a Foucauldian model of sexual modernity which emphasises the process through which categories of sexuality, such as the invert or homosexual, were established in science and medicine from the end of the nineteenth century and increasingly influenced the development of sexual knowledge in culture.[7] Sexological notions of the female invert, the congenitally mannish woman with homosexual desires, began to appear, if rather unevenly, in medical, legal and political circles from the beginning of the twentieth century.[8] In the United States, this concept of the mannish woman as lesbian appeared as early as the turn of the century in the popular press, as Lisa Duggan demonstrates. These newspaper reports of 'abnormal affection' between middle-class girls were structured around the themes of masculine identity, impersonation and same-sex passion. Most had tragic endings.[9] In Britain, even professional and official knowledge of sex between women was limited, as Lucy Bland has shown in her analysis of the ideas at play in the complex libel action brought by the dancer Maud Allan in 1918.[10] However, the concept of female homosexuality began to appear in some writing in the 1920s – literary modernism, middlebrow fiction, educational debates, social investigation and works of popular sexology (for example by Marie Stopes) – all aimed at a middle-class readership.[11]

The most prominent of these cultural explorations of sexual identity was by the writer Radclyffe Hall, who took up sexological ideas in her novel, *The Well of Loneliness*, published and prosecuted for obscenity in 1928. The considerable volume of historical work on the *Well of Loneliness* trial has increasingly positioned it as a significant cultural turning point, a moment at which the scientific model of inversion moved from limited professional and literary circles to a much wider public. Laura Doan has astutely debunked the myth that mannish appearance had a widely recognised meaning as lesbianism in 1920s Britain. She argues that it is only after the 1928 *Well of Loneliness* trial that the mannish woman begins to signify lesbian desire in culture, through the figure of its masculine-appearing author Radclyffe Hall, photographs of whom were widely featured in contemporary newspapers.[12]

Is the 1928 *Well of Loneliness* turning point also relevant for popular culture? It would be logical to suppose that newspaper reports of cross-dressing women might start to become tainted by this association between female masculinity and homosexuality. But historians rarely acknowledge the extent to which these new concepts and ideas about sexuality were located within a very narrow slice of society, and even when they do, the implications for historical generalisations about social and cultural knowledge are not pursued. Most people did not read middle-brow novels, and were even less likely to have access to the non-fiction discussions of sex reformers, feminists or psychologists. While it is equally foolish to imagine a cultural wall between high culture and vernacular knowledge (there is plenty of evidence of wide reading habits and auto-didacticism among many working-class people), the sets of cultural meanings and references at the popular level were very different.[13] How and when did modern scientific concepts of sexual identity enter the world of working-class and lower middle-class women and men?

One important route into popular culture is the mass-circulation press, since it reached into almost every home and both reflected and informed the everyday landscape of gender and sexuality. This book discusses the findings of a comprehensive survey of all reports of cross-dressing women over a 50-year period, from the 1900s to 1960, in two mass-circulation Sunday newspapers, the *News of the World* and the *People*.[14] Stories about women's gender-crossing proved to be a regular feature, with over 200 separate reports appearing between 1910 and 1960.[15] The subject was popular in the years before and during the First World War, and into the 1920s, with an average of five stories published per year. There was a huge surge of interest between 1928 and the late 1930s, with 11 reports in 1929, the year of the Colonel Barker case, and up to 9 or 10 in some subsequent years. In the 20 years from 1940 to 1960, however, there were only 35 stories, an average of just one or two a year. Around half of the stories were quite short, but a large number were well developed, occupying two or more columns and including pictures of the cross-dressing woman. What is important about this study is its comprehensive reach. It is not a discussion of a sample of selected case studies, but a survey of the whole range of women's cross-dressing stories in the British popular press, analysed in the context of related press material, including reports of 'sex change', allusions to female homosexuality, reviews of male impersonation in popular entertainment, and reports of male-to-female gender crossing. Tracking the way in which cross-dressing women were reported over several decades of the twentieth century, and how these stories dealt with love between women and cross-gender identification, gives us a method of exploring the changing presentations of sexuality and gender, and the emergence of modern sexual identities.

I assumed that as sexual science made inroads into other forms of literature and into professional discourses, sexological language would sooner or later appear in these popular-press stories as it had in the United States, possibly from the period of the First World War, possibly from the late 1920s. But this hypothesis about the influence of sexology was rapidly challenged when reading the cross-dressing stories. What emerged from the material was much more surprising and intriguing, and altogether more fun, than the dreary narrative of pathologising scientific discourses. The language used in these newspaper reports – 'astonishing masquerade', 'wife's bewilderment' – shows that the 'masquerade' of the cross-dressing woman was presented as a sensation to be marvelled at, a skilful piece of trickery to be appreciated, and a humorous tale of neighbours and workmates who were fooled by the disguise. What is more, there was an overlap with other forms of gender-crossing in popular culture. In their fascination with gender disguise, the stories made connections with the contemporary appeal of the male impersonator on stage. Popular performers such as Vesta Tilley, and later Ella Shields, were celebrated by music hall audiences through the Edwardian and First World War years and continued to be a central part of variety theatre and revue until the 1940s. Appearing in the sensationalist press and on stage and screen, enjoyed in leisure time, the gender-crossing woman came from the world of entertainment, comedy, and marvellous happenings. What is fascinating about women's gender-crossing is how strongly it continued to carry this playful and humorous tone, and how late it was in the twentieth century before it was reinterpreted as sexual deviance.

The newspapers used specific terminology which separated 'real life' gender passing from theatrical male impersonation. The former was always 'a masquerade', the latter always 'impersonation'. Only extremely rarely did these words get mixed up. Interestingly this usage is almost counter-intuitive. 'Impersonation' implies a more complete and thorough-going attempt at deception, yet was the term favoured for the stage, while the more theatrical concept of 'masquerade' was used in the press for the real cross-dressing women. This use of language talks up the convincing nature of the stage act, while perhaps downplaying the challenge of the passing woman performing masculinity on the streets and in the workplace. A word on my own terminology here: I use the term *cross-dressing* to refer to the newspaper stories (it was not a word that appeared in the press, where the ubiquitous term until after the Second World War was masquerade), and *male impersonation* for the stage performance. *Gender-crossing* is a more general umbrella term I use to refer to either or both forms, as well as trans-sexuality. In discussing cross-dressing women I use 'she' and 'her' as pronouns, mainly to emphasise the dissonance between the woman and her masculine social gender.[16] This dissonance was always part of carnival and masquerade. In the twentieth century, women's 'masquerading' was seen in popular culture as a light-hearted frolic, a daring adventure, though it still carried reminders of the rebellious spirit of carnival from older notions of the masquerade. The disorder of gender inversion in popular entertainment can act as a safety valve to defuse possible challenges to conventional morality and hierarchy. Alternatively it might disrupt the idea of gender stability and encourage the imagining of sexual dissidence.[17]

Despite successfully crossing gender boundaries, often for long periods of time, and despite having wives and girlfriends, the cross-dressing women who appeared in the popular press were not condemned for being socially transgressive, but celebrated for their boldness and success. In many ways the press stories appear to continue the long-standing 'tradition' of women warriors and female husbands in British popular culture. The female soldier or sailor of eighteenth-century ballads was admired for both her manly heroism and her womanly steadfastness in love, as Dianne Dugaw shows. Men and women fall in love with her, demonstrating the ambivalent nature of gender and eroticism, but these narratives were normally resolved through public recognition of her patriotic valour and the reward of a happy marriage.[18] Twentieth-century newspaper stories tended to be less heroic but, like the eighteenth-century ballads, had a particular pattern of their own. Class context and geographical location were reliably recurring features. Cross-dressing women appeared in familiar British suburbs, towns and villages, in local public spaces such as the street and the workplace. Journalists often reminded their readers of other recent cases of passing women, and indeed sometimes of eighteenth-century examples including the female soldier Hannah Snell.[19] This re-composing of a tradition and established genealogy of women's cross-dressing represented the practice as being an accustomed as well as an extraordinary part of national life.

This time-honoured theme of the playful cross-dressing woman, applauded for her successful masquerade, did not fade away in the commercial mass media of the twentieth century, raising questions about how we conceptualise both the periodisation and the nature of sexual modernity. Sexual modernity in mid-twentieth-century Britain was marked by the increasing influence and democratisation of expert scientific knowledge and the more precise demarcation of heterosexual and homosexual identities, historians suggest.[20] Yet these features of modernity developed unevenly and by no means supplanted older forms of meaning around the wonders and mysteries of gender and sexuality which, indeed, were magnified by the technologies of print and film in popular entertainment. We need a space to explore the captivating and marvellous representations of gender-crossing within 'the complexities of a modernity made messy'.[21]

The popular Sunday press and the formula of the cross-dressing story

In tracing the changing representation of women's cross-dressing in the press, this book therefore tells a new story about sexual modernity and popular culture. Popular journalism was itself becoming significant in this period as a mass cultural form. The popular Sunday press was an interesting mixture of the self-consciously 'modern' in its technology, layout and advertising, while retaining much that was traditional in its content – gory crime, scandal, popular amusements and home-made fun as well as reviews of commercial entertainment. It was the Sunday press which first opened up a mass market for newspaper readership in the late nineteenth century, and by the interwar years many daily papers adopted similar sensational and human-interest content. The intense commercialisation of the twentieth-century newspaper industry produced more photography, bigger headlines and greater informality of writing style in order to broaden the appeal of newspapers and gain larger circulations, supplemented by competitive selling techniques.[22] The *News of the World* and the *People* were the top-selling Sunday newspapers by some way in this period, with a readership more truly national (despite regional variations) than any other Sundays. The *News of the World* claimed a circulation of over two million in 1912, rising to four million in 1939, while the *People* was not far behind, selling over three million copies in 1937.[23] By 1938 the market for Sunday papers was considered to have nearly reached saturation point, almost every home taking at least one title.[24]

The popular press helped to produce the shared mass culture of modernity, in the process tending to homogenise a diverse range of working-class and lower middle-class views (as well as gender and age differences) into a commercial product, while providing a shared lexicon for the public discussion of sex and scandal. Readers of both the *News of the World* and the *People* were not ashamed to admit that they read these papers for their sensational reporting of murders, disasters, sex crimes and the marital delinquency of the wealthy and famous.[25] The *News of the World* in particular trod a thin line between respectability and salaciousness in its long-standing interest in the seedy underside of British society. Representing itself as a moral newspaper, on the grounds that it reported the punishment as well as the crime, the *News of the World* stressed its accurate and detailed reporting.[26] The *People*, more inclined to assert opinion through editorials and featured columnists, was a little less sensational than the *News of the World* and was seen as slightly more respectable; it was offered, for example, as more suitable reading for young people.[27] Working-class respectability, however thin a veneer, allowed these two papers to publish lubricious scandals about the upper classes and film and stage stars, under the guise of moral outrage, to produce a highly entertaining read.

The popular press is a significant vector for ideas about sexual transgression and deviance. By creating a shared public language, it is an important but underused source for researching the forms of sexual knowledge circulating in the mass media and available to working-class and lower middle-class readers. However, the semantics of sexuality was far from transparent in the pages of the Sunday press. To maintain respectability as family reading while providing sexual titillation, these newspapers used a faux-genteel or ambiguous vocabulary to report sexual wrong-doing in the divorce and criminal courts, with terms such as 'intimacy', 'molested' or 'grave crime' (which might mean abortion, sexual abuse or gross indecency between men). During the 1920s and 30s, both papers became slightly more straightforward and less ambiguous in reporting sexual transgression – indeed this was part of their claim to be modern – and began to use more transparent codes.

All the reports of women's cross-dressing were presented (and read) within the flow of news stories of various types, including crime, accidents and divorce. While each story was self-contained, in describing the activities of the woman passing as a man and the outcome, they were positioned among, and competed with, a variety of other sensational news items and human-interest stories and, on other pages, reviews of theatrical performances (including male impersonation), serial fiction, puzzles and sport. Newspapers are not read in a logical progression like a novel; the reader will prioritise his or her favourite sections, glance over the other pages, choose the sensational stories according to their taste, and find their eye drawn across the page in response to headlines or pictures. Cross-dressing stories sometimes made it to the front page, but were normally found on the crime and human-interest pages amid the divorce court reports, breach of promise cases (in earlier decades), domestic tragedies (suicide or the murder of children by their mothers), or next to crimes with amusing angles. They might be juxtaposed to odd and bizarre stories of sex-related crimes, such as stories of obsessive men who cut off girls' hair in the streets. In later years, the *News of the World* in particular more enthusiastically reported underage sex and rape cases.

In order to make sense of the hundreds of reports of women's cross-dressing which surfaced regularly, I came to appreciate them as stories with a basic formula with significant common features which subtly shifted over time. They were a minor newspaper genre in their own right. There is considerable variety in the stories, and a novel 'extraordinary' element was found for each succeeding passing woman, yet the more developed reports shared an established structure, a familiar cast of characters, and a repeated set of themes. These conventions were well established in the early years of the twentieth century, and were remarkably persistent in the framing of women's cross-dressing stories into the 1950s.[28]

Gender-crossing news stories are initially signalled by their headlines and tone of astonishment – 'amazing disclosures', 'a remarkable masquerade'. The narrative always begins with the sensational *discovery* – the revelation that a man, in a familiar and usually very ordinary setting, had been revealed to be a woman. It explores the mechanism of discovery, which was usually after the passing woman had come into contact with officialdom; for example, had been arrested for a minor crime, or suddenly hospitalised with acute illness.[29] The report then reconstructs her journey across gender boundaries, in particular focusing on her relationship with workmates, neighbours (or wider community) and wife or girlfriend.

Her motives for cross-dressing are established, or turned into a mystery to be investigated.

The example of George Capon, a young wire-worker in the First World War, discovered to be Ellen Capon when investigated at the military recruiting office in 1918 after two years of passing, shows how the quite complex activities of cross-dressing women fit a repeated narrative structure. Ellen Capon, who came from a working-class family of six children in south London, explained her decision to pass as a boy from the age of 16 in terms of a need to provide extra financial support for her family. She told the press: 'I did it as a bit of daring. My mother is seriously ill and I thought I could earn more money as a man than as a woman.'[30] Such economic motives were those most frequently cited or assumed. Escaping from an unhappy marriage was another reason for dressing as a man, and, less often, but treated as similarly understandable, the love of another woman and a desire to set up home together. A common impulse for young women was a love of adventure – this was clearly a factor for Ellen too.

The newspapers often made a great deal out of the initial moment of crossing gender boundaries. Men's clothes would be borrowed from a brother, bought or stolen. Cutting off her hair was often seen as a crucial sign of dispensing with femininity. Ellen borrowed clothes from a friend of her brother's who had just been called up, and the *News of the World* emphasised the moment of gender liminality:

> I decided to make a great feminine sacrifice, and to cut off my hair. I did it without anyone knowing my intention, and as the tresses fell off under the scissors I realised that the disguising of my sex would be exceedingly difficult, more than I had ever imagined. When I had finished the task and put on the boy's suit I must admit I looked a 'boy' to perfection.[31]

Various tests of masculinity were then presented to the gender-crosser, discussed in huge detail in the press. These always included her appearance as a man, ability to pass unrecognised doing masculine work, interacting socially with other men, and adventures in courtship or marriage with other women, all of which trials were normally accomplished with panache. Capon was described as being of medium height, good-looking, with a 'frank, boyish face . . . she stood at ease with her hands in her side pockets as if she was thinking out some working problem' (see Figure 1). She had worked with an older man, and they had addressed each other as 'mate'. 'We were working just as man and youth would do.' At the same time, now that the reader and the people in her community finally possessed knowledge of the masquerader's 'true' gender, previous events were consistently reworked with jokes and humour, based on the fooling of those around her. The cross-dressing woman is positioned as a trickster – she crosses gender boundaries, disrupting the equilibrium of sex and gender, often drawing a moral or commenting on gender conventions.[32] Always portrayed as a skilful operator, her success in passing is marvelled at with a mixture of incredulity and admiration.

Eventually the cross-dresser comes into contact with authority, perhaps arrested for an incidental crime, taken into hospital with a serious illness or, at the

THE GIRL WHO WAS A BOY.

Miss Ellen Harriet Capon, eighteen, of Upper Norwood, who masqueraded as a boy for two years and "walked out" with a young lady. She had been employed in a factory since she was sixteen, and bore an excellent character. Having become eighten, she had to attend a recruiting office, confessed that she was a woman.—(*Sunday Pictorial* exclusive.)

Figure 1　Ellen/George Capon. *Sunday Pictorial*, 20 January 1918, pp. 6–7.
Reproduced with the permission of the British Library.

extremity of successful passing, her sex discovered on death. A protected war worker, Charles Capon was required to attend the recruiting office in Brixton when she reached the military conscription age of 18. Only then did she meet 'some suspicion of my sex' through discrepancies noticed in her papers and appearance, and when she returned with her military protection card she owned up to being a girl and was arrested. In the process of being unmasked, and in order to maintain her façade as a man, Capon produced letters which showed she was courting a young woman. Courtship and marriage were themes which preoccupied the genre throughout the period, and were often flagged up in the headlines. In this case the headlines were mostly general, such as 'London's Boy–Girl', but the *Sunday Pictorial* used the headline, 'Two Years' Pose As Man. Girl "Walks Out" with Another' to draw attention to Capon's story.[33]

Although 'rightful' gender is restored through the process of discovery, the cross-dressing trickster is not disempowered by this. Cases of passing women often came to light via the courts, but any punishment was normally minor and not highlighted in press reporting. Ellen Capon's family accepted her activities, and though her father was criticised by the magistrate for not exercising more control over her, he defended the actions of his daughter: 'She has been a good girl at home, and one can't turn a girl out.'[34] Revelation and recognition also brought some moral commentary in the cross-dresser's favour. A police officer commented to the Lambeth magistrate: 'She had done well towards her parents in respect of the money she had earned', an honourable aim for any working-class son or daughter.[35]

A distinctive feature of the genre is the open-ended nature of the narrative. Right through to the end of the story, Ellen Capon continued to assert her right to, capacity for and orientation towards masculine employment. Like other cross-dressers she resisted any closure in appropriate femininity and made only an equivocal return to women's clothes, saying she would now go and work on the land. Nor (as will be discussed later) was there ever any conventional closure in these stories through the mechanism of heterosexual engagement or marriage for the gender-crosser. The ending of the story is always incomplete, something which would be unusual in other genres. Some sense of order is restored through true sex being re-established, yet the trickster cross-dresser retains a degree of authority and defiance in her achievement.

The number of cross-dressing stories appearing in the press and the longevity of the genre suggests its popularity among readers. As a recurring type of story, flagged up as a 'masquerade' or similar, the reader is primed with a particular set of expectations.[36] She or he is presented with the delights of an 'extraordinary' narrative, which they know will be fascinating and funny. We may speculate that discussing the novelty of gender disguise and its implications with family and workmates is also part of the entertainment and satisfaction for readers. In fact the cross-dressing woman story opens up fundamental assumptions about the origins and maintenance of gender difference in everyday life, potentially very challenging for readers, but packages this within the familiar pleasures of a known and entertaining genre. A distinct (if relatively minor) genre, the cross-dressing story could also be a vehicle for topical debates in a changing historical context of unstable and evolving gender relations. In some stories, as we shall see, gender-crossing opens up contemporary anxieties around gender and modernity – the struggle for women's suffrage, gender relations in the workplace, men's and women's responsibilities in wartime, changing sexual morality, and the nature of masculinity.

While the structural unity of cross-dressing stories remained stable and coherent over a long period, the genre had a dynamic and changing nature. New story cycles appeared during the twentieth century, which both reflected and helped to form popular perceptions of gender and sexuality. The book is organised around these story cycles and discusses their significance and what they show us about particular time periods. Each chapter discusses a group of cross-dressing stories in the context of gender-crossing in popular entertainment more widely. Male impersonation on stage in music hall and variety theatre, and later in film, is the main area of comparison, though there are forays into other forms including popular fiction, fairground side-shows and picture postcards.

The first two chapters discuss the well-established classic formula of the cross-dressing story which flourished between the 1900s and the late 1920s, paralleled by the popularity of the male impersonator on stage. Chapter 1, 'Work and war: masculinity, gender relations and the passing woman' examines the representation of gender and masculinity in the period, discussing the physical appearance of the cross-dressing woman and her performance of social masculinity at work and leisure. We will see how both press stories and male impersonator acts on stage explored and commented on contemporary gender relations during the suffrage struggle, the First World War and its aftermath. Chapter 2, 'Sexuality, love and marriage' moves from gender to sexuality, discussing the gender-crossing woman as female husband. While love between women was largely presented as respectable in the newspaper stories, it might at the same time be strongly passionate, and it also borrowed sexual allure from the male impersonator on stage.

The three central chapters of the book discuss the 10 or 12 years between the late 1920s and the Second World War, a particularly rich period for a diversity of playful gender-crossing on both page and stage. Chapter 3, 'Gender-crossing and modern sexualities: 1928–39' explores the issue of whether the 1928 *Well of Loneliness* trial and the 1929 Colonel Barker case changed the public perception of gender-crossing women. Did British cross-dressing stories begin to hint at more transgressive possibilities? In the early 1930s there appeared an extraordinary burst of foreign stories, discussed in Chapter 4, 'The sheik was a she!': the gigolo and cosmopolitanism in the 1930s'. Here I analyse French female husband stories and their differences from the British tradition; women cross-dressing as gigolos (some of whom were also passing as Arab sheiks), where issues of racial difference and national identity are explored; and the brief appearance in the late 1930s of mannish women in the cosmopolitan areas of London. Another new cycle of stories begins in the late 1920s, parallel with but not linked to the cross-dressing genre. These are stories of *physical* gender-crossing, discussed in Chapter 5, 'The 1930s 'sex change' story: medical technology and physical transformation'. Science and medicine now appear in the narrative, as 'sex change' is treated as a medical problem which modern science is at last able to solve. But we will see that these stories too borrow from the magical world of the theatre and the freak show.

While there are stronger references to lesbian desire in one or two late 1930s stories, it is not until after the Second World War that the classic gender-crossing formula is seriously challenged. The genre was very resilient, but Chapter 6, 'Perverted passions': sexual knowledge and popular culture 1940–60', shows how it becomes increasingly disrupted from the 1940s as pathological accounts of lesbian desire and transsexuality start to become culturally dominant. This is the story of the huge range of meanings available in the first half of the twentieth century around women's gender-crossing, particularly the potent and erotic mixture of playfulness and power. It is about the losses as well as the gains which came along as baggage with modern sexual identity.

Cross-dressing and cross-reading: male impersonation on stage

The presentation and potential reading of the cross-dressing story was mediated by a related but distinct cultural form – the male impersonator act on the music hall stage. Journalists constantly used the language of the theatre to discuss the sensation of the passing woman. The tone of presentation, in their repeated claims of uniqueness and 'remarkable features', compares to the hard sell of fairground buskers and the talking up of acts on the music hall or variety stage by the compère. In the entertainment pages of the same Sunday newspapers, male impersonator acts were reviewed and pictured, echoing the assessment of the 'performance' of the cross-dressing woman.

Male impersonation was a relatively new form on the late nineteenth-century popular stage, having grown out of the widespread convention of breeches parts in legitimate theatre, the travesty dancer in ballet and the principal boy of the panto-mime.[37] By the heyday of male impersonation in the halls in the 1890s to 1900s, it had become a vital and popular comic 'turn'. Typically, the performer wore well-fitting fashionable men's city clothes to parody contemporary masculine types, usually rather sexualised men such as the dashing swell or ladies' man, and his stage counterpart, the raucous 'lion comique'.[38] A range of styles flourished into the First World War and 1920s, but the dominating star of the Edwardian era, Vesta Tilley, developed a more genteel form which relied on detailed mimicry and admiring flattery alongside her gentle satire of masculine types. This type of male impersonation suited the turn-of-the-century commercial development of music hall, increasingly termed variety theatre, run by national chains and attracting additional, more respectable audiences from the suburbs.[39]

Variety theatre continued to be a popular form of mass entertainment after the First World War, though it was beginning a long slow decline as it competed with cinema. Gradually replacing the old music hall type bill of discrete performers with different acts came the 'revue', a series of loosely connected scenes, often involving the same artists in different roles, which might involve gender-crossing.[40] Male impersonators, including the key stars of the interwar years Hetty King and Ella Shields, continued to be successful in variety theatre, developing constantly changing acts, and, like other performers in this period, appearing on radio and in film. The audience for the mass entertainment forms of music hall and variety theatre was broadly similar to the heterogeneous readership of the popular press, and included children, young people (for whom the halls were a venue for court-ship as well as socialising) and adults of both sexes (though married women had less leisure time for the theatre).[41] Cinema likewise attracted a mass audience from the turn of the century, which increased considerably from the 1920s, challenging the viability of live theatre.

Male impersonation as a music hall or variety act had its own conventions and rules as a theatrical 'turn', which included the efforts of the artist accurately to imitate masculine appearance, the use of humorous, patriotic and sentimental songs to emphasise the type of male character portrayed, and normally some level of parody (as well as celebration) of masculinity. Unlike 'real life' cross-dressing, of course, the audience response and pleasure relied on the awareness from the beginning that the performer was a woman. The newspaper cross-dressing stories owed their sensation factor to knowledge of 'true sex' only with hindsight.

What does this association, this to-ing and fro-ing between the street and the stage, tell us about the meanings attached to women's gender-crossing? Cross-dressing gained value as an amazing story from its grounding in everyday life, in a type of milieu familiar to many readers: manual employment, working-class districts and suburbs, a context of neighbours and friends. Perhaps in its association with the fantasy life and escapism of the theatre, cross-dressing did not count as completely 'real', making the reversal and undermining of gender less challenging. Or did it? Swapping around with gender was surely dangerous and transgressive, however theatrical, in a period when gender identity was deemed to be fixed by nature and gender relations were politically contested. The cross-dresser can be both man and woman, and her skill can be admired. Playing with gender, as the male impersonator does on stage, is fine in a licensed space. But the boundary-crossing between real life and theatre is also troubling. George Capon cannot be turned back into Ellen Capon as dutiful working-class daughter so easily as Burlington Bertie reverts to Vesta Tilley in the dressing room.

Part I
1900–late 1920s

The traditions of gender-crossing

1 Work and war

Masculinity, gender relations and the passing woman

In 1912, the *News of the World* devoted three headlines, two columns and a photograph to

> the bold escapade in which a Chiswick girl has just been detected. Since last August Adelaide Dallamore, 23, a servant, has been working in West London as a plumber's mate in workman's clothes, and during a large part of that period her girl chum has been sharing her lodgings as 'Mrs Dallamore' (see Figure 2).[1]

This report is a classic example of early twentieth-century cross-dressing stories – the 'bold escapade', the typical masculine working-class occupation, and the relationship with another woman. Press stories always pursued detailed descriptions of the 'man–woman's' appearance – height, build and facial hair – and assessed her social performance as a man – strength and skill in masculine work, appropriate leisure pursuits such as drinking and smoking, and courtship and marriage with women. The first half of this chapter will show that each of these themes continued to be important in press reporting between the 1900s and the late 1920s and beyond, suggesting that these were core elements in the contemporary understanding of masculinity. These stories of passing women are really about the performance of gender in daily life. How cross-dressed women acted and were judged as men demonstrates the ways in which masculinities are continually contrived in various everyday settings and relationships and how the mirage of masculinity was produced, not only by those who were passing as men yet had female bodies, but also for biological men engaged in the process of constantly reinventing manliness. Cross-dressing women were both disruptive and respectable. Newspapers represented them as exciting, sensational figures, yet applauded them for successfully following what were quite conservative ideals of masculine behaviour. Within a familiar story formula they were safely entertaining, yet sowed the seeds of the insurrectionary idea that gender was not innate but a social sham.

The early twentieth century was a time of transition and crisis in masculinity and femininity. The second part of this chapter shows how the cross-dressing story was also a means of exploring feminist challenge and the disruption of gender

WOMAN AS HUSBAND.

AMAZING ROMANCE OF TWO CHISWICK GIRLS.

Eight Months in Male Attire.

People will do much for friendship's sake, but not often does it happen that a girl, for love of another girl, will put on man's clothes and live and work as a man, playing "husband" to her friend's "wife." Yet this is the bold escapade in which a Chiswick girl has just been detected. Since last August Adelaide Dallamore, 23, a servant, has been working in West London as a plumber's mate in workman's clothes, and during a large part of that period her girl chum has been sharing her lodgings as "Mrs. Dallamore." They are such devoted "pals" that, rather than yield to a threat to separate them, they adopted this startling device. This strange romance came to light at Acton when Dallamore, living at Annandale-road, Chiswick, was charged with disorderly conduct. Mr. Brown, the court missionary, said the girl had been living with another young woman, the two passing as husband and wife. Each was very fond of the other, and the parents parted them, but prisoner thought the best plan would be for her to dress as a man and live with the young woman, so that no young man should come forward and keep them apart. Dallamore was originally arrested on a charge of disorderly conduct, the police believing her to be a man. The mistake was afterwards discovered. She was then

CHARGED WITH MASQUERADING AS A MAN.

She appeared in the dock wearing male clothing, and it was noticed that her hair had been cut short.—At the resumed hearing the girl was in woman's attire, and the missionary said she had promised to go home and live as a girl.—She was bound over, the magistrate telling her she had

the "husband," sniffing suspiciously, "Yes, love!" exclaimed the "wife," wiping her eyes. "But they shall never, never part us!" After all her experiences the "girl-husband" is all in favour of being a man. "It is so much easier to live as a man than a girl. For one thing I could earn better money. I was free to go anywhere I liked and do what I pleased. I found a man's clothes much more comfortable to wear than the tight garments of a woman, and in my male attire I was free from annoyances. I used to write to an advertising tailor, obtain a self-measurement form, and get my clothes in that way. No one ever suspected me. I even played football with men, and went rowing on the Thames. I got on well with my work-mates, and was quite strong enough to do any task they wanted."

MISS ADELAIDE DALLAMORE.

Figure 2 Adelaide Dallamore. *News of the World*, 7 April 1912, p. 9.
Reproduced with the permission of the British Library.

certainties during the years of suffrage agitation, the First World War and postwar social consolidation in the 1920s. It is striking, however, that despite considerable social changes, there are significant story-telling continuities in the representation of passing women in these decades.

Appearance, clothing and the equivocal body

Masculine gender is established in two interconnected ways. It is expressed physically through body management and also in social interaction with other people, with other men at work or during leisure, with women and in the family.[2] In the press stories both these layers are keenly examined: the 'look' of the masculine and the acting out of social masculinity. The stories were always presented as entertaining and constructed with humour. They often explicitly drew on the reader's familiarity with male impersonation on stage, offering complex and frequently contradictory messages about the very nature of gender.

Women's and men's clothing was so distinctly gendered in this period that abandoning skirts and adopting trousers and short hair was a crucial step towards acceptance as a man. What people wore was central to how they were read by others, not only for their gender but also for their age, class and occupational status. The press was obsessed with the physical appearance and clothing of cross-dressing women. The photograph of Adelaide Dallamore published by the *News of the World* in 1912 showed her to be a convincing young man. The paper described her as 'a good-looking girl, sturdy, and rather short of stature. Dressed in workmen's clothes, with her smooth, boyish face and rather low-pitched voice, she would easily pass as a young man.' Dallamore had obtained men's clothes by mail order from an advertising tailor. After work she would exchange her working clothes 'for a better suit' and her soft collar 'for a hard "stick-up" one' and go out for walks arm-in-arm with her wife.[3] In another case, Paul Downing, a black American, was arrested in London in 1905 after working as a farm labourer in Kent. Unlike many of the other passing women, Paul Downing was described as tall and strong: 'A huge negress ... of powerful build'.[4] The perception of Downing as a man was aided by contemporary racial stereotyping of black people in terms of their physicality and capacity for hard manual labour. '"Paul Downing" was a striking figure – a woman over 6ft in height, and of magnificent physique, with a not unpleasant face and fine teeth.'[5]

The newspaper photographs of the short cropped hair, the confident boyish face and the man's suit of the passing woman, the spectatorial effect underlined by her masculine stance, gesture and accessories such as cigarettes, echoed the publicity postcards of popular male impersonators on stage. The descriptions, too, recall those made of male impersonators. Ernest Wood, a young Soho waiter discovered to be a woman after her death in 1924, was said to dress 'immaculately' in fashionably cut clothes when off duty: 'She was very proud of her appearance, and when walking looked a positive dandy.'[6] The reports of Paul Downing framed her appearance in terms of blackface minstrel entertainment. 'She has a coal-black complexion, dazzling white teeth, is well built, and has a very pleasant manner.'[7]

Both kinds of gender-crosser were assessed for their competence at mimicking masculinity.

Yet the cross-dressing story was crucially different to stage impersonation. Its sensationalism lay in the fact that this performance of gender had gone undetected. The music hall male impersonator was judged on her capacity to imitate masculinity at the time of her performance, in the full knowledge that she was a woman. Hetty King's skill at crossing gender was relished by the audience and her peers: 'Old pros, who had seen the lady over the years, have raved to me about her painstaking, perfect portrayals of the characters she created for her songs: the man about town, the down and out, the army sergeant.'[8] Male impersonators' performance of masculinity was precisely defined and often caustically observed; in some acts it was overblown and comically exaggerated. Real life cross-dressers, on the other hand, aimed to pass so well they would go unnoticed, their masquerade more of a homage to masculinity.

Reviewers emphasised this contrast between the performer's gender and her skill in male costume, an approach which could work to secure the idea of innate gender difference. The press was always willing to help Vesta Tilley construct her image as the best-ever male impersonator alongside her genteel, feminine and irreproachable private life as Mrs Walter (later Lady) de Frece. While 'delightful . . . to look upon in her male attire, those who have the privilege of her friendship know that she is even more delightful to look upon when attired in the garb of the sex which she may truly be said to adorn' declared the *News of the World*'s reviewer in 1919.[9]

Male impersonation had multiple and sometimes contradictory effects. It suggested the social construction of gender, as artists displayed their skill at performing masculinity down to the last gesture. Yet while the inversion of gender and the parodying of masculinity challenged audience assumptions, it was, through the ubiquity of the genre, also normalised. J. S. Bratton argues that the boundaries of male impersonation were increasingly policed in the early twentieth century, as reviews emphasised performers' smart and feminised appearance using terms such as 'dainty' and 'dapper'.[10] Male impersonators might be unsettling in their gender-crossing, but the music hall context stressed their theatrical skills and the woman underneath.

Both the male impersonator on stage and the cross-dressing woman on the street were consciously and deliberately *performing* gender. But in her successful and *undetected* mimicry, the cross-dressing woman undermines the idea of essential gender difference. Her masculinity was not a product of biological maleness, nor presented as theatrical artifice. Because she takes in the people around her with a few authoritative tricks, she reveals to the reader the taken-for-granted daily staging of masculinity by all men, the normally hidden reiteration of 'performative' gender.[11] Hegemonic masculinity seemed to rest on a slim thread indeed (and have little relationship to the sexed body) if these slight, short men, who lacked facial hair, could be accepted in the daily relationships with workmates and neighbours familiar to many readers, over months and years.

The sensational nature of the cross-dressing story rested on this troubling knowledge. Alarm at this dissonance between the sexed body and the appearance of gender was instantly transmuted into an entertaining puzzle for the reader. Which aspects of appearance or behaviour might or should have revealed 'true' gender sooner than they did to those around the passing woman? The stories tried to contain the implications of cross-dressing, both by asserting that 'true' sex would somehow always find its way out, and by dragging women's cross-dressing firmly back to the relative security of the theatrical frame of reference, belatedly assessing her past performance of masculinity.

The occasional story tried to emphasise the 'really a woman' element, rather like the on and off stage performance, implying that cross-dressing was very difficult and contrary to a woman's feminine instinct. Some newspapers told the tale that Charlie Richardson, discovered on her death in 1923 to be Annie Miller, had rented a separate room in which she had kept her women's clothes and went back there sometimes to wear them. The *People* used this as the twist for its headline: 'Astounding Masquerade Revealed by Death: Woman in One Neighbourhood – Man in Another'.[12] Other stories used the language of the stage more explicitly, explaining cross-dressing as a talent for acting. In 1910 Dorothy Morgan, a runaway girl of 15, 'masquerading as a youth . . . was found in the train dressed in boy's clothing, and seems to have essayed to play the part very completely'.[13] A London story from 1926 told how a 22-year-old woman dressed as a man was accused of attempted arson after being found in the garden of a house. Rose Edith Smith, it transpired, was a theatre attendant from Vauxhall. 'Her face was covered in grease-paint, while a moustache had been "lined" in with soot.'[14] Theatrical terminology signalled that cross-dressing was to be judged by the tenets of the theatre – the skill of the performance, the success of the pose, the humorous qualities of the account. Presented as entertainment, the qualities of sensation and display to be enjoyed, the disguise to be marvelled at, the act of gender-crossing was not to be taken entirely seriously and its implications for the making of gender were thus avoided. It is a diversion, a mere 'escapade', as the language of the press headlines reiterated time and again. Even breaking the law is secondary to the main show of the passing woman as star performer in a human-interest drama. The cross-dresser is lent the protection of the performer, the joker, giving her licence to perform outside the boundary of the theatre.

Yet the more stories emphasised theatrical skill, the more evident it becomes that gender can be unravelled and is not an essential quality possessed by the body. The 1910 story of Elena Smith, who had passed as a man in New York for five years, demonstrates this double bind. 'Mrs Smith disguised herself as a man in order to win a wager that any woman possessed of histrionic talent could pass unsuspected as a member of the opposite sex.' Working as a businessman and living the life of a man about town (unusually for a cross-dresser, and more like a stage male impersonator), she 'was constantly at theatres, music-halls, restaurants, races, saloon bars, and even boxing bouts'. Exposing the everyday performativity of gender, Elena Smith said she wanted 'to laugh at both sexes for their shallow, artificial tricks and insincerities' (though she expounded at length on the egotistical and self-centred character of most men).[15]

Gentle humour was a recurring stylistic device in these accounts. Humour, like the theatre and the telling of stories, creates a sanctioned public space to light-heartedly explore what may otherwise be difficult and disturbing topics such as gender, class and sexuality.[16] Comedy and laughter can work to dissipate unease around 'strange' behaviours and relationships, while retaining a narrative *about* this potentially disruptive knowledge. Joking drew attention to the realisation that faking gender was easy, while diffusing anxiety about this knowledge. In the interview with Adelaide Dallamore and her wife Jessie Mann a comic tone develops with some light-hearted exchanges between the two girls about Adelaide's men's clothes. '"Do you remember what an awful job we had tying your first necktie?" The girl plumber burst out laughing at the recollection', and explained that it had taken an hour and a half to get it tied properly.[17] The reported laughter signals to the reader that this is a funny story about the comedy of dressing up and the inversion of gender. The boundaries between male and female clothing styles are so tightly drawn that young women would have no idea how to knot a tie. Yet it also shows that, just like the male impersonator, they can learn how to do so. Gender boundaries are not so impermeable and with a little practice it is easy to pass for the opposite sex by exploiting the everyday presumption that gender is aligned with dress.

As in music hall, comic postcards, funny stories or everyday jokes, stock elements of humour were developed in the cross-dressing stories. There was repeated verbal humour around how to speak of the passing woman, and play with gender pronouns: the classic comment being 'I still cannot call him "she".'[18] The equivocal body provided various jokes. A perennial focus on the beardlessness of the passing woman appears in the story of Annie Miller or Charlie Richardson in 1923. The local barber told the *News of the World*:

> I remember now that she had little hair to shave. There were a few bristles on the upper lip, and some fluff on the chin . . . One afternoon when she came in, a customer suggested that they should toss who should pay for two shaves. 'Charlie' agreed and won. She was delighted, and passed the remark that she had suddenly become lucky.[19]

The responses of the participants – recounted with hindsight – alert the reader to the shifting control and power over the comedy of inverted gender. Who is in charge, and who is the butt of the joke? The local community – the workmates, barbers and publicans of the masculine social world – have been gently tested on their recognition of gender markers and have failed, giving rise to mirth. Now that they know the truth and look foolish, they often re-work the tale. When those in authority such as vicars or doctors are taken in, this is even more amusing. Such characters are classic foils of working-class entertainment where their capacity to represent social order is both demonstrated and undercut. In this particular story Charlie has her own joke that it is hardly worth paying for her shave – only now can bystanders and readers appreciate the whole extent of the jest. She is in charge, playing practical jokes with us and escaping the consequences, in the process turning what could have been gender anxiety into laughter.

Some stories feature the cross-dresser in the character of the clown. These passing women get into trouble with the law (sometimes repeatedly), may be swiftly unmasked, or fail to gain community prestige as successful men.[20] The humour in the story of Paul Downing was partly created by the physical comedy of her odd behaviour. She was arrested in 1905 on Blackfriars Bridge in London 'on suspicion of being a wandering lunatic . . . When arrested the woman was racing after omnibuses on the bridge in the wildest manner, claiming that "his" wife was to be found in one of them.'[21] There is a clownish, theatrical quality to her rushing around in panic, evoking the exaggerated gestures of the stage comedian. Even after her true sex was revealed in the infirmary, she continued to maintain that she had a wife who was in London, for whom she was searching. That the crazy fantasy continued after the 'unmasking' works humorously here, as does the incongruity of a woman claiming to have a wife at all. The trope of 'madness' as a funny and entertaining spectacle was well established in popular entertainment.[22] Similarly her 'spells of religious fervour' are represented as amusing, signalled by the sub-title 'Sermons to the Hens', since they are wonderfully out of place. Having been taken on as a labourer to help on a chicken farm, Downing, a big black man, 'was a success for a short time, but suddenly developed acute religious mania, and insisted upon preaching to the chickens'.[23] It is absurd that she was preaching to birds rather than to people – once again, the exaggerated nature of her actions is both theatrical and crazy. There are also references here to specific jokes from the minstrel show tradition, in particular the supposed fondness of black people for stealing and eating chickens.[24] Paul Downing's evident mental instability and distress give an undercurrent of sadness to this story. While these clowns are not so successfully manipulative of their situation as the majority of cross-dressing women, they are comical and paradoxical characters.[25]

In most of the longer stories, however, the cross-dressing woman is represented much more powerfully as the daring, audacious and successful trickster. A key quality of the classic trickster figure is their capacity for boundary-crossing of all types, between high and low culture, between life and death, between masculinity and femininity, often drawing a moral or highlighting a knotty social problem. As a trickster, the passing woman is in charge and she wins out, escaping scot-free despite her dubious activities and disdain for all sorts of social rules, meanwhile having a laugh at others' expense.[26]

The story of the boyish waiter, Ernest Wood, illustrates all these classic elements of cross-dressing humour and trickster joking. She had worked as a cellarman and waiter in the Italian restaurant trade since being taken on as a boy of 14, and was revealed to be female ten years later in 1924, when dying of consumption in Westminster Infirmary. To everyone it was 'the biggest surprise'.[27] 'The discovery came to me as a complete revelation.'[28] As his employer told one paper: 'you see I still refer to him in the masculine gender. In fact, half the members of my staff still refuse to believe in the disclosure. It seems impossible even to me.'[29] As various people recount what they knew of Ernie, it transpires they were all fooled in different ways as they failed to read correctly the evidence in her physical body. Mr Girio, the head waiter, said: 'We never suspected that he was really a girl. The voice was light, but Ernest always laughed off any reference to his unbroken tones by pointing to his chin, and saying that he didn't even require to shave yet.'[30] Since Wood was in her mid-20s, the joke is really on her male colleagues, while the knowing reader can feel superior to the participants in the drama. Wood had flown across the boundary between life and death, a classic trickster ploy, leaving employer, workmates and girlfriends to wonder about her motives, and what they had wrongly assumed was the irreconcilable difference between masculine and feminine. Gender mix-ups continued in death. A couple of newspapers reported the problem of how to register Wood's death, since her female name was unknown. An official at the Infirmary said he might be buried as 'Miss Ernest Wood'.[31] The loss of some parts of her history adds poignancy to the tale. Yet Ernest has the last laugh: she keeps her masculine name and her mystery after all, and the mixed gender name retains her playful, boundary-crossing, trickster identity.

Performing social gender: masculinity at work and at leisure

While the display of a masculine appearance was absolutely vital for passing women, the newspaper stories suggest that effective masculine identity over a period of time was established through work, rather than simply in the visual presentation of a manly body. There was some humorous examination of the dissonance between the feminine traits expected in a woman and her actual gender performance as a man. In marvelling at the passing woman's success, the thrust of each story was on respectable masculinity. Press reports homed in on how each cross-dressing woman negotiated and adopted social masculinity in her skill at male work, the ability to 'be a good fellow' in socialising with other men, and her success as a breadwinner.[32]

In some types of work skill and strength were significant, but the virtues of working hard and pulling your weight in relation to workmates were always mentioned in the descriptions of passing women. Employment skills might be developed by informal systems of apprenticeship for the younger 'men–women'. Ernest Wood worked as a cellarman at Pinoli's restaurant in Wardour Street between the ages of 14 and 23. Newspaper reports told of how she used to roll heavy barrels around and help to catch rats. Both of these feats were cited to show Ernest's successful mastery of masculine skills, and indeed her manly character. When interviewed, the rat-catcher expressed surprise that Ernest had turned out to be a young woman: 'Never did he show the slightest fear of the rats; in fact, he killed lots of them with the rat gun, and would pick them up when dead without hesitation.'[33] Clearly anything less would have revealed an anticipated 'natural' feminine squeamishness. When she moved to the Astoria hotel the proprietor thought Ernest was too weak for cellar work and made her a waiter instead.

Described as 'an excellent waiter . . . very polite and very attentive', Ernest evidently made a success of this role.[34]

Adelaide Dallamore, who had previously been employed as a domestic servant, resourcefully worked her way into being a successful plumber's mate, at the same time puncturing the notion that there were mysterious or difficult skills associated with men's work. Replying to a notice in a window that a plumber's mate was wanted she was asked if she had ever done any plumbing: 'I said "Yes" (though, of course, I hadn't) and they gave me the job.' She told the *News of the World* in 1912 that it was not difficult. 'A plumber's mate has only to wait on the plumber at his job, handing him his tools and just doing what he's told, and I got on all right.' Again she rejected suggestions of innate female weakness: 'My first job was on the roof of a new house – no, I didn't feel dizzy at all.'[35] Her wages were raised but she moved on to a larger firm of plumbers in Chiswick with 20 pairs of men and lads where she was 'very happy'. As a young man carrying out orders rather than initiating activities, she was able to learn on the job. 'I got on well with my workmates and was quite strong enough to do any task they wanted.'[36]

Older 'men' had to carry off a male work persona more convincingly, with fewer allowances made for inexperience. Middle-aged Charlie Richardson (Annie Miller) worked in a rag-and-bone shop in Hoxton, London, in the early 1920s. 'She showed adaptability, and pleased her employer, who had not the slightest suspicion that her assistant was really a woman.'[37] Locals reported, 'Charlie was very strong, and could lift sacks and heavy weights as easily as a man.'[38] Paul Downing had wandered across half the world in search of her wife, this claiming of space itself a privilege of masculine gender freedoms. 'The woman has certainly crossed through many States in America and through France, Spain and Belgium, and her strength and skill would enable her to carry deception so far as to work as a common sailor.'[39] All male jobs were represented as physically demanding, though there were subtly different types of masculinity in play in different occupations, including the social skills and rapid responses demanded of waiters.

The adoption of habits such as smoking and swearing was also part of the whole masquerade of masculinity, as was male bonding in leisure pursuits such as sports and drinking, frequently carried over from the workplace to the neighbourhood. Only a few pursuits, associated with courtship or youth, including dancing and cinema-going, were carried on in mixed company.[40] While work relationships were made within a set hierarchy of skill, authority and role, outside leisure activities were reliant on individual capacity to create a persona, for instance in the public house. All the newspapers carried some discussion of Charlie Richardson's penchant for drink and tobacco and described how her masculinity was established in the local community as much as in work.

> The Landlord of a public house in the neighbourhood . . . told the 'News of the World' that she drank double whiskies and would often treat men in the bar. But it was not alone for that they liked her. 'She had a pleasing personality,' remarked the landlord. 'She was always ready with a jest, and was "hail fellow well met" to everyone. My customers liked "Charlie." They used to

enquire after her, and they seemed annoyed when she did not come in. She was always a moderate drinker.'[41]

Charlie was assessed on her successful interactions with other men, and on the comparative respectability of her version of working-class masculinity. Heterosexual relationships with women were also vital to establishing manliness.[42] Ellen/George Capon immediately told the officials who came to take her to the military recruiting office in 1918 that she was 'walking out' with a young woman and produced a letter to prove it.[43] Older men–women explained themselves in terms of marital status whether or not they had a wife on the scene. Charlie Richardson/Annie Miller did not have a female partner, but posed as a man separated from his wife. She retained the moral high ground, by telling workmates that the wife had turned out to be a 'bad lot'. The *News of the World* drew attention to her actively heterosexual presentation: 'Annie Miller still further kept up the strange role she had assumed by making herself agreeable to her own sex. She would pat the hands of a barmaid, touch her chin, and flirt in mild fashion.' Adopting the male prerogative of making one-sided sexual advances, Miller affirmed her masculine status in a public space in relation to a woman who, as a barmaid, was particularly vulnerable to the uninvited male touch.[44]

Some of the younger men maintained a wholesome reputation by keeping relatively aloof. Ernie Wood was accepted as one of the lads at work. Mr Girio, the head waiter told how 'He mixed freely with us all and took part in all our jokes. I cannot say I remember hearing him swear, and I must admit that waiters do occasionally swear.'[45] Not swearing was thus constructed with hindsight as a marker of gender and respectability. After the day's work was done Ernest's colleagues observed that she preferred to keep herself to herself, and rather than going out with the lads, she usually went out with a girl. Her girlfriends described her leisure preferences for the cinema and variety theatre, and sometimes open-air political meetings.[46] Yet one or two manly activities were mentioned: Ernie was said to breed dogs in her spare time, and the *News of the World* reported that she had once had a fight with a man and made his nose bleed.[47]

These passing women were presented as being of honourable character in most respects, despite the fraudulent assumption of gender and sometimes the mystery and secrecy as to their motive. They were bold, forthright and fearless, and honest workers, as the ideal man should be.[48] Some, as we will see later, were praised for their patriotism in the First World War, or for protecting the honour of others, especially their wives. An important demonstration of respectable working-class masculinity in this period was the capacity to maintain economic independence through employment, and to be a good provider for the household and family. All of the successful cross-dressing women achieved this, at least until laid low by fatal illness. Ellen Capon was presented as an upright young man who had sought war work for honourable motives, to earn higher wages to help her sick mother. Ernest Wood was said to be a thrifty lad, who had put money by to send to her aunt at Wigan.[49] Adelaide Dallamore, the plumber's mate, lived as a young married man with a new wife, Jessie Mann. Their household in west London was run effectively on two incomes, as Jessie went out to work in domestic service as a daily help. She earned 8 shillings a week, to Adelaide's 12 shillings. Adelaide reported that they had lived comfortably on a pound a week – the average income of unskilled working-class families in this period, and adequate for a couple, though not for a family.[50] Yet respectable working-class masculinity could also overlap with 'rough' behaviour at times. Adelaide Dallamore defended her household and marriage with physical violence after her girlfriend's irate father and brother tracked them down, leading to a 'scrap' in the street, 'an altercation which ended in blows'. Adelaide described it as an honourable use of force: 'There was a little trouble in the street. I stood up for my "wife," and struggled with her brother.'[51]

In the stories just discussed, passing women performed working-class masculinity based on a combination of physical appearance, competence at the workplace and male bonding in the wider community. Accounts of the few middle-class cross-dressers generally contained less emphasis on physical determinants or on the establishment of social masculinity among other men. Middle-class men worked in clean, sedentary jobs, rather than depending on their physical strength, a kind of work which could seem effeminate.[52] Their markers of masculinity included education, authority and professionalism.

One of the most detailed stories in this period is that of Harry Lloyd, discovered to be a man on her death in 1910, aged about 74, after over 25 years of masquerading in the suburbs of north London. While she was one of the most successful passing women, Lloyd's masculinity was more ambivalently demonstrated than some of the others, and this seems to be tied to the family's class status as educated and lower middle-class. Her physical appearance had significance in the story's presentation, but only at the moment of death, when it supposedly gave her away, implying that biological truth will out. The local doctor, who knew Harry Lloyd by sight, was called to the house as she died by Lloyd's daughter.

> He [the doctor] did not recognise 'him' at the moment, and he said to Miss Lloyd, 'I thought it was a man I was called to see.' She replied, 'Yes; it is my father.' Witness told her that he had never seen a more feminine expression on a man's face in his life.[53]

A subsequent physical examination established, to the astonishment of Lloyd's adult daughter, that her elderly and respected father, a widower, was actually a woman. The *News of the World* declared that this was 'a mystery that will ever be famous in the annals of inexplicable romance', and faithfully relayed the discussions in the coroner's court, which sketched in various pieces of information about Harry Lloyd's life as a man.

Harry Lloyd had supported her family as a married man and then widower, by giving lessons in foreign languages. This was very similar to the work she had done many years earlier as a young woman (Marie Le Roy), and not gendered as particularly masculine. There was evidence that she had also worked for an auctioneer in Edmonton for some years, had been the manager of a lodging house, and on her wife's death certificate she was recorded as a newsagent. These were white-collar jobs which fitted the class status of her home (a four-roomed house in Enfield) and her educated respectability. In later years, perhaps as her health deteriorated or because the supply of students declined, Harry Lloyd was driven to doing odd jobs around Enfield: selling newspapers, delivering bills for tradesmen, and selling tea and cakes in the local small arms factory. Here she was nicknamed Joe Chamberlain by the men as she wore a monocle. The daughter (now 26 years old) had become an elementary school teacher and had supported the home and her elderly father since 1907.[54]

All these stories, from across 30 years of newspaper reporting, demonstrate interesting continuities in the masculine ideals against which cross-dressing women were measured. The reports repeatedly focused on certain markers of masculinity – those outward signs which workmates and neighbours should have noticed, had they been more observant, and those which composed the everyday social requirements of respectable manliness. Discussion of appearance, clothing and facial hair created opportunities for humour and at the same time dislocated shared assumptions about the fixed nature of gender. Success in performing a conventional masculine role and gaining the recognition of her peers as a man earned the masquerader nothing but admiration from the press. The entertaining mystery and comedy of these stories of gender inversion packaged their disquieting knowledge in a familiar form while still conveying their challenge, a challenge all the more pointed in a period of rapid change and anxiety in gender relations.

Changing gender relations onstage and in the street

Following several decades of feminist agitation for greater legal and social equality for women, the contested political demand for women's suffrage erupted into militancy and disorder in the years before the First World War. The war brought a huge mobilisation of men into the forces, produced shocking battlefield casualties, and instituted greater freedom and independence for women in employment and the public sphere. Postwar readjustment and a desire for stability in the early 1920s led to anxious discussion of women's position in the family, challenges to masculine privilege from increased gender equality in legislation, and the emergence in the media of a modern feminine ideal. Both newspaper cross-dressing stories and the portrayals of male types by stage impersonators addressed contemporary troubles in gender relations and the changing expectations of men and women.

Male impersonation on stage was a mirror image of passing women stories in the press. The original swell song, and its burlesquing by male impersonators, gained impact from deflating the counterfeit 'gent', both for his class pretensions and for his sham masculinity.[55] It celebrated (though also trenchantly critiqued) the 'bad boy' types of masculinity: the man pretending to a higher social status, the drinker, the womaniser, the man who avoided a hard day's work in favour of a spree on the town or at the seaside. Audiences enjoyed both their identification with these recognisable male types, and also the mockery of them. The dashing swell, the 'masher', the over-dressed gentleman, the narcissistic clerk, the strutting soldier: these were the antithesis of the respectable independent workman upheld in the press stories' presentation of cross-dressing women. While Ella Shields specialised in fake gents and also in blackface numbers, Hetty King was best known for her military characters. Vesta Tilley portrayed all these types, and also poked fun at curates and policemen; as easily deflated authority figures, these were classic material for working-class humour. All parodied the drunken man staggering home, another comic descent from respectability.

Theatre historian J. S. Bratton suggests that, despite their framing within the safely commercial world of variety, the 'distorted, mocking, exaggerated images of masculinity projected by these women from the music hall stage' should be read as carnivalesque, as frequently provocative and at times threatening.[56] The political significance of male impersonation was as 'a space for testing and contesting gender imagery [during] the cultural upheaval that surrounded the women's suffrage agitation'.[57] Even the more anodyne style adopted by Vesta Tilley and others during the 1900s could still be disruptive and edgy in its powerful androgyny, while the 'swell' songs had considerable depth and potential for subversive interpretation.[58] Theatre historians have discussed the possible audience reception of these songs, and we can speculate that the presentation of 'real life' cross-dressing in the press might evoke similar responses. Both men and women in the audience shared delight, fuelled by class resentment, in the swell song parodying of masculinity.[59] Mocking the puffed-up 'gent' parallels the fooling of authority enjoyed by readers of newspaper cross-dressing stories. Other audience pleasures may have been gender-specific. Men might have been flattered by the mimicry of masculinity generally, enjoyed the male impersonator's display of the latest masculine fashions, or taken some songs as celebrating their own social group rather than as caricature. They would have enjoyed the parody of other types of men they regarded as beneath or in competition with them, sharing a feeling of superiority in relation to the poor clerk, or the posing but skint gentleman. 'Casting a woman as "one of the chaps" also served to reduce distance . . . between the sexes, suggesting that she might be manageable on male terms', Peter Bailey argues.[60] Framed as playful theatre, the role nevertheless packed an underhand satirical punch.

While women too enjoyed the male impersonator's accurate imitation of the attractive young man, her assumption of masculine power and independence, even though temporary, was even more seductive. The male impersonator sang of the joys of walking the city streets, of parading in her male finery but being the subject, not the object, of the gaze. She offered women in the audience a fantasy of female appropriation of masculine pleasures including betting, drinking and assertive courtship. If the usual swell song, sung by men, celebrated forms of male behaviour such as sexual triumphalism and alcoholic excess, the parodies delivered by boisterous male impersonators could be highly charged and particularly enjoyable for groups of women in the audience. The equalising effect of a woman piercing the self-importance of swell masculinity, putting down male pretension, satirising those tiresome young men who might or might not be good husband material, was a powerful form of entertainment.[61]

Both passing women and male impersonators continued to draw attention to the constructed nature of gender, a particularly troubling concept in the period before the First World War. Like male impersonation, the cross-dressing stories were a means of cultural engagement with contemporary problems in gender relations, such as women's suffrage, which were being bitterly fought over in more formal social and political arenas. The cross-dresser's role as a trickster is relevant here. In this period, the trickster gender-crosser of the press questions the nature of gender difference, while at the same time pointing to the socially approved versions of masculinity. Boundary-crossing between the two genders gives her the capacity to compare the two and to pronounce on each as seen from within. She also, at a deeper and less explicit level, says something about the nature of women, their huge capacity to do more that they are socially permitted to do, and to fulfil male roles at least as well as the men.

Gender-crossing and gender politics

In the years before the First World War several cross-dressing women were quoted on their thoughts and experiences of living in the male gender. They followed an emancipationist narrative, declaring that work and life as a man was generally to be preferred to woman's lot, and this contributed to the wide-ranging debates about women's position and the suffrage campaign, reports of which regularly appeared in the same newspapers.[62]

Some passing women reflected at length and rather trenchantly on their experiences. Having deconstructed the assumption that men's work was more difficult and demanding, Adelaide Dallamore commented on the benefits of male employment as healthier as well as more highly paid. 'I think men have a much better time than women. I know I was much healthier working ten hours a day as a plumber's mate than ever I was in service!' She was clear about the key advantages of masculinity – higher wages, more comfortable clothes and social autonomy.

> It is so much easier to live as a man than a girl. For one thing I could earn better money. I was free to go anywhere I liked and do as I pleased. I found a man's clothes much more comfortable to wear than the tight garments of a woman, and in my male attire I was free from annoyances.[63]

This assertion of the liberating benefits of masculinity appeared adjacent to a news report that Emmeline Pankhurst had been freed from jail following imprisonment for window breaking, suggesting that Dallamore's activities might be interpreted as a populist version of women's emancipation.

Critical comments about women's wages in particular continued in later years. Ellen Capon justified her cross-dressing on grounds that to her, were self-evident: 'I thought I could earn more money as a man than as a woman . . . Of course, everybody knows that a man can make more money than a woman in industrial employment.'[64] Her family knew what she was doing (she continued to wear men's clothes at home) and supported her. Ellen clearly relished masculine work and its freedoms, telling the magistrate that she would now go and work on the land. Annie Miller also had economic motives and nursed resentment at sex discrimination. Left an orphan in her teens she 'drifted into the rag trade, but failed to make headway, and, rightly or wrongly, believed that her sex was against her' and suddenly vanished, reappearing as Charlie Richardson.[65]

Several women noted the freedom from male harassment that gender-crossing gave them – indeed one young woman had adopted male disguise precisely to avoid this. Flora Langley had gone to New York to make her fortune, believing that 'every girl with education, perseverance, and enterprise had a fair chance to earn something more than mere bread and butter.' Unable to find office work she became a waitress, but to escape the 'terrible New York men, who worry a girl to death' she disguised herself as a young man. After discovery she complained to journalists that no girl with a pretty face or figure could avoid 'being annoyed to desperation by men'. The experience led her to believe that the independence of American working women 'was a fairy tale' and no further advanced than in Britain, a sour commentary on the nation which was supposed to exemplify modernity.[66] There are different possible readings of these stories which highlight the greater freedom and privileges of life as a man. They provide a revelation about the structural barriers impeding women's lives, but also, at times, a warning that there is no mileage in trying to challenge gender roles.

Military masculinity

Both male impersonation acts on stage and cross-dressing reports in the press shifted to uphold patriotic masculinity during the First World War, as gender-crossers adopted uniform or attempted to join the forces as men. Stage performance of military masculinity long preceded the war, and, like the press stories, evoked the well-established folk tradition of warrior women dating back to the eighteenth century.[67] Patriotic celebrations of sailors and soldiers, especially those in the ranks, was widespread in the music hall and developed by male impersonators, including Vesta Tilley and Hetty King, in the 1900s.[68] But it acquired a new edge with war and a new audience segment, troops home on leave. Vesta Tilley revived her song 'Jolly Good Luck to the Girl Who Loves A Soldier', which became enormously popular, and introduced new ones on wartime themes, such as 'A Bit of a Blighty One', which honoured the wounded soldier (still enjoying his 'saucy little nursie'). Her 'The Army of Today's All Right' was used on recruitment posters and she was supposedly responsible for so many enlistments that she became known as 'England's Greatest Recruiting Sergeant'.[69]

Ella Shields too was a hit during wartime. The *News of the World* emphasised the patriotic identification of the troops, noting her 'tremendous reception' at the Shepherd's Bush Empire in 1917: 'Of the four numbers she gave perhaps the one to appeal most was a "Tommy" song. This . . . almost caused a riot, the khaki members of the audience acclaiming, as one of themselves, a perfect representation.'[70] While wartime music hall songs and performers allied themselves with the British Tommy and stressed national solidarity, they presented not only the

glorious side of war and the glamour of joining up but also sentimental treatments
of the hardship and emotions that went with it. Other impersonators gently guyed
the soldier's response to life in the trenches.[71] One of Ella Shields' numbers
attacked upper-class profiteering and avoidance of call-up, decrying the shirker
(clearly a 'swell' in this case) while also understanding his feelings.

> The other coves get all the fun, and all the glory too
> I'd give my shot-silk socks to take my turn
> But someone must supply the brains to get the bus'ness thro'
> And see that all the bally home fires burn.
> I'm Cuthbert, I'm Cuthbert, a very knowing card
> I'm Cuthbert, I'm Cuthbert, The army I am barr'd. I'm starr'd![72]

The popular press censored the worst news of the war and sought to support
government war aims and propaganda requirements during these years. In
parallel to the glamorisation of military masculinity on stage, women who
attempted to pass as men in order to join the forces or do munitions work were
applauded for their patriotism. Historians have assumed there was an upsurge of
gender-crossing by women to enlist in the First World War, but in fact there were
no known cases of women successfully joining the forces as men in Britain.[73]
Indeed there were relatively few press stories of women even attempting to enlist.
In those that were reported, passing women's patriotism was generally praised as
an example to men, shaming their less wholehearted commitment. Although the
conditions of disclosure were particular to the context of wartime, most elements
followed the pattern of civilian cross-dressing stories. A woman who worked as a
man in the Barrow Naval Construction Works for three days was held up as 'an
example of courage and earnestness' to other men in munitions factories.
Described as a middle-aged widow, who 'passed muster' for a time in an establishment employing 20,000 men, she worked alongside men carrying planks and
timber. But her workmates noticed 'the delicacy of her frame' and questioned her
about shaving. A soldier told the press that: 'she "worked like a brick" and did
twice as much work as some of the other labourers'. The fact that she had stayed
in a lodging house for men, without inconvenience, also attracted interest.[74]

Press accounts of young women seeking to join up as soldiers showed how the
compulsory medical examination required by the modern army led to their exclusion from this form of masculinity. When 32-year-old Albert 'F', a married man
with two dependent children from Hornsey in London, was called up in 1916 and
faced with a medical inspection at Mill Hill Barracks, he asked to see a doctor in
private, claiming cardiac trouble, but when refused 'confessed that he was not a
man but a woman'.[75] Described as polite and well-spoken, she was 'a rather short
and slight man with a high-pitched voice', yet her masculinity was not doubted by
her employer, nor by the soldiers and conscripts at the barracks.

> The voice was soft and rather gentle . . . but no notice was taken of that.
> Plenty of young fellows – and she looked like a young man of twenty-four –

have effeminate voices, and when a great many men are being dealt with practically together, individual characteristics like that are passed without comment.

Indeed the glamour and skill of the theatrical male impersonator was attached to her.

> A soldier who saw her said, 'She was the most perfect male impersonator I have ever seen. Not one of the women who wear men's attire on the stage – and I have seen all the best of them – could approach her. We were absolutely deceived.'[76]

In her everyday working life, Albert was a convincing and valued employee. Various accounts were given of her career history as a printer which all stressed her ability. Her employer told how:

> She was engaged first . . . in outdoor advertising work, but it was really not a good enough job, as I soon realised. I offered to teach her the process of aerographing, which is rather technical . . . But she learned the process readily, and in a very little while was able to earn very high wages even for a man.[77]

He explained that she filled the role of foreman in his absence, with the other men under her direction: 'The war took five young men, and I appealed at the Tribunal for "Albert" on the ground – which was perfectly true – that "he" was my right-hand "man".'[78] Enquiries endorsed Albert's story – that she had adopted male guise in order to escape her husband – and a military report 'described her as worthy of every consideration'. She was subsequently invited back to the barracks where the colonel: 'expressed his sympathy and, shaking hands, described her as a "perfect little brick"'.[79] Albert F, then, earned praise from the military for being prepared to fight for her country, and broader recognition of her success as an honourable man.

Both Albert F and the cross-dressing Barrow munitions worker were absorbed in different ways into the wider story of national heroism. The soldier hero is the most potent expression of masculinity, embodying '[m]ilitary virtues such as aggression, strength, courage and endurance [which] have repeatedly been defined as natural qualities of manhood'. His role as the ordinary yet heroic citizen, prepared to defend the nation, means he is also the focus for wider community identifications of national identity, patriotism and imperial power.[80] Those cross-dressing women who attempted to join the forces were engaging with the ultimate forms of masculinity as both ideal and embodied expression. The admiration shown for them endorsed the power and significance of martial masculinity and the nation's wartime struggle.

One or two trickster cross-dressers did not succeed as military men and presented a more clownish relationship to the war. Martha Hodson, born in 1891, repeatedly passed as a man in various towns in the north-west and was constantly arrested for stealing men's clothes and other offences between 1910 and 1915. In January 1915 she was charged with stealing a gentleman's outfit from a house where she was employed as a servant. She tried to enlist as a soldier at a recruitment office in Manchester but her courage failed her when she found a physical examination was required, so she walked to Lancaster where she was arrested.[81] In October of the same year she again stole her employer's clothes and again tried to enlist, described as 'her latest freak'.[82]

Gender-crossing in the military was taken up by the press as another forum to discuss women's appropriate patriotic role in wartime. To what extent should they step into masculine occupations?[83] In the week after the Albert F story hit the newspapers, a journalist wrote that she was not surprised that the latest man–woman had tried to become a soldier and observed that, in wartime, women were hindered by gender from properly utilising their patriotism. 'The Craving they Endure in this Day of Big Things' was one sub-heading. 'Nowadays any woman would wish she could possibly become a soldier, "do her bit", avenge the friend she's lost by killing a few brutes of Germans with her own hands! Isn't it a deadly job to be a woman in wartime?'[84] This suggested that the qualities of vengeance, violence and national feeling were not only masculine, but fully shared by women, and that any woman of spirit would wish to play her part in the war effort.

Despite the barriers to women actually enlisting as men in the British services during the First World War, they could read about women of other nations who took a fuller part in the military. In April 1916, readers could hear of the 'Rebel Amazons' who took part in the Easter Rising. 'A striking figure in the rebellion is an elderly woman, stated to be of high title . . . A Sinn Fein leader. She appeared in uniform – green tunic and trousers and carried a rifle with a fixed bayonet.'[85] A domestic servant from Leyton who cut off her hair and intended to enlist in 1916 said she had been inspired by the Russian girls. This was a reference to the Russian women's regiment, the Women's Legion of Death, whose 'Wonderful Gallantry' was noted on the front page of the *News of the World*. The woman journalist provided an emancipation narrative, noting that they were catcalled in similar ways to the suffragettes. They retorted: 'We are not girls; we are soldiers.' The women drilled and practised shooting just as their male counterparts did and were enthusiastic for battle: 'When word came that they were to be moved nearer the front, their hurrahs lasted many minutes.' Having witnessed these Russian women soldiers, the writer was convinced that: 'women ought to step into the breach, guns in hand. It is their country as much as the men's'. [86]

Postwar renegotiations of gender

The years immediately following the First World War are seen as a particularly important period of gender relations, as society coped with conflicting pressures: a desire to return to business as usual; a need to work out a new relationship between women and men following partial enfranchisement and some significant if limited equality legislation; and the adaptation to peacetime following women's wartime mobilisation and the considerable military casualties suffered by men. Related anxieties were specifically expressed about the falling birthrate and women's willingness to be mothers, the competition for employment in a period of severe recession, and women's social independence and political influence.[87] Adrian Bingham argues that the popular press was less negative about women's emancipation than feminist historians have asserted. As well as expressing anxieties about sex equality going too far, newspapers welcomed some manifestations of women's changing lifestyle as expressions of modernity. The new physicality of the modern young woman (as sexually appealing girl, of course) and her achievements in sport and public life were also celebrated.[88]

In mass entertainment, male impersonation remained in demand in the variety theatre, providing variations on the same male types – the swell, the aspiring clerk and the man in uniform – as Ella Shields' and Hetty King's continuing high profile shows. The new double act of the singing and dancing sisters Beatie and Babs in 1919 offered both old and new trends in male impersonation. Beatie's part of the act was in the style of the flirtatious pretty girl playing a boyish young man: 'Beatie dances beautifully, and is a dapper little knight of the pigskin in her jockey's jacket, breeches and saucy cap.' Babs on the other hand was half-scolded for her success.

> Babs is really a very good-looking young lady, but she has contrived, deliberately and with malice aforethought, to make herself the ugliest and most villainous-looking toreador . . . The disfiguring transformation from the dainty drawing-room artist is simply staggering.

Her more assertive presentation of masculinity – 'she struts and stumps . . . and bellows' – disquiets the reviewer, though he notes the 'overwhelming reception' for both young women. 'It is laughter all the way for the people.'[89]

Women playing men in film were usually attractively androgynous rather than pursuing the accurate mimicry of the stage impersonators. *The People* emphasised the contrast between two images of the film star Marion Davies, one in feminine dress and one in male uniform in her new film *Beverley of Graustark*, with the weak pun: 'Her Self – "Maid Man"'. '[T]o see pretty, shy-looking Marion Davies as she is here, it almost seems incredible that she can so transform herself as to look like this, in order to play the leading part of Beverley . . . !'[90] Though dressed in full military uniform with medals, Davies sported make-up and lipstick. Military uniform continued to appear in the years following the First World War in a range of contexts – for example, Edith Day appeared as a dashing legionnaire in 1927 – while some actresses played other male uniformed types including vicars in revue and film.[91] The highly successful British comedian Beatrice Lillie came to fame as a comic male impersonator during the war years. Although she moved away from gender-crossing in her later career she appeared as a male lawyer in a revue in 1922, depicted in a sketch on the entertainment pages of the *News of the World*. The same edition of the paper noted that for the first time a woman (Miss Ivy Williams) had qualified as a barrister.[92] Lillie also donned male attire to save the fortunes of a theatrical company as the star of the successful 1926 film *Exit Smiling*.[93] In this, as in other films and revues, actresses often crossed gender for only part of the plot, which might promote a romance narrative, or, in comedy, self-reference the world of variety and impersonation. In the film *Manhandled* (1924) Gloria Swanson performed impersonations of Bea Lillie and Charlie Chaplin.[94] As well as comic cross-dressing, the films of the 1910s and 1920s also presented a wide range of tough and athletic heroines, many wearing male clothing to pursue action-packed narratives. These cowgirl stunt queens and other boyish stars engaged in escapist adventure plots, often saving the life of the hero, and they only gradually gave way to more worldly and glamorous leading ladies.[95] While still a vital and complex form, male impersonation in both British and Hollywood film inevitably made less reference to the specifically localised and class-based forms of masculinity than had been possible in the music hall.

The major cross-dressing press stories published in the early to mid-1920s – including those of Charlie Richardson and Ernest Wood discussed above – engage with the same themes and are written in the same trickster tone as those before the war. In some of the shorter stories, however, often involving young women running away from home, there was some equivocal negotiation around gender freedoms and boundaries. Seventeen-year-old weaver Hilda Hardcastle, from a village near Leeds, disappeared one night in 1923 in her brother's clothes. 'Hilda had often wished she was a boy, because, she declared, boys had a better time and more freedom, and she needed a bit of excitement.' She walked for three days through Yorkshire, evading police and sleeping in the woods, but failed to find work as a boy. Spotted while writing her diary, a miner guessed she was the missing girl and reported her to police. Since Hilda expresses the wish that she had never started the adventure, this could also be read as a warning to other young women.[96]

There was also a spate of cross-dressing stowaway stories during these years.[97] Again, these emphasised the adventurous spirit of the girls concerned, and some titillation perhaps around the fact that they were hidden in a ship full of men. Some were accompanying their American sweethearts to the United States, in the troop transports at the end of the war. Others were acting more autonomously. A 'big strapping' Southampton girl worked her passage as a sailor on board the *Pittsburg*, but was arrested as an illegal immigrant and her sex discovered in Hoboken, New York.[98] These stories frame an interesting variety of female independence and masculine assistance. Revealing feminine weaknesses (such as severe sea-sickness) are often what betrays them – a comforting restoration of gender assumptions for the reader.

Mistaking the gender of adult women because of their mannish clothes could be treated as a joke in this period but might also be more troubling. A serial cross-dresser who appeared several times in the press in these years, Mabel Joyce (also known as Hilda Holland) was charged in 1920 with disorderly conduct in west London after a police constable saw her book a bed in a men's lodging house. She was dressed in army clothes, and described herself as a chauffeur, but he was unsure of her gender. The recounting of this tale evoked laughter in the courtroom, and the headline in the *Illustrated Police News*: 'Are You a Man or a Woman?'[99] The joke is on the policeman's uncertainty rather than on Mabel

Joyce, but this was a new phrase in the stock headlines of masquerading. Exactly the same question appeared in a contemporaneous story, which raised more directly the disturbing question of whether postwar women were turning into men. '"Are you a man or a woman?" was the extraordinary question put by the County Court judge at Brighton to a no less extraordinarily attired person in court.' Mrs Beatrice Walker, a widow, had appeared in court wearing breeches and leather gaiters, and at first refused to declare her sex.[100] There are elements of comedy in this and several similar accounts, and because of the rudeness or obstreperousness of the woman in court, they contain the pleasures of authority being flouted. But the tone of the reports, which was ponderous and disapproving, shows they are going too far in behaving like men. These gender-crossing women are not treated as protected tricksters; instead the story reflects fears of what the modern assertive woman with her aspirations and independence might be like in her worst form.

Conclusion

How was the cross-dressed woman understood in the period from the 1900s to the late 1920s? As we have seen, she was a focus for contemporary puzzling over gender – what it meant to be masculine or feminine. Newspaper stories picked up on contemporary concerns in gender relations such as the struggle for women's suffrage and the wartime readjustment of gender roles, in a constant inquiry into the nature and implications of gender difference. Yet what stands out is the continuity of the cross-dressing genre over the first quarter of the twentieth century. The First World War has little fundamental impact on it. The stories of Ernest Wood and Charlie Richardson in the 1920s and those of Adelaide Dallamore and Harry Lloyd in the 1900s, are strikingly similar in their formula – the curiosity and admiration expressed for the passing woman, the assessment of her skills in performing masculinity, the humour and light-hearted tone of the stories and the figuring of the cross-dressing woman as a trickster.

We can learn much about the nature and performance of early twentieth-century masculinity by studying these stories of ersatz men. Women passing as ordinary working-class men showed how masculinity was established in everyday life in its most ubiquitous form. In these stories masculinity – an unstable, contested and complex lived role – was boiled down to a few necessary elements: the appearance of being male, being a sufficiently skilled worker, socialising with and being accepted by other men, and being prepared to demonstrate loyalty and patriotism.

While physicality was important in demonstrating masculinity, especially of the working-class man, many of the passing women whose stories have been analysed here made relatively unconvincing men, at least with hindsight. Although adequate bodily characteristics had to be confidently presented, it was the performance of masculine qualities, character and social role that was crucial. Muscles could be developed and skills acquired. Skill, self-control, independence, competence at work and homosociability led to their acceptance as sufficiently manly men. The relational establishment of gender was important. Successful relationships with other men at the workplace or in leisure activities were repeatedly examined in the press, as were heterosexual relations with women in courtship and marriage. Their demonstrated masculinity was then projected back onto their bodies, and only after 'discovery' was the mismatch of physical characteristics such as voice, facial hair and stature really taken seriously. If femininity is more obviously constructed in daily life, through a greater focus on clothing and appearance, masculinity is also, of course, a performative confection, with even physical embodiments being projected through assumption and fantasy rather than a necessary reality.

The stories of cross-dressing women also show how difficult it is for men to get rejected from the club of masculinity. They suggest that men as a gender grouping, while vociferously upholding the significance of manliness in public, also tend to protect their failures to live up to this by accepting individuals who do not quite fit as still being 'one of the lads'. Some passing women received comments on their physical appearance, but none was excluded as effeminate on this basis and few revealed in this way. A few were described as sickly, or suffered injury or illness, but this was common enough for working men for it not to be seen as particularly emasculating, it seems.

We have seen that passing women were admired for their capacity to perform types of masculinity which seem highly conservative – the kind of respectable masculinity expected of the responsible working-class and lower middle-class man. In choosing to highlight the ways in which passing women successfully fulfilled the best ideals of masculinity, the press partially obscured the transgressive potential of cross-dressing. It was not only class-specific masculinity that was celebrated and debated in gender-crossing stories. It was also British masculinity.[101] Passing women reflect a divergent cultural geography, being found in large cities and in rural areas. While many stories came from London, this could reflect the anonymous nature of big city life, and the focus of press attention on the capital. But there were important commonalities in location nevertheless. Most of the stories concerning masquerading women were located in fairly mundane working-class suburbs and small towns. Here they blended into well-established communities and respectable working-class masculinity, seemingly easily. Gender-crossing women were also tied into British national identity by their espousal of patriotic values and their readiness to support war aims, either on the music hall stage or, for some, by attempting to enlist. While the would-be soldiers were used by the press to make jingoistic points about the duty of British men to fight, these stories also served to align cross-dressing women with the highest form of manliness and national service. The newspaper stories reinforced their longstanding and significant place in British culture by their frequent reiteration of previous cases of celebrated women soldiers and sailors, going back as far as Hannah Snell in the eighteenth century, thus constructing a British tradition of cross-dressing with a place in the national psyche.[102]

The body of the cross-dresser was retrospectively read and deconstructed like that of the male impersonator – for appearance, for gesture and authenticity. Passing as a man earned applause for the difficulty of the feat of taking on what were commonly believed to be the inborn biological attributes and physical presentation of the opposite sex. By making the parallel with stage performance and male impersonation, the press suggested this was a temporary and light-hearted escapade, accomplished by a minority of exceptional women, who were particularly determined or gifted with theatrical skills or capacities beyond the average. But a closer analysis of newspaper reports might give the opposite message – that it was easy and possible to pass as a man. Indeed some individual passing women, such as Adelaide Dallamore, explicitly said so. At the very same moment that cross-dressing reinforced ideal masculinity it also undermined its authority as 'natural' and exposed its fragility.

Did cross-dressing women reinforce gender conventions after a brief period of carnivalesque froth and fun? Or did they pose a more troubling presence behind the humour and light-heartedness? On balance, I would affirm the second inter-pretation for this period. Their representation as tricksters was a journalistic deci-sion. But it unleashed a wide range of anarchic possibilities, including the licence to expose the deep-seated illusion of gender fixity. Having moved between mascu-line and feminine, they were poised to comment on one of the most persistently unsettling fractures in British society – the meaning of gender and the position of women. On this they sometimes offered equivocal parables, but generally they celebrated freedom and possibility. They also emphatically laid bare male privi-lege. With the enduring power of their ambiguity and joking actions, passing women consistently brushed away authority, not because they altogether escaped punishment in the courts, but because they did not take it seriously. A familiar figure in a recognised formula story, the trickster cross-dresser was appealing in her androgyny, her lack of respect for the proper conventions and her jesting individualism. She incited popular delight in the outlaw.

2 Sexuality, love and marriage

The gender-crossing woman as female husband

Courtship, romance and even cohabitation and marriage between a masquerading woman and her female partner were central to the entertaining strangeness of almost all cross-dressing stories.[1] Headlines drew attention to this particularly extraordinary aspect of the disguised woman's life. The Adelaide Dallamore story highlighted the same-sex love angle as: 'Woman as Husband. Amazing Romance of Two Chiswick Girls'[2] while sub-titles such as 'Woman Woos Woman' or 'Fond of Girls' (this last was Ernest Wood) were common.[3] This chapter examines the ways in which sexuality was represented in gender-crossing narratives. From the 1900s to the late 1920s, love-making (in this period meaning kissing and cuddling, or 'spooning') between women was presented in popular culture as intrinsically harmless – it was certainly not seen as sexually deviant. In many female husband stories, as the first part of the chapter will show, love between women was portrayed as both passionate and honourable. Yet within both the press stories and music hall male impersonation there were many levels of address to the audience and reader around love between women, and I will suggest that the erotic appeal of the male impersonator was also at play in the telling of real life cross-dressing stories. While the humour and context of both forms were based on heterosexuality, they were open to a range of readings. The second part of the chapter will discuss various types of text to show that there was a continuum of possible readings of the gender-crosser, ranging from the respectably sexy to the hidden knowledge of pornography. This wider sexual hinterland is demonstrated first for women wearing male military uniform and then for the potential connection between cross-dressing and sex between women.

Love between women in the press stories

The loving relationships between the cross-dressed woman and her female partner were explored in detail in some press stories. Full descriptions were given of the passionate and loving nature of these attachments between women, which were also idealised in immensely positive terms as respectable and honourable. These virtues were strongly invoked in the accounts of the female marriages of Adelaide Dallamore and Harry Lloyd. Adelaide Dallamore, the plumber's mate, lived as a young married man with a new wife, Jessie Mann. They had 'set up house together in Chiswick' as Mr and Mrs Dallamore, and on discovery in 1912 declared to the press that they had done this because of their love for each other. '"We have always been very fond of one another," [Dallamore] said, explaining the reason of [sic] the escapade.' Jessie's family wanted to part the couple and were urging Jessie to marry a man she did not like and so 'we agreed that the only way out of the difficulty was for me to become "a man," take Jessie away quietly, and live with her as a "husband."'⁴ According to Adelaide's account, they had lived an exemplary married life together, spending most of their leisure with each other. They went out walking after work, sometimes went to the theatre (where, who knows, they may have enjoyed male impersonation on stage) but spent most evenings quietly at home. They read many books together and Mr Dallamore tried her hand at writing short stories, though none to her satisfaction. They thus typified wholesome and respectable artisan marriage and instructive rational recreation. They were 'a sort of model couple' and said they never quarrelled once.

Their passion for each other was made clear throughout the account. Their actions in challenging Jessie's parents and eloping were described in the language of romance from the beginning of the report: 'not often does it happen that a girl, for love of another girl, will put on men's clothes and live and work as a man, playing "husband" to her friend's "wife"', which went on to describe them as 'such devoted "pals"'. Dallamore told the *News of the World*: '"We've felt more like lovers to each other than friends, haven't we, dear?" The "wife" readily assented; it was plain even to a stranger that the affection between the two girls was much more than common.'⁵ The newspaper treats this as an extreme form of female friendship, an unusually strong but not unacceptable bond between two women, and uses a language of love which suggests a parallel with heterosexual courtship and marriage.

Harry Lloyd's decision to pass as the husband of Eliza Lloyd and to bring up her daughter following Eliza's death, was presented as displaying the highest masculine virtues of honour and chivalry. There was only a brief description of the long-ago marriage, which had appeared to be a 'strange match' to the neighbours. This may have been due to differences in education or age – Harry would have been in her early fifties, while Eliza was much younger. Eliza's child had been born illegitimate in Hackney Infirmary and in piecing together the evidence in 1910 the coroner assumed that Harry Lloyd 'was attached to Miss Lloyd's mother [i.e. Eliza Lloyd], and that in order to protect her honour in her lifetime passed as her husband . . . [which was] a very pathetic and kind reason [born of] . . . unselfish love.' Any sense of scandal or wrongdoing was associated with Eliza Lloyd's heterosexual veniality in having a child out of wedlock. Harry Lloyd's masquerade repaired this socially and was an act of unselfish protection: 'the little Frenchwoman, with the impulsive chivalry of her race, assumed the garb of manhood to shield a woman's honour'.⁶ Since the prime motive was assumed to be protection from social censure, and as Harry Lloyd was at the time of death passing as an old man, a widower who had lost his wife 20 years earlier, sexual feelings seem very much in the background.

Yet further threads appear in this account as it moves into the style of a detective story. The earlier life of Marie Le Roy, who, it was argued, had become Harry Lloyd, revealed plenty of evidence of her recurrent passions for other women, though the reporter professed to be mystified as to why she should wish to live with another woman as her husband. In the 1870s, Marie le Roy, the educated daughter of a French army officer, had mixed in freethinking circles around Charles Bradlaugh and Austin Holyoake in London. For three years she had worked as a governess to Mrs Holyoake's children and became 'exceedingly attached' to her. Mrs Holyoake told the *News of the World* that 'her devotion to me was quite remarkable. Though she was so tiny I got to look upon her as "a big brother".' As a young woman she was represented as an independent 'new woman', wearing her hair short and appearing quite mannish-looking with her square jaw, although physically petite. In subsequent years Marie Le Roy lectured and taught French at the Freethinkers' Hall of Science. One member described how she had then gone to live with another woman Freethinker in Hackney. 'These two had been very much attached to each other at the Hall of Science.' Plenty of evidence of passionate attachment and strong feeling between women was expressed in this story, yet this is not mobilised as an explanation for how she came to live with Mrs Lloyd as her husband. This is a 'romantic mystery' which 'still remained unsolved'.[7]

The female couples in these narratives are permitted to express intense feelings of love for each other and reject heterosexuality without criticism or censure. Unusually, there is no conventional resolution to the stories. Most domestic dramas and comedies (including cross-dressing trickster plots such as *Twelfth Night*) end with a wedding or other means of reinstating gender, family and patriarchal hierarchies.[8] But in these twentieth-century stories from popular culture there is no satisfactory closure, leaving profound questions about gendered behaviour and love between women still hanging in the air. In the Dallamore narrative there is no formulaic heterosexual resolution such as Jessie's marriage to the man she had earlier rejected, and while the marriage between the two young women is broken up, their relationship is shown to be close and strong, and both assert that it will continue.

The Dallamore and Lloyd marriages develop ideal conceptualisations of both masculine and feminine character. The cross-dressing husband is shown to be honourable in her conduct, fulfilling the chivalrous and protective roles of a man, while both partners are credited with loyalty to each other and deeply loving affection. Long-term marital relationships between women were accepted in Victorian bourgeois circles, as Martha Vicinus and Sharon Marcus show.[9] Across all classes, marriage primarily signified social recognition, stability and kinship, and was only secondarily seen as a location for sexual activity. These cross-dressing women were certainly respectable, in so far as they fitted into the social ideal of marriage. Yet intense homoerotic feelings were strongly conveyed in these accounts and the active pursuit of same-sex love through passing as a man was also represented as a mystery and a conundrum.

The erotic appeal of the male impersonator

In her general sexual appeal, humour and sentimentality, the male impersonator on stage offers one important context to help unpick the varied meanings of same-sex love at play in the female husband stories. The theatrical gender-crosser acted out different kinds of sexualised characters and situations and appealed in a number of ways to both women and men in the audience. Both the popular Sunday press and the music halls trod a thin line between the claim to respectability and the attractions of vulgarity. This was an issue facing the music hall as it modernised into self-styled 'variety theatre', controlled by big business, offering ever-improving environments and trying to attract a more middle-class audience. Theatres had long been associated with heterosexual immorality, in the persons of the actresses themselves and the prevalence of prostitution in and around theatre buildings. It was enormously difficult for female performers to retain respectability, such was the generally low reputation of the profession in its presumed proximity to vice.[10] The turn-of-the-century campaigns to improve morality in the music halls focused on the flesh-revealing costumes of the chorus and ballet girls and the rampant soliciting by highly painted women in the bars and promenades. Indecent lyrics and the sexual suggestiveness of some performers were also abhorred.[11] Following the trials of Oscar Wilde in 1895, the association of the theatre with aestheticism and homosexual degeneracy, and the use of particular theatres for gay cruising, was also a periodic if less clearly expressed concern for some commentators.[12]

The press often used the theatre as code for a world with lower moral standards and 'fast' living. It was a liminal space where the sexes mixed freely and where people (especially women) performed in revealing clothes. Long before the ubiquitous bathing belles of the interwar years, it offered an acceptable opportunity to depict lightly clad young women. The *News of the World* ran a photograph in 1914 of five or six 'Lady Music-hall Artistes' playing football clad in shorts; their cross-gendered display a vehicle for showing their legs.[13] Show-business gossip received increasing press attention in the early decades of the twentieth century, ranging from discussion of actresses' future roles and their weddings to titled gents, to their disreputable behaviour in night-clubs and subsequent divorce proceedings. Still a key provider of mass entertainment, variety theatre was usually reviewed in the entertainment pages of the Sunday newspapers in positive or anodyne terms. Like the Sunday press itself, popular theatre was, if only on the surface, respectable entertainment for all the family.

Above and beneath this surface, multiple forms of address offered titillation from the stage and page, in the 'knowing' delivery of songs and the coded hints of sexual activity. Peter Bailey has developed the concept of 'knowingness' to suggest that although music hall songs may have seemed innocuous on paper, it was in their delivery that propriety and social hierarchy were challenged. The performer could argue for an innocent reading of the words of their songs (as Marie Lloyd famously did), but make opportunities for ambiguity through a repertoire of winks, gestures and catchphrases, a kind of collusion with the audience to create a shared sense of defying respectability. Audiences could enjoy filling the gaps with sexual meanings as they pleased, at various levels of sophistication.[14]

How far can we extend this concept to the newspaper readership, to make an analogy between stage innuendo and the use of euphemism and the potential for multiple readings of press accounts? Obviously there is no live performance to add sexual suggestiveness to the words of newspaper reports. Reading alone, or in the family group or pub, was a different experience from that shared with a large theatre audience. But the use of humour and the mysterious angles in the cross-dresser's story might signal that further levels underlay the superficial presentation of the account.[15] We should also bear in mind that the pleasure of 'knowingness' may not include knowledge of anything concrete. Part of the reward for many in the audience or readers of the press, from the mysterious or half-heard joke or odd circumstance, is the pleasure of sharing in a moment of possible transgression, however vaguely defined. Vulgarity or the forbidden is signalled, even if we cannot get to the bottom of it.

Women presented all kinds of turns on the variety stage: as acrobats and animal tamers, and as performers of sentimental and romantic songs. The male impersonator was just one of these women, each of whom was displaying and selling her skills, and dispensing various kinds of parasexuality: that is, a freely projected but closely managed sense of sexuality, a glamorous promise offered from a distance.[16] The male impersonator employed a heterogeneous erotic appeal, presenting all kinds of sexual pleasure and amusement. In the first place, her physical presence had in common with other women performers the sexual appeal of the female body on display. It was customary for music hall singers to reveal their arms and décolletage, but wearing tight-fitting men's trousers emphasised instead the shape of the legs, hips and buttocks and provocatively half-hid the curves of the breasts, waist and hips within the masculine cut of the suit. This offered voyeuristic satisfaction to the men in the audience, and identification, glamour and homoeroticism for the women to savour. Even if the assertive, rumbustious impersonator became increasingly feminised and restrained in her female masculinity in the early twentieth century, it does not follow that this more androgynous breed of male impersonator was less sexually attractive to the audience. The principal boy type may have been no less unsettling in her inexplicable allure of both feminine and masculine than the big roaring male impersonators of late nineteenth-century legend – these were simply different varieties of erotic appeal.[17]

The songs of the male impersonators, as they parodied various male characters, addressed the audience in an explicitly sexual manner. In the case of the swell, or ladies' man, the burlesque was of a highly sexual man, and thus charged with suggestive eroticism, even if the aim was to deflate his power. Peter Bailey writes that the swell song (as performed by men) was about the sexuality of display, and while he notes that the meaning of his patter, and his 'stage business' with accessories such as walking sticks and handkerchiefs is largely lost to us now, it was undoubtedly sexualised.[18] When male impersonators adopted these gestures and accoutrements in parody and strutted and postured onstage they were certainly borrowing a sexual charge. Laurence Senelick argues that, because they were gender-crossing, women performers could go further in their portrayal of these dubious masculine types and their assertive sexual swagger and attitudes, than would have been possible for the men performers themselves.[19]

In this period 'knowingness' – whether in the reception of music hall acts, on saucy postcards, or in the popular press – was predominantly reliant upon heterosexual readings. Both respectable courtship and more raffish 'picking up' were recurrent themes in male impersonators' repertoires. Some of their songs conjured up the tensions and feelings of heterosexual courtship, recounting barriers to romance and how they were overcome, or the heartbreak of losing sweethearts. These songs, such as Vesta Tilley's ballad 'The Girl I Left Behind Me', sung by the male impersonator about another (unseen) woman evoked the sentimental intensity of youthful passion and romance.[20] But in parts of their act, male impersonators recurrently savoured the delights of watching the girls' dresses blow up in windy weather and celebrated the pleasures and perils of the 'experienced' girl: 'Been married *twice*, is game for *more*'.[21] Ella Shields' bluffing Percy, 'the great and mighty monarch of the boulevard', picks up a 'very hot' lady in 'gay Paree', who spends all his money on food and wine and then tries to rob him:

> Percy's curly hair, he thought had conquered her
> Until he saw her try to gain the pocket with his watch and chain;
> Then Percy slapped her wrist and said, 'You naughty, naughty girl!
> Oh, maiden, have a care! Not there, my child, not there!'[22]

After the honeymoon, working-class marriage, as explored in popular songs and jokes, revolved not around sexuality but around the problems of domestic relationships, the revelation of a spouse's true character, the nagging wife and the drinking dissolute husband.[23] Male impersonators gleefully related the shock in store for the wild young blade.

> Of lots of girls you are the beau
> When you're a single man . . .
> But when you're married, when you're married,
> You live upon a highly proper plan;
> You give up girls and giddy life,
> Or if you don't there's certain strife,
> They only let you have one wife when you're a married man.[24]

Sexual humour in the press stories

While press stories were less raucous in their presentation than music hall songs often were, I suggest that knowingness and sexual humour leached into the portrayal of cross-dressing women and their activities in courtship and marriage. Marital conflict around erring husbands featured in a few short reports, creating slapstick humour on a familiar theme. Thirty-seven-year-old Alice Elbourne drew a crowd around her in the streets of St Pancras in London, when she dressed up in men's clothes in March 1914. Arrested for disorderly behaviour, she told the magistrate she had done it to catch her husband, who was going out with another woman.[25] A recurring joke which drew attention to the potential for heterosexual hanky-panky was that of the cross-dressing young woman who shares a bed or bedroom with unknowing young men. In 1915 this formed part of the story of Martha Hodson, who was variously reported as having shared a bed with her land-lady's son for six weeks, with the landlady's husband, or at another lodgings with a young man who was engaged to be married.[26] Ernest Wood similarly 'occup[ied] a bedroom with half a dozen or so other lads with whom he worked'.[27] As well as the sexual innuendo of a young woman half-dressed among a group of young men this also speaks of the cross-dresser's skill as a trickster. In this potentially intimate situation, her sex was not revealed or suspected, and her peers were fooled.

The multiple conquests of the swell-about-town are brought to mind in the story of Ernest Wood. Described as a dandy and 'rather fond of the ladies', she had three girlfriends, one of whom she referred to as her fiancée.[28] Her manager, Mr Broggio, described how she 'seemed particularly sweet on' one of the kitchen girls: 'she would even chaff her and say, "When are you going to take me to the pictures?"'[29] These bamboozled girlfriends were subsequently covered in confu-sion as they groped for appropriate gender pronouns and sought to minimise their foolishness. One of the girls Ernest was 'walking out with' was Rina Bachini, a 'pretty, vivacious Italian dressmaker', who said she found it impossible to believe he was not a boy.

> We used to go out together, but we were not sweethearts; you must not think that. Sometimes he came here to see my mother. He was very polite. I wanted to improve my English, and that was one reason why I went out with him. He spoke so beautifully. But he had another sweetheart. She is a Miss Taylor . . . I think he was rather fond of the ladies.[30]

The other girls said much the same. Gladys Smith went out to the pictures with Ernie: 'Ernest's conversation was always entertaining, and he never became at all foolish, nor did he ever try to make love. He simply seemed a very good pal who was anxious to be as nice and friendly as possible.' She had seen him with one or two other girls. 'But as we were not sweethearting I never thought anything about that sort of thing.'[31] The gentle humour draws on the comedy of the courting couple and their sexual ignorance – which the reader has to be knowing enough to appreciate.[32]

The Adelaide Dallamore story also utilises humour along with the powerful sentimentality found in the music hall. The *News of the World* described some light-hearted exchanges between the two girls as they recollect the difficulty in tying Adelaide's first tie. The joking may divert attention away from the transgressive possibilities of two girls rejecting conventional family life because of their passionate love for each other. At the same time it opens up space for further reading, as their reported laughter works to emphasise the warmth of the relation-ship. The homoerotic appeal of the male impersonator, as well as the strength of

Jessie's feelings, are evident in her appraisal of Adelaide's appearance: 'And you looked so nice in men's clothes! Better than in skirts!'[33]

In a rather melodramatic final paragraph, the couple responded sadly when questioned about the break-up of their home: '"Why couldn't they have left us alone? We were so happy together, weren't we, darling?" said the "husband", sniffing suspiciously. "Yes, love!" exclaimed the "wife", wiping her eyes. "But they shall never, never part us!"' This sentimentality also works ambiguously. Its histrionic flavour could suggest they are merely playing at marriage – playing not just in the sense of performing the roles of husband and wife, but also that this is inconsequential – it is just an entertaining game after all. On the other hand, it also conveys the strength of their feelings, the pleasure and satisfaction they derived in their marriage and Jessie's assertion that their relationship will continue.

In the Dallamore story and other accounts, the relationship between the cross-dressing woman and her wife or girlfriend is idealised as a perfect romance. 'We were supremely happy together . . . We never quarrelled once', said the Dallamores.[34] Several newspapers published a comment by one of Ernest Wood's girlfriends, that: 'He seemed to understand girls better than most boys of my acquaintance do.'[35] All the wives and girlfriends emphasised the unusual understanding and considerateness of their partners, implying that women can make extremely attractive lovers – thoughtful and romantic. This ability is a measure of the cross-dresser's skill as a true trickster, becoming the handsome and sentimental lover of fantasy who unites characteristics of both sexes in her movement between them. It is also a comment on the limitations of heterosexual partnerships, a critique of conventional marriage.

Just as the male impersonator is sexually attractive in her androgyny, so the cross-dressing woman in the press stories contains the liminal appeal of both sexes. Since each was constantly shifting between being a man among men, a man with a woman, and a woman with a woman, what kinds of cultural spaces were there for more risqué or eroticised readings? The fluid relationship between the theatre and the popular press as forms of entertainment means that female husband stories are part of a continuum of increasingly hidden knowledges about sexuality – both heterosexual and same-sex. Knowingness about sexuality in this period moved along a tremendously wide sliding scale which included the gentle jokes about courting couples found in the press, the suggestive innuendo in many popular songs, and the bawdy sexual humour within ostensibly innocent Edwardian comic postcards.[36]

In order to investigate the different levels of address (and potential for multiple readings, ranging from the innocuous to the explicitly erotic), we need to examine the reading contexts within and beyond the theatre, such as picture postcards and pornography. As Sharon Marcus observes, 'pornography and mainstream culture share an erotic repertoire'.[37] The image of the woman in military uniform will be discussed first, tracking a range of mainly heterosexual meanings. Then a similar continuum of homoerotic reading contexts for two women together in courtship and marriage will be followed. In understanding how the mechanism of knowingness worked in print culture, Anna Clark's concept of 'twilight moments' is useful.

This refers to the conceptual gap between the socially approved and the abject or forbidden, wherein lay sexual desires and sexualised readings only half-understood by individuals or only partly acknowledged in culture.[38]

Women in military uniform

In Chapter 1 we saw that women who cross-dressed to enlist or serve in war industries were applauded for their patriotism and lent the cachet of military hypermasculinity. Male military uniform has been widely discussed as imbued with the symbolic meanings of national spirit and imperial power. It identifies those who wear it as patriotic elite men representing the nation and their solidarity with weighty war aims.[39] Encasing the highest form of masculinity, uniform acted as a powerful and remarkably elastic sexual signifier. The well-established erotic charge of military uniform – the bright red tunics of guardsmen, the smart headgear, neat lines and shiny metal accessorising of other troops – gave a gloss to heterosexual masculinity and was a socially recognised provocation to women's libidinal energies.[40] It also possessed a longstanding, if more hidden, potency in relation to male homosexual desire.[41]

What of the woman in masculine uniform? Feminist historians have focused on women's military uniform as an empowering public signifier for those who wore it and as an effective way of establishing women's right to contribute to the wartime national struggle. They have also drawn attention to the masculinising look of uniform on women, especially in this period when it was new, and to the frequently hostile response this provoked in attacks on women's claim to a stake in the public sphere.[42] In discussing postwar responses to women in uniform Laura Doan suggests that the 'female body dressed in masculine or male uniform produces surprisingly diverse spectatorial effects'.[43] What has been noted far less often – though it was clearly a very significant part of the cultural reception of women in uniform – is the widespread response to women in military attire as attractive and erotic.[44] There was an expanding public sexualisation of women in uniform during the First World War, a heterosexual dynamic extending from the jolly fun of the male impersonator as a Tommy (private soldier) to more illicit sexual meanings.

We have seen how this worked on the music hall stage. J. S. Bratton stresses the enthusiastic reception of male impersonators in uniform: 'Reviewers found realistically correct uniforms and parodically or provocatively modified ones equally appealing.'[45] 'Ella Shields . . . in uniform is well-nigh irresistible', declared the *News of the World*.[46] The spectacle of women's volunteer corps drilling and marching in uniform drew large crowds and much newspaper comment, especially in the first two years of the war.[47] The uniforms were often described in detail: '[T]he smart khaki Norfolk coat, short slit skirt, and soft felt hat worn by the officers are quite charming, and most becoming to a pretty woman, besides being thoroughly practical.'[48] The *Daily Mail* presented a more equivocal and also more sexual picture of women in khaki: 'in short skirts, with their hair either cropped or hidden under their felt hats, and slapping their riding-boots with their whips'.[49] Photographs of women in military uniform or doing masculine work in trousers were commonly featured in the popular press, addressing a public appetite for such images, as well as being an easy resource in a period when actual war news was censored.

But women's adoption of masculine uniform, while found attractive, was not always, in practice, straightforwardly celebrated. The wearing of military uniform by those not entitled to do so was a criminal offence at all times, and it was further regulated during the First World War by the 1914 Defence of the Realm Act. Theatrical male impersonators were not prevented from incorporating military uniforms into their acts, however, and all the main stars did so.[50] While these performers were positively appraised, and women in ordinary male clothing attempting to enlist were described as demonstrating pluck and patriotism, individual women wearing male military uniform in civilian contexts were sometimes arrested and punished. Their behaviour was interpreted in a number of ways, not all of which are transparent, but which were often associated with heterosexual immorality.

The fears of the authorities were expressed in a 1915 case when 'Masquerading Marie', a young woman of 21, was arrested on the streets of Stratford, east London, and charged with 'masquerading in a sailor's uniform, her action being likely to bring contempt on His Majesty's uniform'. She told the court the uniform was her husband's and she had been to have her photograph taken in it: 'It is only a joke.' But the magistrate warned her she was lucky to get off with a caution rather than a heavy fine. The Bench 'were obliged to take a serious view of this sort of thing' in wartime. If people wore uniforms which were not their own, 'we know exactly what happens. They defraud the public perhaps; it may lead to the grossest misconduct, and even to spying'.[51] Her husband was present in court and clearly did not take the judicial telling-off seriously, since he laughed when she was given a caution.

There seems to have been a strong clash of interpretations here, between the state's perspective on women in men's uniform and that of the general public. What was going on when Marie Hodge decided to have her photo taken? She was not trying to pass as a man. Her actions have echoes of fancy dress and theatrical activity; indeed are redolent of the publicity postcards of famous actresses, including male impersonators. In a domestic context there appears to have been some deliberate appropriation of the sexual power of the uniform, combined with a desire to commemorate this action. It was not uncommon for women to have photographs taken of themselves in military uniform.[52] When women put on their boyfriends' or husbands' uniforms they could be expressing all kinds of motives and feelings such as pride in their men's loyalty and patriotism, while creating a memento for their husbands or themselves. They were also generating a frisson of amusement, sexual pleasure and personal power, both for their partners and themselves, by replicating the image of the male impersonators.

An understanding of the sexual magnetism of the woman in uniform was also at work in public heterosocial spaces, as other crime stories suggest, and was punished by the authorities as potential, if not actual, sexual misconduct. The young women arrested in military uniform were strikingly consistent in claiming the immunity of the jester as an alternative framework for their actions, sometimes successfully. Jane McGregor admitted that she had had drinks in two public houses in Chatham while wearing the uniform of an officer of the Royal Engineers in January 1917. She assured the magistrate that 'it was only a joke'.[53] Two girls, dressed as a sailor and soldier, were prosecuted for being drunk and disorderly after going out late at night with three soldiers in Birmingham, though the charges of wearing military uniform were dropped. Their behaviour, 'jostling people about, bumping into windows and behaving generally in a disorderly manner', was clearly linked to immorality, since the women were in the company of men late at night, were young and were drunk.[54]

As judicial anxiety around these cases involving women in pubs indicates, cross-dressing in military uniform had some power in the commercial market for heterosexuality. When Emily Wilkinson, aged 29, was arrested in Victoria Street (London) for 'insulting behaviour' (i.e. soliciting), she was wearing the full uniform and cap of a captain in the Army Service Corps and reportedly said, 'I could get off better with the boys when in uniform.'[55] She was defiant on arrest, saying 'I am Capt Wilkinson, and you cannot touch me.'[56] A dramatic case was reported from Hull, involving two young women, one an actress, both sentenced to hard labour for keeping a disorderly house. Police watched as they 'ran out into the street dressed in the uniforms of 2 naval men who had undressed in the house.'[57] Several of these cases took place in dockyards and naval towns and were obviously addressing the particular sexual interests of some groups of men.

The sexual significance of women in military uniform is also apparent in popular iconography, such as picture postcards which were important as a mass visual form, produced for a pan-European commercial market and widely used from the turn of the century. They are significant for this study because they link very different types of market and image – the glamorous publicity postcards of actresses on the one hand, and the undercover erotica market on the other. Suggestive jokes and imagery involving women in military uniform, especially from the Women's Auxiliary Army Corps, frequently appeared on comic postcards of the First World War. These had punchlines such as: 'Would you prefer a slap in the face – or a WAAC on the knee?', and offered varying degrees of approval or hostility towards women's military roles, coupled with sexual innuendo.[58] Women in male uniform also featured as a minor trope in heterosexual pornography during the war. Erotic postcards printed in France, but also circulating in Britain, pictured semi-naked feminine women trying on soldiers' caps and posing provocatively with guns, greatcoats and stockings.[59] What kinds of sexual dynamics and power relations were operating here? Masculine uniform on a sexualised feminine body flatters male power, and the contrast between a stiff uniform and female curves and make-up heightens gender difference and heterosexual allure. At the relatively respectable level of parasexuality, this appeal was that of the principal boy look, but at a more transgressive erotic level it might be linked to clothing fetishism or a submerged male homoerotic desire. Cross-dressing undoubtedly has a place in heterosexual eroticism, but, like the complexities of heterosexual desire generally, this is an under-researched topic in the history of sexuality.[60]

The polymorphous sexual appeal of the woman in masculine uniform also had an erotic charge for women. The double glamour of the boyish performer on stage in military uniform may have worked on all kinds of levels – evoking heterosexual feelings for a boyfriend in uniform, or a particular attachment to that performer and her roles. The woman who commissioned a studio or private photograph of herself in uniform may have had a variety of motives, not least her own pleasure in adopting the signifiers of masculine authority and sexuality. The sense of power and social recognition lent by wearing uniform was an effect which women themselves readily commented on during the First World War.[61] When pictured with another woman, homoerotic readings demand consideration. The context may have been fancy dress: cross-dressing was always a favourite choice for costume parties. It may have been a desire to identify across gender and imagine oneself passing as a man. It may have been an expression of same-sex desire, demonstrating sexual assertiveness through masculine clothing. In middle-class circles we know that some women who developed uniformed organisations, such as the women police, were not only constructing a self-image as powerful women, but also signalling their own sexual identity as women who desired women.[62] What is much more difficult to reach, however, is the leverage that this reading or spectatorial effect had for working-class or lower middle-class women.

Women's cross-dressing, popular culture and homoeroticism

Without being tied to a specific sexual identity in this period, women's gender-crossing was undoubtedly presented and enjoyed as resonantly homoerotic. Pleasure in homoeroticism should not be elided with awareness of homosexual practice.[63] There was certainly no clear conceptualisation in early twentieth-century popular culture of sex between women. There has been little historical investigation either into same-sex relationships among working- and lower middle-class women, or into perceptions about such relationships in British mass culture.[64] As far as we know there was no equivalent for women of the drag balls or meeting places for cross-dressing queer men.[65] Successful passing women, in fact, present an entirely contrasting picture. Their lives were lived in isolation from other women who cross-dressed, albeit within a recognised cultural tradition. Both cross-dressing stories and male impersonation projected powerful representations of love between women and a passionate homoeroticism which came only gradually, in later decades, to be reductively identified as lesbianism. Cross-dressing in combination with female marriage might convey various meanings to different readers, including an honourable love relationship, passionate homoeroticism, or a sexual practice made explicit in the twilight world of pornography, without being fixed into any particular one of these.

There is plenty of evidence of women's homoerotic response to male impersonators. Clearly there was a wide female fan base for these performers. As for the other leading actresses of the day, many picture postcards were sold to promote male impersonators throughout the Edwardian period and into the First World War and were avidly collected by fans.[66] Turn over these postcards and we find messages from one friend to another: – 'Dear Flo, As promised here is the P. C. of your Hetty.'[67] Of Vesta Tilley: 'Have you ever seen her she is splendid and so smart' (see Figure 3).[68] 'Another one to add to your collection . . . Vesta is coming here to open the new Hippodrome in December.'[69] 'I think you will like this card something like the last.'[70] There is also evidence that male impersonators were wooed by admiring women – they certainly inspired obsessive crushes among their female fans. Vesta Tilley wrote: 'Each post brought piles of letters, varying from an impassioned declaration of undying love to a request for an autograph . . . or a piece of ribbon I had worn.' 'During one of my tours I received masses of most beautiful flowers from a girl who apparently followed me from town to town during the whole trip' and who took a box for each performance.[71] The wide-spread shared culture among women of admiring and following the stars of male impersonation produced compelling erotic pleasure but was not seen as sexually transgressive behaviour.[72]

Theatrical postcards normally depicted the male impersonator alone. This was a solo act and she rarely appeared with another woman on the music hall stage. As a 'masher' or romantic lover the male impersonator addressed an imaginary woman. Yet in pantomime or light comedy roles, women dressed as men did appear as the lovers or consorts of feminine women, and this was sometimes pictured in theatrical postcards.[73] Such publicity photographs were designed to promote performers' careers, and while making play with parasexuality, did not suggest there was anything particularly risqué about the roles they were performing as a female couple. Indeed the image of two women romantically posed together, one cross-dressed as a man, was a common motif for general picture postcards. These postcards, published on the continent, were popular before and after the First World War, and while they drew on theatrical poses and sometimes costume, used anonymous models. Sent through the post in the ordinary way, these seem to have been presented and enjoyed as any card of a pretty or glamorous woman pictured alone would have been. At one level, they were as innocently sweet and romantic as similar depictions of cute pairs of children or baby animals were.[74]

Yet the theatre, as we have seen, was figured as part of the demi-monde, where greater sexual laxity was to be expected and feared. The milieu of the stage may well have included heterosexual prostitution and male homosexuality in the public imagination, but in this period (at least until the 1918 scandal associated with Maud Allan) this general sense of immorality did not stretch to sex between women. Martha Vicinus argues that theatrical transvestism was one source of modern lesbian identity and style for women in elite and bohemian networks.[75] Some performers who worked as male impersonators, such as Beatrice Lilley, were part of homosexual circles during the 1910s and 1920s, but gossip about their sexuality would not have been generally known to their working-class audiences.[76]

One newspaper story about a male impersonator who also cross-dressed off-stage evokes the seamier side of the theatre world, though in ways which are quite difficult to unpick. It concerns a woman named René La Vie who was charged in July 1911 with loitering in Croydon High Street, dressed in male attire for a

VESTA TILLEY

*Have you ever seen her al
so splendid & so smart.*

Figure 3 Postcard of Vesta Tilley, 1907. From the author's collection.

supposedly unlawful purpose. A police constable described how he had seen her in male attire after 10 p.m. speaking to a man outside the Grand Theatre, with whom she went into a public house. She then came outside and spoke to another man. Her hair was cut short, giving her a boyish appearance, and she had been seen earlier in the week smoking cigarettes and a calabash pipe. It is likely that she was arrested on suspicion of soliciting (or even importuning if the police had believed she really was a man). René La Vie told police she was doing it for a bet. She was a male impersonator on the stage and the men she had been speaking to were members of the theatrical company. Some of the issues about the seedy relationship between the theatre, homosexuality, prostitution and sexually independent actresses were suggested in this story, but lesbianism was not among them and respectable closure was achieved when La Vie's story was accepted and the case was dismissed.[77]

Cross-dressing did carry 'lesbian' meanings in pornography. Risqué continental postcards certainly circulated in Britain, though the extent to which they penetrated popular consciousness is unknown. Lisa Sigel suggests that pornographic postcards were openly sold in corner shops and on the streets of Edwardian London, and were part of a new commodity culture. Postcards and peepshow exhibitions made sexual imagery available to working-class consumers, including women and children.[78] Vendors of indecent pictures did not see them as inappropriate; one young woman used an entertainment defence, arguing that the postcards she sold were either 'comic' or high art.[79]

Most erotic postcards reflected hegemonic formulations of sexuality – the white female body in various states of undress, exoticised and sexualised images of people of colour, or heterosexual bedding scenes. However, other cards were more transgressive, depicting interracial sexual desire, fetishism and same-sex eroticism.[80] In some images a woman and her cross-dressed partner appear in contexts – the wedding night or undressing scenes – in which sexuality between women is made explicit. We can see this kind of soft porn as lying at the end of a continuum which begins with the eroticised figure of the male impersonator. Ambiguity and humour also adhere to these images. One series of 10 cards depicts the wedding night of two women, one cross-dressed (see Figure 4).The feminine partner removes her outer clothes and reveals one breast, while the woman dressed as a man is positioned as the active pleasure-seeking suitor, blindfolded for a time to suggest forbidden desire.[81] The tone is light-hearted mimicry of the wedding night. While the two women end up under the covers in bed together, their feet are poking out in a row at the bottom, not entangled up in each other. One reading could still be that of respectable sisterly bed-sharing. This type of soft porn offers lesbian possibilities for those who wished to read them. The involvement of two women in a wedding night series, which in other pornographic narratives inevitably leads to sexual intercourse, indicates that a knowledge of sex between women was explored within erotica if only as a minor trope. In Paris or Berlin, in the context of a more developed lesbian sub-culture and more explicit cabaret performance, these images would have had a more widely recognised meaning as female homosexuality.[82] This type of card was probably less common in Britain, but it does show that a knowledge of lesbian sexuality existed, however restricted in its circulation.

The sexually explicit postcards rarely carry hand-written messages, unlike the picture postcards of theatrical male impersonators or glamorous romantic female couples. The latter were widely understood and acceptable as part of popular culture, and were publicly circulated by mail and shared among friends and family. The more daringly erotic cards were known of or owned anonymously by a minority, and illustrate twilight forms of knowledge – exploring and laying bare the sexual possibilities behind the glamour and eroticisation of male impersonation, cross-dressing courtship and the female husbands of the newspaper stories.

Sex between women in the press

Possible awareness of these more hidden knowledges occasionally surfaced in press stories, in hints of disquiet about the love relationships between cross-dressing women and their girlfriends. Some anxious comments about the Dallamore couple were made by the perplexed journalist, who referred to their marriage at different points in the article as: 'the bold escapade', 'the strange menage' and 'the weird story'.[83] An earlier report quoted Adelaide Dallamore's sister, who said she 'was under the delusion that she was a man', suggesting family condemnation.[84]

Figure 4 Postcard from a series depicting a wedding night with a cross-dressing woman as husband, probably published in the 1900s. From the collection of Sarah Waters.

Jessie's family also disapproved. They had tried to part the couple before they eloped, and then reported their whereabouts to the police (who declined to take any action), tracked them down and tried to bring Jessie away. It was this which led to a street fight between Adelaide and Jessie's brother, and the subsequent arrest. Within both families, then, there was a sense of unease and a feeling that the masquerade had gone too far.

An atypical example of greater knowingness came in a 1911 *News of the World* article which told the life of Catherine Coombe, who had cross-dressed for 40 years and been unmasked back in 1897. A newly discovered manuscript by the author Charles Reade had recently been published in the *English Review*, and was abridged by the *News of the World*.[85] With this fictionalised version of the 'weird, androgynous Catherine Coombe', the newspaper imported terminology normally alien to cross-dressing stories. After marrying a painter, Tom Coombe, his young wife Kate decides to dress as his son, Fred, and work alongside him. But a young woman, Nellie, soon falls in love with her, 'to Tom's explosive amusement'. The story takes a light-hearted joking tone, with some melodramatic scenes. But the author also raises explicit questions about the morbidity of the relationship between the two young people, since 'Fred' fully reciprocates Nellie's love.

> The naughty hussy revelled in a novel excitement . . . Here we have, I grant, a phase of human emotion baffling analysis, and wholly escaping definition. Such a passion is in truth hybrid, perhaps morbid, perhaps insane, yet not outside the region of recorded fact. That it must yield nothing more satisfying than Dead Sea fruit does not militate against its existence.

Fred's desire for Nellie is described as pathological and barren, terms evoking late nineteenth-century concerns about degeneration and women's rejection of marriage and motherhood. Yet in the same paragraph it is also restated as nothing more than innocent fun: 'these lovers would sit down like harmless tabbies to the tea-table and muffin-worry, billing and cooing right pleasantly'.[86] This treatment of the story is a couple of steps removed from normal journalistic reporting of cross-dressing, since it is culled from a literary journal and fictionalised by the author. It may be the case that a more literary, educated awareness of sex between women via, for example, French literature, has been drawn into the popular press with this borrowing from the *English Review*. Originally written in the 1870s or 1880s, it may also reflect late nineteenth-century anxiety about the New Woman and her friendships in its use of language such as 'this strange androgyne'.[87]

The passion between Fred/Kate and Nellie is seen as mysterious, something found on the borders of human knowledge. As the 1911 Catherine Coombe story suggests, the twentieth-century recognition of sex between women depended upon the reworking of *fin-de-siècle* anxieties about sexuality, degeneracy and the arts. The concept of female homosexuality remained very opaque in the popular press. This obscure and hidden quality was also evident in the reporting of the sensational 1918 case in which the dancer Maud Allan sued the right-wing MP Noel Pemberton Billing for the libel that she was a lesbian. Part of the evidence was the planned appearance of Maud Allan in the play *Salome*, written by 'the moral and sexual pervert' Oscar Wilde and originally published in 1895, the year of Wilde's trial. While Allan's counsel tried to emphasise that the play depicted heterosexual passion, it was alleged by the other side to be 'full of homosexual inclinations'.[88] Maud Allan became 'the bearer of the Wildean decadent legacy'[89] in a number of ways, but it is at this point that the idea of active female sexuality, combined with the name of Oscar Wilde, begins to signal desire between women. The idea that there was a female parallel to Wildean vice was to resurface 10 years later, when the *Sunday Express* condemned Radclyffe Hall's novel *The Well of Loneliness* through a comparison with 'the Oscar Wilde scandal'.[90] 'Decadence' was a derogatory catch-all term for sexual vice by the 1920s, especially that linked to the avant-garde. While it derived from sexual science, eugenics and the debates about national degeneration, it did not necessarily imply any specific theories, but was used to indicate pathology and perversion in general.

Shadowy images of female homosexuality appeared more frequently after the First World War, but they continued to hark back to the 1890s and 1900s, to the *femme fatale* of *fin-de-siècle* decadence.[91] The Maud Allan trial suggested that the lesbian could be imagined as hyper-feminine and glamorous, linked to bohemian artistic freedom or to the decadent social elite. Sexological ideas of the mannish invert, which were beginning to influence some middlebrow writing from the end of the war, made no appearance in the popular press until *The Well of Loneliness* trial in 1928 and thus could not taint the cross-dressing story.[92] Sexual desire between women was represented as a feature of upper-class degeneracy, not as part of the working-class communities to which cross-dressing women belonged.

Reflecting fears about female sexual subjectivity, the decadent woman was invested with considerable seductive power, for example as the predatory wife-snatcher, threatening the private home. This seducer trope was used in the attack on Maud Allan's sexual character in 1918 when it was suggested that she had a dubious friendship with a married woman, Margot Asquith, wife of the prime minister.

> Did you go to Downing-street? – I did. – Did you dance? – No. – Did you see Mrs Asquith there? – Naturally, when I was her guest. – Have you met her anywhere else? – Yes. – Has she ever been in your dressing-room at the Palace? – Never. – You would recognise her, of course? – I have eyes.[93]

How clear were these codes for female same-sex love in the Sunday newspapers? The censored reporting and complexity of the evidence brought in the Maud Allan case meant the nature of the central allegation remained obscure in many press accounts, as Lucy Bland has shown.[94] The *News of the World*, alone of the popular Sunday newspapers, did publish in full the explicit language of the indictment that Maud Allan's 'private performances of an obscene and indecent character, [were] so designed as to foster and encourage unnatural practices among women, and that the said Maud Allan associated herself with persons addicted to unnatural practices'.[95] The report in the *People* was so abridged as to make the proceedings tantalising but unintelligible.[96] For many readers, no doubt, the Allan case was another story about the titillating sexual misdemeanours of the elite, however vague these were, with little connection to everyday life. Allan moved in upper middle-class circles, and her profession as a dancer rendered her a high-profile figure who was also on the moral margins.

Apart from the somewhat opaque reference in the Maud Allan case, the threat to married life posed by the predatory lesbian was first set out in the popular press in the reporting of the 1921 parliamentary debates on a clause which proposed to criminalise sex between women in the same way as male homosexuality.[97] The *News of the World* omitted the more explicit language and parts of the debate, but presented vivid images of the lesbian as asylum inmate or marriage wrecker. One MP (Sir Ernest Wild, later to preside over the Colonel Barker trial) told the story, which earned the sub-heading 'Married Life Was Ruined', of a man whose 'wife had been taken from him by a young woman'.[98] Among the cases known to 'all lawyers who have had criminal and divorce practice'[99] may have been one of 1915, reported in the *News of the World* with the judge's eugenicist comment as the headline: 'Not Fit to Marry'. The wife, an actress, held that her artist husband had agreed that their marriage 'should be a platonic union' and that her friend, another actress, should live with them. On the wedding night the wife 'slept in a room with her lady friend, petitioner sleeping at his wife's cottage, as had been previously arranged'. Some time later, after a violent quarrel, the wife asked her husband to leave, though he maintained that 'he never threatened to "ruin" her by going to all her friends'. The judge strongly condemned the wife's 'perfectly scandalous' and 'immoral' conduct which may be understood as both her refusal to have sex with her husband and her preference for intimacy with her woman friend.[100] This bohemian world of the theatre and the arts may have signalled further sexual possibilities to knowing readers.

In 1924, a good five years after the Maud Allan case, the *People* decided to alert its readers, in more explicit fashion than hitherto, about this modern moral danger, also promising to enlighten them about the real issues in the Allan case. '[A]ll sorts of accusations are made; these the public do not understand because, in detail, they are never printed. There is an air of mystery around it all; and London wonders and asks questions, only to be told vague things.' Again, there is an emphasis on mystery; homosexuality was an enigmatic concept which could not be properly known. In the first article, 'The Smear Across London', feature writer Hannen Swaffer wrote of a 'definite cult' of 'decadent' people (of both sexes), addicted to 'perversion' and 'the unnatural' who congregated around the theatre and literary world. This 'slime' was 'poisoning London . . . and menacing our future'.[101] The following week Leonora Eyles fleshed out these allusions a little further and applied them specifically to women.[102] The difficulty of writing about sexual relationships between women in the popular press in this period is emphasised by the awkward grammar and vocabulary of her title: 'Another Phase of "the Smear": Women Friendships that People Talk About.'[103] Adopting the glutinous and sexually loaded word 'smear', as well as the term 'decadence', throughout her article, Eyles spliced together a number of concerns, including a growing awareness that 'decadence' was also found among women, and the effects of this awareness on innocent friendships between professional women. She wrote about 'raves' in girls' schools, and the views of a psychoanalyst who blamed this 'sudden orgy of decadence' on the war and sex antagonism. Describing a very middle-class world, she implied that the vice was most likely to be found 'among artists, theatrical and society people'.[104] These articles sensationally introduced some middlebrow anxieties to a popular readership by suggesting a new threat of perversion, to be found among both women and men in a kind of modern gender equality.

Given its greater emphasis on features and opinion pieces, it is not surprising that it was the *People* that first revealed key images of same-sex female desire from the middle-class imagination to a working-class and lower middle-class readership. The types of women Eyles describes are all middle-class or elite, and as professional workers and divorcees they are undoubtedly also modern. Yet the Sunday press remained disinclined to draw much attention to lesbian stories, and these scenarios had little direct purchase in relation to the everyday life of working- or lower middle-class readers.

In none of the examples discussed above from the 1910s and 1920s are the women represented as particularly mannish in appearance. Maud Allan's stage persona drew upon long-established conventions of seductive femininity as well as on modern dance styles. Although Eyles quoted a psychoanalyst who appeared to draw on the British sexologists in linking female decadence to feminist politics, he did not cite their ideas of gender inversion. The same-sex seducers of the 1921 parliamentary debate and related stories of broken marriages were dangerous precisely because they were not distinguishable from normal women, according to most commentators, though their assertive sexuality and power to lure wives away may be read as masculine. Cross-dressing women of the 1920s thus remained immune from any association with this figuring of lesbian desire.

Conclusion

The gender-crossing woman was a fascinating and titillating sexual figure. Principally understood through heterosexual codes and frameworks, the female body dressed as a man was not primarily presented as an indicator of sexuality between women in popular culture. Yet that possibility was not closed down either. The cross-dressed woman was sexualised on both stage and page. She carried the eroticisation and glamour of the male impersonator; the common tropes of sexuality and courtship in working-class humour were attached to her masquerade; and she was a part of the intangible connection between the theatre and illicit sexuality. However, none of these aspects of her allure was corralled into any concrete meanings in this period. Hence she could be saucy, attractive and troubling in her attachments to other women, while remaining harmless and acceptable, even within female marriage.

Flirting and romance between women when one was gender-crossing was amusing and sweet on stage, in the popular press and on picture postcards. The predominant reading was probably that she was acting out the part of a man and playing at heterosexual love, rather than seriously courting another woman as a woman. But the pleasures of homoeroticism were presented as part of the performance or story, which also contained sexual humour, parodied the sexually swaggering man, and subverted heterosexual romance and marriage. We have seen that more illicit readings were possible, since the cross-dressed woman in military uniform and in bedroom scenes with a feminine woman was clearly identified as sexually provocative in prostitution and pornography of the period. But these texts and contexts had limited resonance in popular culture, where there was no shared and acknowledged conceptualisation of lesbianism. These explicit sexual practices were extremely well hidden from the average reader of the Sunday press, but a continuum of sexual knowledge through a range of popular texts did exist, even if access to it was limited by class, education and gender. While there were occasional glimpses of female homosexuality in the popular press after the First World War, it was represented as being part of an upper middle-class or bohemian world and never associated either with working-class culture or with cross-dressing or mannish women in these Sunday papers.

The eroticism attached to the courtship, love and marriage of the woman cross-dresser and another woman cannot be, and was not, understood as 'lesbianism' in this period in popular media and entertainment. Yet there was a rich layer of potential readings through which to enjoy this same-sex eroticism. The expression of love between women was clearly and directly set out in many newspaper stories of romantic love and cross-dressing marriage. These stories, which mixed intense female friendship and respectable courtship and marriage, were presented to the reader with multiple forms of address and potentially open readings. The playing out of heterosexual scenarios by male impersonators on stage generated a potent response from women in the audience, who relished the attacks on male privilege, and enjoyed the sense of identification with an assertive woman and her para-sexual homoerotic charge. The press stories presented readers with a strong tradition of cross-dressing which included the convention of a relationship with another woman. Combined with the reading across from the stage of glamour, eroticism and equivocation about heterosexuality, this tradition also legitimated same-sex passion. These representations and performances of desire between women were both diffuse and powerful in the early decades of the twentieth century.

Part II

The 1930s

Entertaining modernity

3 Gender-crossing and modern sexualities, 1928–39

The story of 'Colonel Barker' (Valerie Arkell-Smith), prosecuted for fraud and for marrying another woman while passing as a man, generated unusually extensive coverage in the press over two months of court appearances during March and April 1929. After a failed marriage and a subsequent heterosexual relationship in which she had two children, Barker adopted masculine clothing and spent much of the 1920s masquerading as a war hero, former boxer, restaurateur and man of independent means. She married a younger woman, Elfrida Haward, in a church wedding, and following the breakdown of that relationship took up with at least one other woman. On a previous occasion she had been tried on a firearms charge without her sex being discovered, but she was revealed to be a woman in 1929 when arrested for contempt of court following fraudulent business dealings. Colonel Barker's masquerade has been treated by historians and cultural theorists as the key example of women's cross-dressing in the twentieth century, occurring at a significant moment of cultural change around sexuality. Involving as it did, a marriage between two women, it followed hard on the heels of the trial for obscenity of *The Well of Loneliness* in 1928, a novel by Radclyffe Hall which dealt with the feelings of a mannish lesbian and her relationships with other women. In *The Well of Loneliness*, Hall turned the sexological discourse of female inversion into an accessible fictional text.[1] She created a powerful story of a mannish woman (already so masculine as a baby she was named 'Stephen') who discovers her desires for other women and achieves professional success as a writer. A 'true' invert or homosexual, she forms a relationship with a more feminine woman, whom she nobly relinquishes to a normal heterosexual future rather than the outcast status which is the lonely destiny of the invert.

To what extent did *The Well of Loneliness* trial initiate the cultural recognition of a link between female mannishness and lesbianism, and did this have any impact on the presentation of the Colonel Barker case? The significance of the Colonel Barker story for historians also rests on the judge's final summing up, when he condemned Barker's 'perverted conduct' which had 'profaned the House of God, outraged the decencies of nature, and broken the laws of man'.[2] This was the first explicit reference to homosexual immorality in a female-to-male cross-dressing case.

Some have analysed Barker's sense of self within the developing discourses of sexual inversion. Did her passing as a man reflect a cross-gendered identity: was she, in late twentieth-century terms, a transsexual or a mannish lesbian?[3] James Vernon argues that we cannot read contemporary identities back into the past and examines how Barker presented herself within the discursive framework available. He also suggests that, although the language of sexual inversion or lesbianism was not used in the trial, it is likely that many made this association.[4] While there is evidence that those in literary and artistic lesbian circles made a connection, what is more important for my enquiry is the question: did these ideas have any meaning at the level of popular culture after 1928–9? Or was the Colonel Barker case not linked with lesbianism because it was incorporated into the well-established tradition of women's cross-dressing, as Laura Doan argues?[5]

In the secondary literature, the Colonel Barker case has generally been treated in isolation from other cross-dressing stories. This chapter will discuss the significance of Colonel Barker, but aims to de-centre this case by placing it in the wider context of cross-dressing stories from 1929 to the Second World War, their continuities and changes. The reporting of the Colonel Barker case undoubtedly challenged the cross-dressing genre – but did it fracture it? Were new sexual knowledges created in the reporting of subsequent cases? The second half of the chapter will examine the wider reading contexts: allusions to desire between women in other press stories, the development of male impersonation in theatre and on screen, and the treatment of gender-crossing by men in the interwar period. We will see that the British cross-dressing story of the 1930s remained largely impervious to the new potentialities for linking female masculinity to same-sex desire or inversion.

Colonel Barker

Of course the press interest in Colonel Barker had begun long before the judge pronounced his damning phrase. In the *People* and the *News of the World*, coverage of the Barker story largely followed the existing cross-dressing formula, but departed from it in some interesting respects. After setting the scene with the initial revelation and usual exclamations of astonishment at the successful masquerade, both papers devoted the equivalent of a whole page to Colonel Barker and published several pictures, developing the previous week's interviews into lengthy stories. They presented her life from childhood, including her tomboyish pursuits in adolescence, her war service in the VAD and WAAF, her brief failed marriage, her subsequent 'common-law' liaison with Australian ex-serviceman Pearce Crouch (with whom she had two children) and her adoption of increasingly mannish clothing while still living as a woman. This detailed life history was unusual for cross-dressing stories and was facilitated by numerous interviews with her workmates, former valet, acquaintances from her sporting and political activities and her wife of three years, Elfrida Haward.

The considerable press interest in the Barker case was due to the sheer scale of her activities, and to the unusual criminal charges. She had contracted a formal marriage in church, rather than simply setting up home as a married couple, and her spurned wife was prepared to talk to the press. Barker's masquerade was a hyper-intense version of cross-dressing. She passed not only as a military man, but as a decorated First World War hero – as an officer and a gentleman. Her story involved firearms and fraud, the pretence of a middle-class life in the country and in a Mayfair hotel. In that sense it was another world in class terms – unlike most cross-dressers, her activities were not those of readers' everyday lives.

Both papers paid much attention to Barker's physical appearance. Each included Elfrida Haward's account of Barker's swimming in a river and public pool wearing a normal man's bathing suit (which in this period was a one-piece costume covering the chest).[6] Barker's landlady highlighted the unsettling feelings produced by gender inversion and translated them into humour with her remark that 'I can never say "she"' – a comment classic to the genre.[7] There were also the jokes about shaving which we have seen in earlier stories. Barker had clearly fooled her valet (employed during a more affluent period) who was convinced that she shaved and had also accepted Barker's explanation of her odd physical appearance by the need to wear corsets after her wartime injuries. Although the hotel staff (where she later worked as a receptionist) said they never saw Barker shave and were suspicious, this did not translate into unmasking. There were also reports that these colleagues had 'chaffed him' about her small hands, and high voice, examples of humour where Barker was the butt of the joke. According to the *People*, they also nicknamed her Ella Shields, a nice intertextual reference.[8] With hindsight, Barker's physical presence was represented as less convincing than the marvellous disguise of earlier cross-dressers. Nevertheless, the suspicions of colleagues were disarmed by the presence of her wife (by the time she worked at the hotel, this was Barker's second common-law wife). Heterosexuality acted to stabilise the evidence of her less convincing body.

Barker was from the solid middle class, and so distinct from the usual run of passing women. Part of the power of her story lay in the way she appropriated privileged forms of masculinity – military glory, middle-class affluence, her assertive engagement in village activities as a member of the local gentry. Like Harry Lloyd and Albert F, she was also credited with honourable motives for her disguise, especially the need to support her son after her relationship with Pearce Crouch broke down. The theatrical nature of Barker's enterprise was emphasised, as with other cross-dressers, by explicit reference to her period of time as a travelling actor.[9]

In these first reports, the press largely kept to the usual expressions of admiration for the successful cross-dresser, even more so because of the extraordinary nature of her activities.[10] The sheer scale and colourful nature of Barker's masquerading lent her the aura of the trickster, though this was punctured to some extent by the *News of the World* recounting the occasions on which her cover had been broken. She had had to flee from Andover after village society became aware of legal documents referring to her in a female name. Barker, of course, was eventually disgraced by official court proceedings, and so was not an altogether successful trickster. Nor did her cross-dressing yield any piquant or pointed observations about gender relations, as we have seen for earlier trickster cross-dressers. But the *News of the World* story ended in typically sentimental vein by drawing attention to Barker's son and speculating on how the little boy might receive the news.[11]

The *News of the World* accounted for her actions by reference to the 'shattering of a romance' (with Pearce Crouch, the father of her children). But the *People's* story took a subtly different slant. After the usual puff that this was 'the most fantastic, daring and successful masquerade ever undertaken', the paper went on to say: 'And it is, incidentally, the presentation of a psychological problem which defies solution.'[12] This was novel language to use about women's cross-dressing, and appears to echo some of the phraseology used about Radclyffe Hall's *Well of Loneliness*. While not (at this point) censorious, it drew on the kind of middlebrow journalism the *People* sometimes used and suggested a new set of parameters through which to understand cross-dressing. However, the psychological angle was not followed up in the lengthy reports which followed. Another break with tradition was in the use of a photograph on the front page of Barker wearing skirts and hiding her face from journalists when leaving Holloway Jail.[13] (Photographs of Barker in male disguise appeared on inside pages.) Previous coverage of women cross-dressers rarely depicted them in skirts, and if they did it was in jaunty before-and-after style, not, as here, carrying notions of shame, distress and wishing to hide.

A further distinction between the two papers was the *People's* focus on Barker's marriages as being of key interest. According to this newspaper she had had three or even four wives. All the headlines (over three pages) drew attention to her actions as a female husband: '"Col. Barker's" Red-Haired "Wife" Vanishes: She Was "His" Second' (front page); 'How the Man–Woman Wooed and Won' (page 5); 'The Woman who Spoofed "Her Wife"' (page 7).[14] The front-page story explored the mystery of Barker's most recent common-law wife, a topic not covered by the *News of the World*.[15] The journalist suggested that readers should find the wife's deception particularly intriguing. 'Three years of "marriage" to a "man" who was a woman – and the "wife" never suspected anything!'[16] We have seen that the courtship and marriage of cross-dressing women was a perennial press interest, and often negotiated through light-hearted humour. While the *News of the World* described Barker's marriage to Haward, it did not foster an interest in the deception of marital sexuality in the insistent way that the *People* did.

In its next report, following Barker's initial court appearance, the *People* took the opportunity to dismantle her powerful image as a cross-dressing trickster, describing how she had broken down in tears in court, thus turning into a woman again. A common thread in cross-dressing stories was the assessment of passing women with hindsight for signs of femininity which should have given them away. Normally in the genre, this enhanced the admiration for their success in adopting masculinity. But the *People's* headline was cruelly misogynistic, stripping away her previous androgynous power by emphasising her weak femininity. 'How "Colonel Barker" Really Became A Woman Again: The Unhappy Masquerader Does Just What One Might Expect of the Sex – She Weeps!'[17]

The final act of the Barker drama was her trial and conviction on the marriage charge at the end of April 1929, which carried further weight since it was tried at the Old Bailey rather than in a magistrates' court. In the *News of the World* report, Barker regained her imposing masculine appearance and cool demeanour. The paper headlined its story with the judge's 'Scathing Condemnation of Marriage Travesty' and reported Sir Ernest Wild's comments that Barker was an 'evil example' to others, an 'unscrupulous adventuress' who had 'profaned the House of God, outraged the decencies of nature, and broken the laws of man'. The story included the detailed courtroom questioning of Elfrida Haward, and her assertion that, although she had previously known Colonel Barker as a woman, everything about her marriage appeared to be 'perfectly normal'.[18] Despite its earlier probing interest in Barker as female husband, the *People* took the extraordinary decision to utterly ignore the denouement of the case, and no report of the trial appeared in its pages.

Sir Ernest Wild was a 'knowing' judge in his denunciation of Barker's 'perverted conduct' – and as such, atypical. He had been involved in the legislative attempts to make lesbian sex a criminal offence in 1920–1 and was elsewhere preoccupied with the moral deterioration which he believed was developing on the streets of London. When sitting in judgement on cases of male homosexuality he violently denounced the activities of defendants.[19] But while Wild certainly had female inversion in his sights when pronouncing on Barker, how far were the popular press willing to elaborate that for their readers?

We might speculate that the *People* was using the Barker case as an opportunity to point towards some of the implications of mannish women arising from the *Well of Loneliness* trial in a familiar and traditionally entertaining format, but lost its nerve and did not follow through its reference to the 'psychological problem'. These Sunday newspapers sensationalised sexual immorality but preferred to skate over the detail with the tested language of hints and innuendo. Their language was that of 'grave crimes' and 'outrages', rather than explicit denunciations of the James Douglas type.[20] The Colonel Barker trial was largely reported within the familiar cross-dressing genre. But it was preceded by *The Well of Loneliness* trial, drew Wild's forthright comments and was interestingly anomalous. Barker challenged powerful forms of masculinity rather than upholding respectable working-class masculine ideals. She was not quietly passing in a suburban district; her story was far more flamboyant and theatrical than most. It was of the tradition and yet outside it, in Barker's class milieu and her decidedly disreputable behaviour, in the judge's comments, and in some aspects of press reporting. What was the effect of the Barker case on the cross-dressing story? Were these suggestions of psychological problems and perversion carried into subsequent coverage of women's gender-crossing?

British cross-dressing stories 1929–39

Subsequent 'man–woman' stories were often flagged in headlines as having a direct link with the Barker case. When Kathleen Keeping was convicted of breaking into a house at Chiswick with a male accomplice and stealing articles worth £100, the *News of the World* announced: 'Masqueraded as Man: Girl's

Action Probably Stimulated by Barker Case'.[21] Several papers took an interest in the 16-year-old housemaid Elsie Taylor, after she was discovered in the same month as the Barker trial to be taking men's clothes from her employer and cycling to Skegness at night.[22] The huge press interest in the Colonel Barker case reignited the genre and there was a rise in the number of cross-dressing stories, from around three or four per year in the late 1920s to 11 during 1929, and between five and eight in each of the following five years. Some of these stories were set abroad, especially in France, and since they have particular common features, this group will be discussed in the next chapter. But right up until the late 1930s, the domestic stories of cross-dressing women set in Britain largely retained their respectability as well as the characteristic humour and playful style of earlier years.

William Holton: 'Ideal Lover, Husband, And – Parent!'[23]

Alongside Colonel Barker, it is instructive to consider a major report which followed soon after, the 'Extraordinary Story' of William Holton, already outlined in the Introduction (see Figure 5).[24] After cross-dressing for at least 15 years, it was reported, and doing a variety of male manual jobs in the towns and villages of the west Midlands, most recently as a timber haulier, 42-year-old Holton's sex was revealed after she was admitted to the Evesham Poor Law Hospital seriously ill with enteric fever.[25] Appearing in the press just two weeks after the conviction of Colonel Barker, Holton's was presented as a similar story, but largely told within the classic framework of the genre. 'Another Man–Woman: Amazing Fortitude of Masquerader: Illness Betrays Secret', trumpeted the *News of the World*.[26] The regional press, with local pride, claimed 'An Evesham "Col. Barker": A Man–Woman Timber Haulier'. Their investigations 'revealed a sequence of events perhaps more amazing in some of their characteristics than those brought to light in the notorious "Col. Barker" sensation'.[27] Indeed Holton was not only successful in passing as a man, but had a long-term relationship with her common-law wife, Mabel Hinton, who professed complete ignorance of the masquerade and believed Holton had fathered her second child.

The story was given generous coverage in both the *News of the World* and the *People* – the best part of a page in each, plus photographs of Holton and said wife and children. Beginning with an account of the discovery, the narrative followed the usual conventions of content, tone and style, though like the Colonel Barker story there was greater development of the intimate details of physical disguise, marriage and parenthood. Interviews with Holton's wife, workmates and neighbours told of her appearance, physical strength, capacity for hard manual work and social relations with workmates, emphasising her skill at passing as a man over a long period of time. Most contained extensive details of how she met Mabel Hinton and discussed their married life together, including its vicissitudes. The usual speculation as to why the gender deception had been carried on, and who Holton 'really' was, was amplified by the mystery of how she had successfully masqueraded not only as a husband but also as a father.[28]

MAN-WOMAN'S POSE FOR 15 YEARS.

"HE" WAS AN IDEAL LOVER, HUSBAND, AND—PARENT!

"The People" has discovered evidence that the Man-Woman of Evesham, known as William Sidney Holtom, carried on "his" amazing masquerade for fifteen years, mostly working at jobs such as a navvy's, which require great strength.

Holtom's sex was only discovered when "he" was taken to the local infirmary with enteric fever, and was found to be a woman. "He" is forty-two, and is registered as the father of a child eighteen months of age.

From "The People's" Special Correspondent.

Evesham, Saturday.

"I swear before all that I hold holy and sacred that I never once suspected that my husband was not a man. I cannot bring myself to think otherwise even now."

In those astonishing words, spoken to me, Miss Mabel Hinton summarised her life at Evesham with her woman-husband,

MR. HOLTOM.

Figure 5 William Holton. *People*, 12 May 1929, p. 3.
Reproduced with the permission of the British Library.

As in earlier stories, Holton's appearance had been sufficiently masculine to be convincing. A neighbour described her as 'tall, thin and very strong . . . she used to shave occasionally'.[29] The *People* described her as 'of medium height, with dark hair, a fair complexion, a masculine voice and handsome features'.[30] The *News of the World* published a photograph of Holton as a splay-legged workman, awkwardly dressed up in her best suit and tie and with brilliantined hair, next to a separate picture of Mabel Hinton in fashionable hat with the baby. There were some discrepancies which served to construct a playful dynamic around expectations of gender, as individuals tried to rationalise what they now knew with hindsight. A woman who had known Holton for some years had 'always remarked that he had a squeaky voice, but I never suspected the truth'.[31] Closer curiosity was displayed in the mechanism of her physical disguise, recalling Barker's creaking corsets. When found at Evesham Poor Law Hospital to be a woman, the *News of the World* reported that Holton's chest was bound with wrapping.[32] As with previous passing woman stories, the neighbours did not suspect, not did her workmates, and much of the humour turns on their astonishment.

Holton's masculine work persona glowed through the pages of the *News of the World* as workmates described their bewilderment. It was said of Holton that 'she had cheerfully undertaken heavy manual labour of a kind which would have taxed the endurance of the strongest of men'. 'Holton used to work as hard as any of us', related some of the men who had been on the hauling work with her. 'She managed the horses wonderfully.'[33] The *Daily Express* pointed out that timber hauling was an arduous task, and Holton had been employed removing 'enormous trees' from the Cotswold hills to Evesham, driving teams of four, five or six shire horses.[34] Holton had stopped working in the timber business two years earlier, after a workmate had been killed under the wagon she was driving. Although her nerves had given way and she had subsequently been under continuous medical treatment, this was not treated as an essentialising womanly weakness. In this respect Holton exemplifies the contradiction that heavy manual labour produces a culture of 'hard man' masculinity yet at the same time undermines the health and bread-winning capacity of men through industrial injury.[35] Holton had since retrieved her gendered work identity by working as a navvy building a bridge at Evesham: 'she was as strong as any of the men and could sling a bag of cement about as easily as any of the others'. She also did odd jobs and repaired boots, at which trade 'she had no mean skill'.[36] Holton seemed to have specialised in rather heavy and often semi-skilled work around the west Midlands, which reinforced her presumption of masculinity. Indeed hers is the only post-Barker story which constructed employment skills as integral to the passing woman's masculinity in the way earlier reports had done.

William Holton's social masculinity was fantastically over-determined. 'He drank heavily when he could afford it, and smoked three or four ounces of tobacco a week',[37] according to her wife, and 'liked her cider and her pipe' said her workmates.[38] Not only was she a 'Bogus Man Who Smoked Black Twist', but this tobacco was a particular brand 'of a strength that only the most inveterate smokers could tackle' and was specially ordered for her by the local tobacconist. As the *News of the World* put it: 'Strength and skill were not the only prerogatives of the male that she usurped. She could swear like a trooper, and had a rare collection of smart stories which made her popular among her workmates.'[39] Holton socialised in the local pub where the *Evesham Journal* said she 'always preserved a quiet demeanour', playing cards and planning fishing parties with the other men in the neighbourhood.[40] 'Two years ago she accompanied a party from the public house to the English Cup Final, and took part in the festivities with the rest.'[41]

Her working-class masculine virtues included new expectations of home-centred masculinity developing in the interwar years, now reflected in the cross-dressing formula.[42] Though out with the men in the pub in the evenings, Holton was also a thoughtful and sympathetic husband and gentle father. Although she 'refused to go through any form of marriage' with Mabel Hinton, they lived together as Mr and Mrs Holton and she 'worked hard' to provide for her and her child, as well as the new baby. Holton was reportedly delighted that Mabel was pregnant and in 'seventh heaven when "he" learned that it was a boy', naming it William after himself. 'Holton loved her home and was never happier than when she was playing with the children and singing to them or bouncing them on her knee.' There was a traditional gendered division of labour in the Holton household, but fond father William Holton 'found time to sympathise with the arduous nature' of her wife's domestic work. 'You must be tired, my girl', Holton would say, after Mabel had done a day's washing. 'I always thought that women's work was the hardest.'[43] Of course there was some trickster joking going on here. Not only did Holton have unusual insight into opposite gender roles, this comment refers to one reason she later gave for gender-crossing – her antipathy to the domestic work expected of women.[44] The *News of the World* ended the story with the almost identical structural device used in its account of Colonel Barker – evoking sentiment around the children's predicament following the revelation of parental sex. Holton's older child (whom she had step-parented) continued to have complete belief in Holton's masculinity. 'The most pathetic feature of the case is the bewilderment of little Doris Holton, a pretty six-year-old child, who is continually inquiring in a pathetic voice, "Where has my daddy gone to? When is he coming back?"'[45]

It was while working at a coal wharf in Birmingham five years earlier that Holton had met Mabel Hinton, the sister of her employer, who eventually agreed to live as her common-law wife. Both Sunday newspapers borrowed the style and language of the romantic novel in describing their courtship and a later temporary period of estrangement, printing a wonderfully histrionic quote from Miss Hinton:

> At one time 'Mr. and Mrs. Holton' quarrelled, but the nature of the rift is still their secret. 'It was one of the blackest times in my life,' Miss Hinton related, 'and I can tell you I felt as if death would be a relief, for I had grown to love my "man" with all the love in my heart and soul. I worshipped him. Never once did he beat me or spank the children.'[46]

The fooling of neighbours and friends over many years was taken further by Holton's marriage and paternity. The deception of wives and girlfriends creates an amusing situation, as we saw developed a few years earlier around Ernest Wood's girlfriends, but Holton's achievement, as she 'most astonishingly of all, claimed paternity of a child born to a woman with whom she had lived for over four years',[47] capped all the previous stories. This kind of humour is more pointed in the Holton story, probing the puzzle of marital intimacy and paternity. Mabel

Hinton continued to claim that he was the father of her child, even when unmasked as a woman. She protested to the *Daily Express*: 'I always believed him to be a man, and I cannot believe otherwise . . . My baby, born eighteen months ago, of whom I believed him to be the father, was registered as William Sidney Holton. Our life together was perfectly normal.'[48] The wife is bewildered, and sticks to her ridiculous story of innocence. She cannot win, of course. She either incriminates herself or is a fool. The joke here (echoing Colonel Barker and earlier cases of courtship) rests on the wife's sexual ignorance. However the wife's positioning has changed: here she is the butt of the joke, while Efrida Haward was described as a figure of tragic deception.

As we have seen in earlier chapters, the creation of 'knowingness' – whether in the reading of the popular press, reception of music hall acts, or on saucy post-cards – was largely reliant upon heterosexual readings. William Holton's wife, though made to look foolish, is a sexually knowing subject. Her history includes one illegitimate child already, before meeting Holton, and she lives with him out of wedlock. Surely she knows how babies are made. The *People* published a slightly different quote from Mabel Hinton: 'Only one thing in our association together has struck me as odd . . . That is that he would never undress until I had gone to bed.'[49] Rather than closing the story, this comment invites the reader to speculate on what might have happened after Holton stepped into the bedroom. This approach to telling the story marks a shift back towards the more openly bawdy humour of early nineteenth-century broadsheet ballads.[50] Being the butt of the joke disempowers Mabel Hinton in some sense, yet she still has a significant place in the narrative; she holds many of the secrets of this unusual family. Here there was, in fact, a baby, yet the claim for Holton's fatherhood is positively absurd. There are gaps here – a lot of loose ends which do not make sense within a hetero-sexual paradigm. The reader can only assume that Holton produced the baby like a conjuror on stage – it has that quality in the telling. How did she do that?! As suggested earlier, the readings of cross-dressing stories owed a lot to the entertain-ment tradition of male impersonators. Suggestive jokes and the eroticised body were rendered safe through humour and the designation of the stage as a licensed space. In this context, one reading of the Holton scenario is as farce, as one big joke. We can visualise the couple banging on and off the stage, making and finding a baby in the most unlikely ways. Possibly it was born in a handbag.

Not only was Holton a particularly accomplished trickster – subverting the laws of reproduction as well those of social gender – her story also contained the typical 'jokes within the joke' of the character. One of these was an intertextual reference to Colonel Barker. A friend told one newspaper: 'Recently while the Colonel Barker case was being heard, Holton showed keen interest and frequently expressed indignation at the masquerade.'[51] A neighbour said, 'Only last Friday we were talking about the "Colonel Barker" case, and Holton went into hysterics of laughter over it.'[52] Holton's jest can only now be appreciated since we have learned she is a brother-in-arms to Barker. Now that we do know that, how can we trust gender – and how do we know that our well-established friends and neigh-bours are not also trickster gender-crossers? Although the reports in the national papers told of Holton's initial reluctance to speak, she subsequently gave an interview to the local paper in which she took charge of the situation. In this she appropriated the power and what Andrew Stott calls the 'sanctified ambiguity of the fool or trickster'.[53] Now Holton positioned herself as the knowing comic turn with reference to her supposed paternity: '"But I never had anything to do with the matter", said the "man–woman" with a merry twinkle in her eye.'[54] Within the Holton story, Colonel Barker was frequently referred to as 'notorious'. While the reporting of the Holton case picked up some developments from that case, particularly the more pointed humour around marital sexuality, it retained the classic formula, especially the admiration of the trickster's skill, her qualities of ideal working-class masculinity and multiple levels of humour.

Controlling cross-dressing

Many of the 1930s British cross-dressing reports could have been published in the 1910s, so traditional was the world they evoked. William Holton, indeed, still worked with horses, rather than motor vehicles, and was stuck in a rural past. Interwar Britain was a country of contrasts, of economic stagnation and growth, mass unemployment and labour shortage in different parts of the country. These domestic stories seem part of this curious interwar world, both familiar and new. They deployed classic light-hearted humour around courtship and marriage, maintaining the traditional tone of the genre and only occasionally offering more overtly sexual hints. The 1932 story of Jack MacDonald (actually a 17-year-old girl) echoed all the usual amazement of the genre, and featured a picture of her as a fresh-faced young lad (see Figure 6). Briefly married, she had left her husband after two days, passed successfully as a young man and cycled from Scotland to the south of England in search of work. She duped an admiral who had met her on the road, paid for lodgings and found her a job as a kitchen boy at a hotel in Teddington. Her sex was revealed after she was charged with the theft of watches and clothing from guests at the hotel. She smoked, drank and socialised with other young men and courted a young woman, to whom the news came as a shock: '"I can't realise it", she said. "I have been out with her, danced with her, and she was jolly good company. I never once suspected."'[55]

In a 1929 Glasgow wedding case, Mary or Hugh Brown was prosecuted for making a false declaration three years previously, when she married Elizabeth McGowan. This story highlighted a common comic theme in popular humour – fooling the authorities, in this case the parish priest.

> [T]he two women had been friendly for some time . . . On Nov 3 1926, they both went to a Roman Catholic priest in Port Glasgow and asked him to arrange for their wedding. Brown was then attired in women's clothes, but she disclosed to the priest that she was really a man, and gave him a reason for being dressed as a woman. The priest agreed to marry them on condition that Brown came dressed in the clothes of the sex to which she claimed to belong. This Brown did, and the couple were duly married.[56]

GIRL BRIDE BECOMES A MAN

MASQUERADE THAT DECEIVED AN ADMIRAL

SMOKED A PIPE, DRANK BEER, COURTED A GIRL—AND WAS CAUGHT OUT!

BY OUR SPECIAL CORRESPONDENT

Feltham, Middlesex, Saturday.

THE strange career of a Scots girl who left her husband two days after she was married, and masqueraded as a man, was revealed to me to-day by scores of people she deceived.

Adopting the rôle of the smart young man about town, she—

Concealed the fact that she was married;

Courted a Richmond girl;

Drank beer and smoked an ounce of tobacco a day; and

Joined a boys' club.

Her maiden name was Madeline Findlay, a seventeen-year-old native of Grangemouth. Her amazing escapade was revealed to the Feltham magistrates, who bound her over and sent her to a home.

Two Days Married

Madeline married a labourer named Dixon at Hemel Hempstead. But two days of domestic bliss were enough for her. She absconded.

A few weeks ago a polite, good-looking Scottish boy, named "Jack McDonald," confronted Admiral Smith-Dorrien at Berkhamsted, and spoke of his sad plight.

He had cycled from Scotland, he said, to look for work, had sold the machine for food, and was now destitute.

"I was completely deceived," the admiral said to-day. "He was respectable, charming and polite, and I determined to help him. I paid his lodgings for a week and then got in touch with the Church Army officials.

"A Regular Fellow"

"They, too took a liking to the lad, and we christened him 'Jack Tar.' Eventually we got him placed as boots and kitchen boy at a Teddington hotel."

Here "Jack's" natural charm made him the favourite of guests and staff alike.

"Jack" was one of the most popular members of a Twickenham social club. She drank, smoked a pipe, and was a regular fellow. It was at a dance there she met the girl whom she afterwards ardently courted. For weeks they went about together.

The girl, who is employed at a Richmond hotel, told me that the news that "Jack" was a girl came as a great shock to her.

"I can't realise it," she said. "I have been out with her, danced with her, and she was jolly good company. I never once suspected."

Even "Jack's" boy pal seemed stunned by the news.

Admiral Deceived

"Why, she drank and smoked with the best of us," he said. "We were friends, and she fooled me like the rest. But sometimes I wondered," said one of the men she met there. "She was very soft spoken, but her Scots accent coarsened her voice."

"Jack" made a very good-looking boy with closely-cropped, well-brushed hair, and well-cut suits.

She loved to dress in the smartest masculine clothes, and it was this love of personal adornment that eventually proved her undoing.

She went to a fashionable tailor, and under false pretences ordered an entire outfit.

She chose her clothes with meticulous care, and was measured for a pullover, grey flannels and white silk shirt.

Meanwhile, watches and articles of clothing were missed by the staff and guests at

MADELINE as a "man"

the hotel, and eventually "Jack" disappeared.

No one ever suspected she was a girl till Detective-Sergeant Gimblett traced her to Richmond, and while questioning her discovered her deception.

"Jack" tried to persuade the officer to keep her secret.

"Oh, don't tell anyone," she pleaded, but the whole astonishing story was revealed at Feltham police court. The girl was bound over, and sent to a home at Kingston.

Figure 6 Jack MacDonald/Madeline Findlay. *People*, 31 July 1932, p. 2. Reproduced with the permission of the British Library.

This episode is repeated twice in the report, and some anti-Catholicism may be in evidence. The priest is depicted as particularly stupid, as Brown first of all met him dressed as a woman. Deception of the parish priest, a theme which recurs in other stories of female husbands, recalls the anti-clericalism of the nineteenth-century press and of the contemporary comic postcard, where the innocent vicar appears as a bumbling fool, often misunderstanding his parishioners in sexually suggestive ways.[57] It was also clear that this was a story about love between women, and Mary Brown did not disguise her strong attachment to Elizabeth McGowan. It was represented as odd but acceptable in the way that the Dallamore marriage had been back in 1912.

While the general presentation of the 1930s stories continues to be astonishment and playful humour, there are occasional hints of broader sexual knowledge. The aptly named Mrs Wellbelove supposedly told the *People* in 1933 of her 23-year 'marriage' to Bill O'Connor (Lilian Smithers), 'the amazing man–woman of Weybridge'.[58] She described how she was thrilled and delighted with her female husband.

> We set up house together, and Mrs Smithers put on men's clothing. I could not repress a little shout of delight when I saw how perfectly she looked the part of a man! Upon our mutual earnings we managed to live fairly comfortably.

But the story leaked out, and Mrs Wellbelove was obliged: 'to leave for ever my best friend in all the world. There never was anything in our association of which I need be ashamed.' This is an explicit refutation of any possible wrong-doing. But by raising the question of sexual morality at all, this story comes closer to acknowledging the possibility of sex in a marriage between two women. This angle may have been developed, even fabricated by the *People*, given the fortuitous name of the wife.[59]

In the 1930s, the press worked hard to maintain the cross-dressing genre. As a sensational, exceptional story, women's cross-dressing was part of the human-interest formula, together with crime and disaster, which, as the Colonel Barker trial demonstrated, sold newspapers. Maintained in traditional form as an appealing, puzzling entertainment story, with a very polymorphous eroticism associated with the stage male impersonator, it could be justified within a family newspaper. If the genre were to become tinged with homosexuality, then all these elements of humour around women's gender-crossing – which beyond the cross-dressing story also included cartoons and comments on the modern girl and masculine fashions – might be compromised.[60]

The cross-dressing genre even returned to military themes in the 1930s, stressing loyalty to a country or cause. There were several belated revelations of women who had supposedly served in the trenches as men on the Western Front. Each had demonstrated exceptional courage and heroism, some showing up male cowardice.[61] These stories were a popular-press contribution to the wider cultural revisiting of the First World War in Britain in the late 1920s and early 1930s, in poetry, fiction and autobiography. Other military stories were connected to new theatres of war of the later 1930s, telling of Chinese women who passed as men to defend their country against the Japanese and of British women who masquer-aded across gender to fight in the Spanish Civil War.[62] Their skill, heroism and allegiance to their cause or country formed a significant thread of the reports. Almost all these military stories involve heterosexual relationships – the woman as soldier is standing in for a brother or lover, avenging a father, or accompanying a lover. Loyalty to a man and loyalty to the national cause work together in these narratives to restore faith in gender complementarity and patriotic virtues in a decade of increasing political insecurity in Europe.

Heterosexual romance also appeared in some domestic cross-dressing reports in the 1930s, at a time when the newspapers appear to operate more deliberate control over the moral messages and outcomes of the narratives. This is evident in a series of reports appearing in the *News of the World* between August and October 1933, involving the adventures of 'pretty and charming 24-year-old shorthand typist', Hilda Terry, who could not get a job until she dressed as a boy. Although presented as factual reporting, the story was probably concocted. There were no court appearances or other brushes with authority to tie it into social reality, there was no parallel version in the *People* (though this was sometimes the case), and the story neatly follows the young woman through a number of episodes, after she found work as a waiter in a West End hotel. In commenting on men from the perspective of a disguised woman, Hilda Terry fulfils the trickster's role of crossing rigid social boundaries and mediating the sexes to one another, but in a less polit-ical form than the suffrage-era cross-dressers. She is much less assertive and feisty than most other passing women, and is represented as less successful in her attempt to hold down employment. The story tells of how she was obliged to take girls out 'because the men chaffed her about her lack of interest in women' and how, 'to her acute embarrassment, she aroused the infatuation of a young parlour-maid'.[63]

Whether or not Hilda Terry was fictional, or a young woman deliberately encouraged in her masquerade by the newspaper, her story most unusually ends with a heterosexual romance. We have seen in earlier chapters that there is gener-ally no conventional closure in the cross-dressing formula. Maintaining the carni-valesque possibility of gender inversion until the end, the passing woman in many respects retains her defiance and is not represented as cowed or reined in after discovery, even if she is obliged to return to feminine clothes. In no instances is she subsequently married to a man, as in Shakespearean cross-dressing plots, or eigh-teenth-century female soldier ballads.[64] But in this 1930s serial Hilda Terry has a happy reunion with a man she had met earlier and welcomes the return to femi-nine gender identity with relief.[65] This story explicitly stabilised cross-dressing as an entertaining escapade. Feminine feelings and gender identity were presented as natural and fixed, and cross-dressing was not a serious threat to morality and heterosexuality.

The cross-dressing woman story proves to be a robust formula, and the genre was not derailed by the 1929 denunciation of Colonel Barker's immorality. Even subsequent reports about Barker revert to the classic mode. In her later court appearances for stealing she was treated quite leniently, and her motives interpreted as honourable protection of others, namely her son. Her whole life history was retold on these occasions, but Ernest Wild's reference to sexual perversion never reappears and has no continuing purchase in the press.[66] Passing women continue to court girls and set up home together for love. They continue to be represented as daring and skilful, resist being cowed by the judiciary and make fun of other authority figures. Some post-Barker stories do push further around the secrets and mysteries of the same-sex marriage bed, but they do this largely through humour, as before. The *People* appears slightly more inclined to hint occasionally at other possible interpretations and the *News of the World*, in just one or two stories, moves away from the open-ended gender challenge of the trickster towards a more controlled emphasis on innate gender identity and safe heterosexual closure.

Gender-crossing on stage and in film

Newspaper accounts of women's cross-dressing continued to be understood in the context of male impersonation in wider forms of 1930s mass entertainment such as variety theatre. But the explosive popularity of cinema in the era of the 'talkies', and the transatlantic reach of Hollywood film, meant that the sexual attractiveness and power carried by gender-crossing women on screen was in the process of moving away from the local reference points of the earlier twentieth century.

While variety theatre found its profits and popularity under some threat during the 1930s, it maintained an important place in popular culture, if not the dominant force it was before the war, as continuing press interest suggests.[67] Both the *News of the World* and the *People* published the words and music to popular songs each Sunday, as well as reviewing variety performances. Some of the many male impersonators of this period harked back to the glory days of the music hall and the influence of Vesta Tilley (who had retired in 1920), presenting similar sentimental songs, and even impersonating Tilley herself.[68] With the gradual shift towards revue and musical comedy (featuring pretty girls to be looked at) rather than the specialist turns of the music hall, the interaction between variety performers and their audience was probably less intense than it had been before the First World War. There may have been a less challenging and visceral quality to male impersonation than earlier, but well-established acts such as Hetty King and Ella Shields retained their popularity.

Ella Shields continued to be an important exponent of the parodic swell song, burlesquing men who were not so smart, wealthy or grand as they purported to be, especially in her greatest hit, 'Burlington Bertie', first sung in 1914.[69] Completely unable to maintain the fiction of being a 'gent', Bertie was a tramp who had lost his top hat and came from Bow. This type of song might now also relate to a newly widespread social type, the rich man who had lost everything in the postwar recessions, or, equally, reference the top-hat-and-tails performer in the increasingly popular film musical.[70] This classic type continued to be a mainstay of the male impersonator's act. Cicely Courtneidge was pictured in the *People* in 1927 'With The Lid On', sporting the top hat she would be wearing in her appearance in a variety show that week.[71] Courtneidge also cross-dressed in film, notably in *Soldiers of the King* (1933), where she played a music hall star who masquerades as a guard in order to marry an army lieutenant.[72]

There was a renewed interest in exploring male impersonation in early 1930s cinema, using a variety of genres and plots featuring historical figures, seductive vamps, cowgirls and the independent girl-next-door. Although normally tamed into appropriate feminine behaviour at the end of the film, these gender-crossing women could display both glamour and strength for most of it. Marlene Dietrich and Greta Garbo were iconic Hollywood stars in the 1930s, reflecting audience pleasure in their particular qualities and roles. Their European accents and Dietrich's background in German cabaret gave them a foreign sexual allure. Particularly in their pre-Hays Code films, their sexuality was ambiguous, unconventional and autonomous. Both played independent powerful women in roles which explored modern expressions and uncertainties of gender identity. Garbo brought her exotic appeal to *Queen Christina* (1933), merging masculine elements into her glamorous image.

> Her clothing is masculine through the first third of the film, and her relationship with a court lady named Eva is very much that of lover and mistress. She kisses her on the lips, dismisses her from the boring business of politics, and even gets jealous when she learns that Eva is planning to marry. All these elements are written into the script, but the rest of Garbo's masculinity resides in herself – in the brusqueness of her movements, the long stride, the forceful hand gestures, the tone of her voice, and the angularity and big-boned quality of her frame.[73]

Dietrich's sexuality was even more ambiguous, bringing the potentially threatening decadence of cabaret to Hollywood in her partnership with director Josef von Sternberg on several films.[74] Her kiss with another woman in *Morocco* (1930) has been much discussed by film historians.[75] In contrast to German, or even American audiences, most British viewers were unlikely to read the gender-crossing she imported from Weimar cabaret as directly 'lesbian'. Yet Dietrich's insistence on wearing trousers away from the film set as well as on it was noted with a little unease by the British as well as American press: '"Trousers for Ever", says Marlene Dietrich.'[76] In one gossip column 'this strange fad' was explained as a decision of her new business manager. A few months later, when 'clad in a man's lounge suit she took that centre of feminine fashion [Paris] by storm', her choice was dissembled by the news that she was en route to the Riviera with her husband and little girl.[77]

These female stars carried their glamour into the androgynous cross-dressing role, creating a powerful homoeroticism for many women in the audience. Their attractiveness was heightened by the assertive roles they played on screen, evoking identificatory fantasies of confidence and achievement. In this way they continued the powerful allure of the male impersonators from music hall days. The passionate feelings of love towards film stars felt by their women and girl fans echo the declarations made about and to the music hall male impersonators discussed in Chapter 2. This type of crush or attraction was quite acceptable. Jackie Stacey's study of women fans shows they were not self-conscious about it, and nor was it seen as strange or undesirable, until well after the Second World War.[78]

Other gender-crossing film roles were more sexually ingenuous, especially following the 1934 Hays Code which censored any hint of sexual deviance from Hollywood film.[79] Engaging with and providing a magical solution to contemporary economic problems, Gracie Fields, the most famous British variety and film actress of the period, posed as an American (male) singer to convince a lord to reopen a shipyard in *Shipyard Sally* (1939) and restore local employment prospects.[80] In transferring to cinema, male impersonation lost some quality of immediacy and relationship to everyday life. In films shown across the western world, gender-crossers could no longer parody locally recognised male types. However, the heroines who dressed as men in the movies moved the practice into modern mass entertainment and drew on the glamour of Hollywood stardom. These gender-crossers retained some familiar traits: they were coded as sexually powerful when borrowing from the cabaret form and they displayed the trickster qualities of explaining the psychology of the sexes to men and women as they playfully leapt across gender boundaries. They were assertive agents of their own destiny.

The mannish invert? Lesbianism in the press, 1928–39

Despite the prosecution of *The Well of Loneliness* with its mannish invert heroine, neither 'lesbianism' as a general concept, nor the mannish woman as a particular sexual type was at all prevalent in the Sunday papers in subsequent years. Laura Doan argues that it is only after the *Well of Loneliness* trial in 1928 that female masculinity begins to signify lesbianism in culture.[81] In the popular press, this association develops particularly slowly and is not automatically made even in the late 1930s. A language of upper-class decadence had already been established to indicate same-sex female desire, and the trial did not initiate an immediate discursive shift to link mannishness with lesbianism. Not all of the Sunday press emphasised gender inversion or female masculinity in their reporting of the *Well of Loneliness* trial. The *News of the World* told readers that the book was found obscene because it dealt favourably with the subject of 'unnatural practices between women'.[82] Stephen, the heroine, was 'depicted as a child with unnatural tendencies' who goes on to have three friendships with women.[83] In contrast, the *People* intervened with editorial judgement from the beginning and emphasised gender inversion. The initially unnamed 'secret' novel 'treats with astounding frankness a revolting aspect of modern life', it asserted, expanding on the 'sexual aspects' of the book with a comment from the publishers: 'It is concerned with the phenomenon of the masculine woman in all its implications.'[84] The paper's description of the plot continued this theme. The parents hoped for a son, and their daughter 'began with a boy's instincts, a boy's thoughts which later developed into the instincts and thoughts of a man . . . Miss Hall seeks not only to explain her pervert "heroine," but also to justify her.'[85] The *People*, always inclined to offer more extended commentary than the *News of the World*, highlighted the association between same-sex desire and the mannish woman, as had the original attack by the *Sunday Express*.[86] None of these reports was particularly long or developed, and unlike the story of Colonel Barker, might easily have been missed.

Neither newspaper pursued an interest in female homosexuality in the 1930s, though they did develop their reporting of male homosexual crimes (discussed below). The only oblique hints of sexual practices between women were attached to the general sexual immorality and decadence associated with the 'smart set' – wealthy young people and theatrical folk. A 1927 account of a society party where several well-known people cross-dressed was cast in a tone of theatrical fun, but accompanied by the ambiguous language of 'queer' and 'freak'. 'Young Men In Skirts! And Some Of The Girls Wore Trousers At Society's Latest "Freak" Party The Other Night'. The Honourable Stephen Tennant went as the Queen of Sheba and the actress Tallulah Bankhead as a male tennis star in trousers to 'one of the queerest of all the "freak" parties ever given in London'.[87] The photograph of American heiress Ruth Baldwin with short hair and mannish tie, which headed the column announcing her death after collapsing at an all-night party in 1937, may have signalled her lesbian sexuality, together with the information that she shared a house with wealthy Betty (Joe) Carstairs. A leader of the 'Bright Young Things' in the early 1920s, 'she always dressed neatly in tailor-made clothes and wore magnificent cuff-links'.[88]

Aside from these elite circles, there was sporadic anxious commentary on masculine women or female couples from more everyday backgrounds, particularly in respect of their active heterosexuality or lack of it. A story of two women friends running an aviation business was headlined: 'No Time for Romance' and expressed some concern about whether they were engaged in heterosexual romance or whether independence and business life were enough for them. Yet such women were also presented as modern young women, who were to be admired for their self-reliance and successful forays into the masculine world of sports and business.[89]

There were occasional stories which dealt with love between women as a potential problem but one which could easily be dismissed as a crush. Middle-class anxiety about adolescent girls' sexuality and how it should be managed in relation to their desires for each other or older women was quite well developed in this period in professional discourses. It appears to have been an incomprehensible yet anxiety-pricking topic within the parameters of the popular press. The *News of the World* published two long reports on the inquest into the 1932 suicide of a schoolgirl following concern about her friendship with her teacher and the discovery by her mother of 'rather indiscreet' letters from the teacher. There was much disquiet hovering around this example of 'hero-worship' although it was neither condemned nor put in the language of psychology.[90] But there was an uneasy sexual prurience at play in the reporting of an American case in the late 1930s, when 'Miss O'Connor, a fine athletic girl, and her bosom friend' appeared in court 'to answer a charge of "a morals offence" at "Happy Camp," just outside the city' where they had been employed as counsellors. A man who admitted he had acted as a 'Peeping Tom' alleged that he saw them 'hugging and kissing in a small cottage they occupied at the camp' but the case was thrown out.[91]

In the 1920 and 1930s, these Sunday newspapers had a set of discourses to deal with sex between women, which was generally imagined as happening far from the day-to-day world of their readers, occurring among the upper classes, the smart set, and the cultural elite. In spite of the trial for obscenity of the *Well of Loneliness*, this theme still remained largely obscured, and was clearly not a topic which the newspapers wished to pursue.[92] While it might seem with hindsight that the cross-dressing stories would converge with the figure of the mannish lesbian in the 1930s, the power of the genre, and the complexity of linguistic and cultural manoeuvring to publish stories on vice without offending readers' sensibilities, meant that the popular press was reluctant to make clear links between them. British working-class cross-dressers retained their traditional place in national consciousness, and toler-ance of the masculine woman as female husband persisted.

The interwar reporting of male homosexuality and cross-dressing

While women's cross-dressing stories remained largely unaffected by suggestions of lesbianism, men masquerading as women were increasingly clearly associated with homosexuality in press reporting, especially from the 1930s. Male homosexu-ality was illegal – including sexual activity itself (gross indecency) and picking up another man for sex (importuning) – while sex between women was not. Cross-dressing and effeminacy was a well-established part of some gay male sub-cultures and, as a visible signal, made male homosexuality vulnerable to police attention and prosecution.[93]

But female impersonation was also an entrenched tradition in the theatre, and this meant that in the years before the First World War, and indeed until the late 1920s, men arrested when cross-dressed on the streets could be reported as funny and entertaining. There was much overlapping language (most obviously that of 'masquerading') between men's and women's cross-dressing stories, as in this headline of a 1911 Huddersfield case: 'Male Masquerader: Dyed his Hair and Donned Female Attire'.[94] To most readers it would appear that the crime of theft was straightforward enough, while his disguise gave added amusement to the story. Police officers were sometimes reported to have dressed up as women in order to trap criminals. With headlines such as 'Police Fashion Parade' there are echoes of the pantomime dame, as well as a desire to poke fun at the police as ambivalent authority figures.[95] Men arrested for wearing women's clothes might claim it was just a joke, done for a lark, or even, for one man, because he was 'in a frivolous mood', and were reported as such.[96]

The mid-1920s was a transition period for both Sunday newspapers in their reporting of male homosexuality. Matt Houlbrook argues that journalistic condemnation of effeminacy emerged in the 1920s, when the weekly newspaper *John Bull* launched an investigatory campaign into the 'menace of painted boys' who hung around certain meeting places in the West End.[97] A similar, if less explicit, concern was voiced by the *People* in 1924 in a veiled warning about 'deca-dence' in the arts. At the ballet and at unhealthy plays produced in the West End, there were 'difficulties' among the audience. 'You cannot, in a newspaper intended for general reading, put it more clearly than that.'[98] A more forthcoming critique of effeminacy in 1925 condemned 'The She-Men', a dangerous cult in the universities today. 'The thing has become something approaching a public scandal.'[99] The *People* mainly focused on this type of general warning and rarely reported the everyday male cross-dressing and homosexual cases which began to appear more frequently in the *News of the World* from the late 1920s. Alongside this anxiety about effeminacy came a retreat by the press from its previous approval of female impersonation on stage. The *People* in 1923 reviewed one female imperson-ator as a 'real beauty', but went on to qualify its praise: 'My readers will agree with me, even if like myself they do not like men masquerading as "ladies".'[100] Although rarely noted after the mid-1920s in these newspapers, female impersonators remained acceptable on stage, in concert parties made up of ex-servicemen and in amateur theatricals.[101]

Codes remained ambiguous to protect press claims to respectability and reports were brief. References to homosexual offences not involving cross-dressing were normally couched in the constrained but hardly opaque language of 'improper conduct' or 'a serious charge' involving two men, 'grave offences against a number of lads', etc.[102] This terminology was also used to report abortion and sexual assaults on women, but the context of the crime was usually obvious. Stronger language was occasionally used from the late 1920s. Joseph Donnison was described in one headline using both the old-fashioned code of 'West-End Pest' and the more explicit 'moral pervert'. Sentenced to two years' hard labour 'for persistently solic-iting men in the West-end for immoral purposes', the arresting officer 'described Donnison as the associate of some of the lowest class of undesirable persons frequenting the West-end, male moral perverts who adopted girls' names'.[103]

The presentation of men's 'masquerading' as entertaining and theatrical more or less ceased in the 1930s and it increasingly became a code for sexual offences which could not be directly named. In a case headlined by the *News of the World*: '"I Am Not a Woman": Masquerading Charge Against Man', 57-year-old Albert Tattersall was actually charged with 'loitering with intent to commit a felony while dressed in women's clothing', the felony being, presumably, importuning.[104] But this construction might still imply some kind of property crime for many readers. Men's cross-dressing reports could more easily be deciphered when they cited the language of condemnation used in court which, as we have seen, was not used of women cross-dressers.

In making the links between gender-crossing and male homosexuality more explicit, the turning point for the readers of the *News of the World* (but not the *People*, which declined to report these cases) was the detailed reporting of the raids on drag balls and homosexual clubs which took place, mainly in London but also in Birmingham and Liverpool, from the late 1920s. The subsequent trials meant that the use by men of women's dress, names and cosmetics was increasingly strongly associated with homosexuality, not only in relation to the individual behaviour of queer men but also with the idea of a homosexual sub-culture in the city.[105] Readers were left in no doubt that this kind of cross-dressing was criminal, sexually immoral and socially abhorred. In a trial concerning the Bycilla Club in Soho in 1936, the 'Magistrate's Strong Comments' condemned this 'Horrible place where effeminate men danced together'.[106] The judge in his summing up of the Holland Park trial of 33 men at a drag ball, some of whom termed themselves 'Lady Austin's Camp Boys', spoke of 'a foul and horrible canker, which, if allowed to spread, would make the Metropolis another Sodom'.[107] By the 1930s it was increasingly evident that men's effeminacy and cross-dressing was a euphemism for homosexuality in the press, and it was frequently labelled as vice and perversion in condemnatory remarks in court. Since women's cross-dressing did not signify lesbianism, even after 1929, it appears that there was a growing divergence between men's and women's gender-crossing in press reporting.

If dressing as a woman and behaving effeminately indicated homosexuality for men, why could dressing as a man not mean something similar for women? A report of the 'Dance-Hall Orgies' by effeminate men in 1927 was directly adjacent on the page to a story of a woman dressed in trousers and behaving oddly.[108] Yet cross-reading for sexual deviance was probably uncommon. Discussion of the social and cultural acceptability of women's cross-dressing highlights the absence of legislation proscribing sex between women (which therefore could not officially exist or be policed), and gendered assumptions about sexuality. Though these were changing between the wars, the idea that female sexuality was passive and responsive rather than assertive, was only beginning to be challenged. The interrelationship of theatrical tradition and judicial immunity meant cross-dressing by women could continue to be treated as a humorous diversion even after ideas about sex between women had been voiced in the courts.

Medical expertise and cross-dressing

If any kind of sexological discourse in relation to women's same-sex desire (or cross-gender identification) was going to filter into the popular press in this period, then it was likely to be through the notion of the mannish invert, as suggested above, and through a medical interpretation of women's cross-dressing. Medico-scientific approaches did begin to appear in reports of men's cross-dressing as it was increasingly linked to homosexual crimes and began to receive new scrutiny. Chris Waters and Angus McLaren argue for the increased medicalisation of deviance in the treatment of male homosexual and cross-dressing cases in the 1930s, as sexological and psychoanalytic ideas were gradually taken up in the criminal justice system.[109] McLaren further argues that after the 1931 case of Augustine Hull, who had successfully passed as a woman and lived with an unsuspecting man as his wife, some experts and journalists began to make a distinction between homosexuality and transvestism.[110] My survey of these particular Sunday newspapers suggests some support for this argument, but shows that the process was slower, more inchoate and less sophisticated than McLaren suggests. Medical reports were called for in some cases of men's cross-dressing throughout the

period, though whether in order to determine sex, look for evidence of homosexual practices or measure sanity was not usually stated. Male offenders dressing
as women, even to carry out property crimes, were increasingly likely to be investigated for sexual abnormality by the late 1930s. A Reigate burglar, William Fish,
was fully dressed as a woman when arrested and charged with breaking and
entering and stealing a handbag in 1930. Although a medical report was
mentioned, there was no reference to sexual or psychological issues.[111] However,
when the same man was tried in 1936, again for housebreaking, and again wearing
women's clothes when arrested, evidence was called from various doctors and
psychologists. They agreed that he was stealing women's clothes and jewellery to
feed an obsession, and a medical psychologist described his uncontrollable urge to
wear women's clothes as 'sexual deviation' and 'perversion', an example of 'effeminate psychology'.[112] There was a similar shift in the judgements made of men who
committed suicide while cross-dressed, from verdicts of unsound mind or temporary insanity, to increasingly medicalised language, as in a 1934 case when a
doctor referred to 'a condition known as fetishism' (sic).[113] In most reports of male
importuning or cross-dressing, however, any exploration of psychological motives
was far less sophisticated: 'moment of mental aberration' or 'abnormality' were
common terms, as well as 'perversion'.[114]

Doctors and women's cross-dressing

While there is evidence that modern scientific expertise was beginning to be used
to categorise, account for, and process men in the criminal justice system, this was
certainly not the case for women cross-dressers. Doctors frequently appeared in
women's cross-dressing stories in the press, but not as experts on transvestism.
They might play a brief role as part of the mechanism of discovery, when a passing
woman went into hospital or died. Annie Miller (Charlie Richardson), Ernest
Wood and William Holton were all forced to attend the local infirmary when
stricken with acute illness, at which point their gender-masquerading of many
years was revealed.[115] Albert F's cross-dressing was discovered through a medical
inspection when she was called up in 1916.[116] Doctors occasionally had a professional role as arbiters to establish biological sex. Mary/Hugh Brown was required
to be medically examined by the parish authorities after she had confused the
priest and her wife's parents as to her gender.[117] And doctors did give expert
evidence in court on the mental health of clearly disturbed women and girls who
cross-dressed, normally using pretty unsophisticated formulations. In a number of
cases this was framed using the notion of 'delusions'. This referred to a fixed
conviction that they were of the male gender (even after being unmasked) but was
only normally used when symptoms of insanity were apparent. After being
arrested in 1915, the cross-dressing Mabel Joyce was said to be under 'melodramatic delusions', probably on account of her tall tales of masquerading across
nationality, and having been a spy and cowboy.[118]

But, undermining these professional and discursive powers, doctors frequently
appeared as objects of comedy, having been fooled as to the true sex of their cross-
dressed trickster patients. Charlie Richardson (Annie Miller) had already been

treated for a poisoned leg as an out-patient at the hospital, without her masquerade being detected. The press report made a certain amount of play around the fact that this doctor 'never tumbled to it' although 'a woman's leg is unlike a man's'.[119] Although William Holton was eventually unmasked in hospital, she too had successfully deceived the local doctor up until then: 'No other person, not even the doctor who attended the supposed husband for 15 months, suspected "his" real sex.'[120] As the butt of humour, doctors' powers were deflated, but in any case they had a fairly limited role in regulating women's cross-dressing and certainly did not act as a channel for the spread of modern psychological ideas within the pages of the Sunday press.

'An unhealthy friendship': the Harrogate wedding

Psychological explanations were absent until another female husband case of 1937, when one young woman was prosecuted after marrying another in Harrogate. It is interesting to compare this 'Woman Weds Woman' story with that of Mary/Hugh Brown and Elizabeth McGowan from 1929. Both cases involved the attempts of two young women to marry in order to be together. Both had successfully fooled the vicar. The 'bridegrooms' were each charged with the same crime, of making a false entry in the marriage register – the same charge as Colonel Barker. But in 1937 the press and courts were much more concerned with the sexual nature of the women's relationship.[121]

Joan Coning, the 20-year-old 'bridegroom', who worked as a nurse, was prosecuted after marrying Ruth Barker, aged 25, whom she had known for four years. According to the prosecutor,

> Both girls were interested in music, and they visited each other's homes in the usual normal way. This friendly association between the couple had been going on for about 12 months . . . when Miss Coning suddenly told Ruth Barker that she was a man. This assertion was apparently accepted by Miss Barker.

In 1933 Joan's parents were away and the two girls stayed together at her house. The prosecutor's account was fairly circumspect.

> I have no desire to go into details as to what took place . . . but the things that did happen indicate that Miss Coning's mental outlook on certain matters was a little peculiar. These events . . . did nothing however to undeceive Miss Barker with regard to the statements which Miss Coning had made to her [that she was really a man].

Joan Coning's defence lawyer pursued the same theme, with the aim of shifting the blame away from his client on to the older woman, Ruth Barker. He said:

> 'These two girls . . . met in 1933, when Miss Coning was 16 and Miss Barker 21. One was on the threshold of sex development and the other was obviously

past that stage. I am not going into details, but these girls became so friendly that the elder girl stayed at the house of her younger friend while the latter's parents were away, and occupied the same bedroom for some nights. They also went on holidays together at Rhyl, and again occupied the same bedroom. The friendship developed and developed,' [he] added, 'and I could probably tell a story which your worships might not credit, and it has culminated in this episode.'[122]

A few moments later he described it as an 'unhealthy friendship' – which was becoming a code in middlebrow literature by the 1930s for a potentially lesbian relationship between two young women.

In this story, the practice of cross-dressing is finally connected to the possibility of sexual relationships between women. Knowledge of the latter is assumed to be shared by the courts, the public and the newspapers' readerships by 1937, though it is approached awkwardly with a vague use of language: 'unhealthy friendship'; 'things that happened' when two girls shared a bed. In his summing up the chairman of the magistrates 'observed that it was a very sad and serious case'. He took into account Miss Coning's age and previous good character and 'what the bench supposed must be her peculiar mental outlook'. This final formulation of 'peculiar mental outlook' was the closest attempt to name the women's sexuality. Ostensibly uninformed by psychiatry or sexology (no doctor was called to give evidence), it centres not only on the sexual activities of the two girls, but also on Joan's cross-dressing and assertion of masculine identity.

It is significant that Joan Coning was referred to in the *News of the World* headline as the 'Eton-Cropped Girl "Bridegroom"'. Laura Doan suggests that after images of Radclyffe Hall with her cropped hair and masculine tailored suits accompanied the trial of her book, perceptions of the mannish woman began to change.[123] As I have argued above, lesbianism tended to be seen as class-specific and this correlation between female masculinity and homosexuality was rarely applied to cross-dressing women in the following years. But in the late 1930s, one element of the cross-dressing or masculine woman's appearance – very short hair – began to be used as a code in the popular press for the masculine woman who was possibly a lesbian. The wider social recognition of sexual relationships between women by the late 1930s – and furthermore the stigma attached to them by the general public – was also signalled by reports of antagonism from local people. In Harrogate, it was reported: 'Women . . . stood outside the door [of the magistrates' court] and booed the "bridegroom."'[124] The only photograph of Joan Coning, published by the *Daily Mirror*, showed her with a coat over her head, indicating her shame – and reminiscent of the picture of Colonel Barker leaving Holloway.[125]

Yet the courtroom and newspaper discussion did not altogether condemn the young women. The '"unhealthy friendship" [which] had been broken forever' was the discourse of the intense schoolgirl crush which had gone too far. The youth of the two girls created the possibility of redemption: they could move on from this with the help of their parents. Joan Coning was bound over for three years to be of good behaviour and to place herself under the care of the lady probationer officer. She 'should be carefully taken care of and watched during those three years to see that no further trouble shall come to her'.[126]

The Harrogate case borrows heavily from contemporary middle-class anxieties about adolescent girls' friendships and lesbianism. Educationalists, child psychologists, middlebrow commentators and novelists had been concerned for some time about the proper sexual and emotional development of young women, and the mechanisms for controlling homosexual behaviour in girls' schools. But readers of the popular press were barely familiar with these debates.[127] It is important to reiterate that this was the only case before the Second World War in which the language used and reported – 'unhealthy friendship' – was even this explicit.

Conclusion

Until the late 1930s, women passing as men in Britain continue to be represented in the popular press as entertaining, fascinating and even admirable. The *Well of Loneliness* and Colonel Barker cases only briefly destabilise the classic cross-dressing story by introducing sexological inversion in the shape of the mannish lesbian. The traditional framing is then re-established through deliberate strategies by the press. Classic generic elements are maintained in new reports of cross-dressing women. Occasional semi-fictional stories are developed, which either deny sexual immorality by the cross-dresser, or emphasise economic motives and a heterosexual resolution, but which in both cases keep the formula lively. The reappearance of military stories, which stress loyalty to the nation and allegiance to a morally worthy cause, also serve to reinforce the respectability of women's cross-dressing in the 1930s.

There are some interesting differences between the *News of the World* and the *People* in their attempts to duck and weave around the topic of homosexuality. The *News of the World* increasingly reported local examples of sexual crimes between men in the 1930s, and the condemnatory remarks by magistrates trying such cases. Its language codes loosened a little, but circumlocution and censorship remained powerful. In any case the courts also shared this preference for using vague terminology to refer to sexual misconduct. The *People* began to approach the issue of same-sex desire through its emphasis on the marital relationships of Colonel Barker and issued portentous but mysterious warnings about effeminacy and decadence through its opinion articles. Once or twice it appeared willing to take up the new discourse of psychology in relation to women's gender-crossing. But the paper, rather astonishingly, declined to publish the outcome of the Colonel Barker trial and the judge's mention of her 'perverted conduct' and fought shy of reporting actual cases of male homosexual crime. Nor did the *People* report the 1937 Harrogate wedding story, preserving its readers from this disturbing new knowledge of 'unhealthy friendship'. The idea of sex between women, and any link to gender-crossing, still remained largely outside the everyday frame of reference for the working-class and lower middle-class readers of these Sunday papers. While the British press was unwilling to acknowledge or discuss the topic of sex between women, continental awareness of lesbianism was rather more open, in popular literature and the press, on stage and in the existence of lesbian bars and night-clubs in major cities such as Paris and Berlin.[128] The British popular press had long been practised in the art of representing unwelcome sexual vices as having their origins abroad, and in the 1930s, as we will see in the next chapter, they began to export the disturbing possibilities of desire between women to France, where they flowered most entertainingly.

4 'The sheik was a she!'

The gigolo and cosmopolitanism in the 1930s

In June 1932, the *People* ran a story about a young woman who had cross-dressed as an Arab man and worked, until she was unmasked, as a very successful paid dancing partner. This sheik was indeed a she. The report began with an explicit reference to the 1921 film version of the desert romance, *The Sheik*:

> Neurotic women of the Sheik-struck type created by certain American films voted Ibn Ben Ali one of the most charming Princes of the Desert they had ever met.
>
> And in the fashionable 'dancings' of Paris, Nice, and the North African seaboard, the 'Prince' had no lack of women patrons queuing up for the 'honour' of being his dancing-partner.

The sheik's true identity was discovered after the police began to make investigations, after 'a number of complaints were lodged by English and American women who alleged that, under pretence of making love to them, the "Prince" had obtained sums of money and valuable jewellery.' The sheik hurriedly left Paris and was traced to Oran in Algeria. He was revealed to be a young middle-class Anglo-French woman who had found her life in a Paris suburb too dull, and so sought adventure in masquerading.[1] This chapter discusses the slew of 'foreign' cross-dressing stories which suddenly appeared in the British popular press after 1929. Mostly set in France, they engage with some established and some more unexpected themes, muddles of names and gender in French cross-dressing marriages, and a further extraordinary group which, as illustrated above, involved women working as gigolos or paid dancing partners, often passing across race as well as gender boundaries. 'Foreign' cross-dressing stories appeared regularly in the popular press from the 1900s, at the rate of one or two a year. Until the late 1920s, they most frequently came from English-speaking countries such as the United States and Australia. The French stories began to appear from 1929, and they account for the relatively sharp rise in the number of foreign stories from this date into the early and mid-1930s, reaching six or seven a year.

This chapter will show that these foreign cross-dressing stories were used to explore the potentially troubling issues of sexual morality and national security.

The relationship between gender, sexuality and national identity flavoured the cross-dressing story in complex ways. A sense of British national identity was collectively imagined in relation to both the colonised people of empire and the foreign rivals across the Channel. Ideas about sexual morality, especially of women acting as symbolic guardians of racial purity, are crucial to the construction of national belonging.[2] Existing and newer themes in popular culture, which attributed greater sensual freedom and attractiveness to foreigners, form the backdrop to some of the passing women stories. Displaced 'abroad', across the Channel, female morality could be somewhat loosened, and cross-dressing narratives could provide a means of exploring those sexual meanings of female marriage which could not be admitted within British culture.

Britain had a complex relationship with France as both ally and rival. As Britain's nearest neighbour and close competitor, France was the key defining 'other' place in the national imagination, and had long held that position politically and culturally, if not still militarily.[3] French national character was defined as effete in comparison to the beef-eating John Bull. Threatened invasion in the early nineteenth century still had a place in the national psyche, joined by more recent rivalry over imperial expansion. Yet there was now a fresh (and perhaps still insecure) relationship of Anglo-French alliance since the turn of the century and during the First World War, and France was established as a friend. This history of conflict between the two countries, and a continuing cultural shaping of British nationhood against stereotypes of Frenchness provided a rich set of connotations for cross-dressing stories in the 1930s.

Cross-dressing marriage stories set in France, that perennial home of sexual misdemeanours, are discussed in the first part of the chapter. Displaced overseas, the risky and potentially troubling sexual possibilities raised by female husbands following the *Well of Loneliness* trial and the Colonel Barker case could be explored without tainting the classic tradition of the British passing woman. The central section of the chapter deals with the extraordinary series of 'gigolo' stories in which concerns about female sexual excess could be expressed in relation to foreign locations and racial others, but not yet acknowledged as British. These narratives are doubly displaced, combining a non-national setting with exotically foreign cross-dressing gigolo lovers. They also reintroduce the decadent upper classes as a further signifier of polymorphous immorality. Finally, these dodgy cross-dressing stories at last make their way back home, to spaces within the UK not seen as fully British, especially cosmopolitan London, indicating the beginning of a shift in how women's gender-crossing is perceived. Drawing on debates around cosmopolitanism developed by Lucy Bland and Mica Nava, this section discusses the attractions of the exotic in contemporary popular culture as the other side of the official censure of racial mixing, and its associations with vice and homosexuality in the metropolis.[4] The portrayal of race and nationality in entertainment in this period provides a context for the sexualising of the cross-dresser. These stories mobilised older traditions in popular culture as well as engaging with new fears accompanying interwar modernity.

French female husbands

Although France was a political and military ally of Britain, the uneasy neighbour just across the Channel generally occupied an equivocal place in national consciousness. Calais and Boulogne were regarded as the gateways to a more licentious sexual culture than was permitted in Britain. France had long been associated, literally and figuratively, with sexual behaviours disowned by the English – a country where prostitution was taken for granted, male homosexuality legally tolerated, and can-can girls made Parisian music hall distinctly more exciting than the British variety theatre.[5] We should see the sudden appearance of French female husband stories in this context, yet also as outlining threats to a respectable bourgeois society similar to that found in Britain. At first sight the stories of young French men courting women, but turning out to be women themselves, presented as extraordinary, funny stories, seem to parallel the classic British cross-dressing reports. But the subtle adaptations of the formula emphasise the sexual attractiveness of the passing woman as suitor and husband, barely mentioning employment or other anchors of respectability, and are more suggestive about the dangers she poses to heterosexuality and social stability.

The stories feature the cross-dressing woman as a Don Juan figure and contain fairytale elements in the way that seemingly perfect marriages were enacted – but then undone. Edmond Burgon was handsome and charming, and a popular figure at social functions in 1929 Orleans. Apparently wealthy, he was 'thought the matrimonial catch of the season, and he was angled for right and left by well-to-do girls and their matchmaking mothers'. He married Jeanne d'Albret, 'not only the belle of the town, but also an heiress', and they were briefly seen as a charming and happy young couple. But the marriage quickly went sour. Jeanne d'Albret left her husband after six weeks and began proceedings for annulment. '[F]or the first weeks of their wedded life her suspicions were not roused, but in the end she made a discovery that forced her to return to her home.'[6] This 'discovery' during the honeymoon period introduces sexual speculation into the story, as of course did the claim for annulment. These stories demonstrate that despite the irresistibility of the suitors, such a marriage was impossible to contract or to sustain. What had seemed an ideal match turned out to be a same-sex union, which was decried and denounced in a number of ways. Annulment proceedings, as mechanisms of judicial control, stress the impossibility of a relationship between two women and the seriousness with which it is regarded by the community. Shame is the appropriate response of the tricked wives, whose reputation is damaged by such an association, and also of the fake husbands who are effectively run out of town. These cross-dressers are heavy-footed tricksters; their schemes backfire and they end up as losers.

What are the wider lessons suggested? That attractive young men could be dangerous if they are strangers to the community; that the threat of disruption to heterosexuality posed by passing women needs to be repelled vigorously. This is a far more extensive warning of the dangers and problems of cross-dressing than is found in the British stories, where the protagonists are sympathetic figures who tend to bounce back and are more likely to be admired than condemned. Without directly addressing the question of same-sex desire they go further in exploring its implications and the appropriate social responses. The attractiveness of the passing woman and the strong sexual desires she awakens in women is represented and problematised. Women's pursuit of lust creates social disturbance, as in each case the masquerading suitor had incited jealousy and rivalry. In Orleans, 'tempers became frayed, and some ladies allowed jealousy to betray them into violent scenes in public'.[7] The French stories rehearse the dangers of female passion, but also censure the cross-dresser for her transgressive desires.

One particular element of the humour in these stories is peculiarly French: a certain amount of 'stage business' around the official documents needed to marry and prove one's identity in France. The headline of one report reads: 'Wife is a Man: And Her Husband a Woman! Courts Tackle Queer Problem'. The journalist cites common clerical errors in French birth certificates and the rigidity of French law for 'the matrimonial tangle'. The woman's name was Renée but incorrectly entered on her birth certificate as René. Coincidentally, her husband, whose name was Aimé, was described as Aimée, so that when they presented themselves to be married, the mayor decided it was in order, with 'the woman figuring as the husband, and the man as the wife, the man taking the wife's name and family'. Unfortunately when an uncle died, they were left his fortune in the name they ought to have borne if the man had been recognised as husband by the law, hence the 'queer problem'.[8] Here we have an elaborate joke against the French, perceived to be a nation of sclerotic bureaucrats, where gender identity lies in the paperwork and not in the body. It is easier to marry in the wrong gender than correct a clerical error, a situation which is implicitly contrasted with English good sense and pragmatism. These stories are playing on national stereotyping, but also on anxieties about modernity, one feature of which is an ever-increasing role for the state in individuals' lives and the overweening power of this bureaucracy.[9] The traditional tricksterish cross-dressing story picks up and pokes fun at the absurd regulations of the modern state.

A female marriage story of 1937 brought together all the elements of the gender-crossing genre, together with a different whiff of lesbianism, in relating how two women had lived together as husband and wife for 40 years on the French Riviera, near Juan-les-Pins. Monsieur Camille Bertin, apparently a man of independent means, had met a young Glaswegian woman named as Hilda Joan Scott in London and brought her to France where he married her. They had three daughters.

> In the 40 years of their married life the couple entertained lavishly, but it was noted as something peculiar that their guests were always women. Never was a man received at their table. Furthermore, the three daughters were brought up to avoid the opposite sex.

Camille Bertin's sudden death led to a judicial enquiry and the discovery that she was a woman.[10]

There is another swipe at the inanity of French bureaucracy. The report explained that it was easy for Bertin to carry out her deception because Camille is a name common to both sexes in France. She just had to alter the entry under sex in her birth certificate. The marriage and the birth registrations remain perfectly legal 'because, for purposes of legalisation, the only things that carry weight in France are the papers presented by the persons wishing to marry or to register births'. This is published later than the other stories of French suitors who get their comeuppance, and written in more sombre style. While the successful deception is represented as amazing, it is not seen as admirable. 'Both women, it seems, had had love disappointments in their teens, and for that reason had become man-haters.'[11] This element of 'man-hating' was unusual – most stories of cross-dressers stressed their integration into the masculine social world – and may have indicated lesbianism.[12] Bertin's will left all the estate to the three daughters, on the condition that they did not marry. The newspaper points out that this is not binding, however, as the French courts regard restrictions on marriage and procreation as being against public policy and therefore illegal. French laws and procedures, though elsewhere ridiculous, here rescue the daughters for a heterosexual future.

The undercurrents of women's same-sex desire, briefly raised by the Colonel Barker case, are transposed to France in these narratives. The further implications of the female husband story for a society based on similar moral codes around marriage and the family, and the appropriate social responses to the disruption threatened by same-sex passion, could here be explored at arms length.

The 'Naughty Continong':[13] the gigolo and sexual desire

At the beginning of the 1930s there suddenly appeared – and only in the *People* – a burst of particularly exotic cross-dressing stories, in which gigolos (paid dancing partners) working in foreign clubs and hotels, who had charmed money and jewellery from their wealthy female patrons, were eventually unmasked as women. They had a number of common elements. They all took place in French leisure resorts or the night-club areas of Paris. The gigolo was always described as particularly handsome, sophisticated and as having an irresistible romantic style. She generally had an 'exotic' background; indeed the stories developed from featuring the gigolo as an English aristocrat fallen on hard times, to Latin lovers and Arab sheiks, involving the young women passing across race and class as well as gender boundaries. The desires of her society patronesses are emphasised; in some stories they fight over 'his' favours, in others engagements are promised. In two accounts, both involving wealthy Americans, the gigolo is cited as co-respondent in divorce proceedings. In each story the deceived women are rendered ridiculous by the press, while the trickster cross-dresser escapes or even claims the high moral ground.

Like the French female marriage reports, the gigolo stories occupy an interesting chronology and location. Appearing at a time of renewed interest in women's cross-dressing following the Colonel Barker trial in 1929, they initiate a shift away from the classic British tradition of gender masquerade, towards a style of reporting which signals sexuality more explicitly. The 1930s gigolos protect the respectability of the British cross-dresser by displacing sexual transgression onto both foreign 'others' and non-national settings. There is no simple dichotomisation of sexuality into what was nationally acceptable and what was louche and foreign. Rather, in the gigolo stories, there is complex interplay between two historically potent ways of 'othering' forms of deviant or excessive sexuality – associating it with continental licence and also with other races, through the trope of the Latin lover or the Arab sheik. The seductive masculinity of these male types borrowed heavily from other areas of popular culture including romantic fiction and variety theatre. This sexualisation drew from different periods of modernity. The first trope of French naughtiness was well established from the late nineteenth century, while the open fascination with exoticised non-European sexualities was a product of interwar modernity.

What is it that makes these stories both un-English and more sexual? Their particular locations – the theatres and clubs of Paris, and the French seaside resorts patronised by wealthy British and Americans – were part of the grammar through which France stood for sexual naughtiness. Gerald Bruce was 'one of the heartbreakers of a fashionable Normandy resort', Deauville, while 'sheik' Ibn Ben Ali held court as a 'most charming Prince of the Desert . . . in the fashionable "dancings" of Paris, Nice and the North African seaboard'.[14] The French Riviera was an ambivalent place of recreation for the wealthy. Made fashionable for English visitors by the patronage of Queen Victoria and the English aristocracy in the late nineteenth century, it was at the same time seen as a place of loose morals, with its gambling casinos and the mistresses accompanying prominent men. Between the wars the liberal freedoms of Paris attracted wealthy bohemians and African-American musicians and performers, such as Josephine Baker. It was a stimulating site of cultural mixing, generating developments in modern jazz and 'primitive' and surrealist art, and offered a reputation for sexual tolerance.[15]

Most of the cross-dressing stories made reference to Paris and its clubs, including the 'notorious night resorts of Montmartre and Montparnasse'.[16] Nightclubs could encompass a range of social and sexual possibilities, from exclusive hotel venues for the elite, to downmarket clubs catering for the underworld or sexual sub-cultures where prostitutes and queer men might hang out, but which might also be visited by the wealthy 'smart set' in search of thrills. Cabaret was more exotic and sexually explicit in Paris than it was in London variety shows, a fact well known and often referenced in British popular culture, as in Marie Lloyd's music hall song 'The Naughty Continong'.[17] The Moulin Rouge translated the provocative spectacle of Paris streetwalkers on to the stage in a theatrical erotic show.[18] Though Sapphic titillation was possible on stage, even in Paris there were limits to how far this could go.[19] In case readers were in doubt, the *People* spelled out the liminal respectability of some of these Paris venues. The career of one gigolo in Montparnasse was brought to an end when 'the police of morals raided a certain night establishment in search of undesirables frequenting it', and found that his passport showed he was an upper-class English girl whose motive was adventure. She had found London and its night life 'too dull' (despite the fact that it was often censured by the popular press), drawing attention again to the greater licentiousness available over the Channel.[20] This was also emphasised in the *People*'s use of language: the terms 'gigolo' and 'apache' (discussed further below), both derived from the French, were used repeatedly in these stories to denote exoticism, and suggested more exciting sexual possibilities than the familiar language of English divorce court reports. The French language itself was used as a referent for sexual knowingness on the stage, as in Marie Lloyd's song:

> Twiggy voo, my boys, twiggy voo?
> Well of course it stands to reason that you do,
> All the force and meaning in it you can 'tumble' in a minute,
> Twiggy voo, my boys, Twiggy voo?[21]

The different levels of continental meaning, however obscure, are those conjured with in the male impersonator Ella Shields' 1925 song 'If You Knew Susie', where innuendo about a day trip to France soon dismantles Susie's 'perfect reputation'.

> When in Boulogne say, she'll nothing wrong say,
> Oh, oh, parley vous with my fi-ong-say,
> But my cherie she's quite all there
> She confesses that she loves the pom-de-terre.

Since 'she stops the traffic with her chassis' and 'On the sofa she's a riot', we can all work out what kind of a girl Susie is, and clearly Shields is one of the lads who knows.

As in all the cross-dressing stories, the gigolo is judged on her performance of masculinity, but here this is a highly sexualised form of masculinity, instantly conveyed by class and racial stereotyping. Early gigolos featured in the *People* were passing across class rather than racial boundaries. The 'young Adonis' Gerald Bruce, 'a strikingly handsome young man in exquisite flannels', created a stir in Deauville. 'The story was circulated discreetly that he was heir to an English title going back to the days of the Conqueror', but in the event Gerald turned out to be a young English parlourmaid, recently employed in a Cheltenham hotel.[22] Subsequent gigolos were masquerading as Arab sheiks, Spanish or French men. Interestingly, this rapid shift in ethnicity mirrors the broader developments in interwar romance fiction, where the English aristocrat as sexually attractive hero was increasingly displaced in the 1920s and 30s by Mediterranean heartthrobs and desert sheiks.[23]

By 1932, the date of the first cross-dressing sheik story, the Arab sheik was well established as part of the language of sex and romance, following the enormous success of E. M. Hull's 1919 novel *The Sheik*, the story of an Englishwoman abducted to the desert, and raped by a handsome Arab sheik. A huge bestseller, it also became a hit film in 1921 starring Rudolph Valentino. The power of this figure was reflected in the intertextual references in the press to 'Sheik-struck' neurotic women.[24] Billie Melman argues that the term 'sheik' came to stand for a new image of masculinity in the popular western imagination after 1919, which was particularly sensual, 'primitive' and virile. The enormously popular 'love in the desert' novels of that period were erotic literature for women – they were about sexual fantasy rather than romantic love.[25] Rather than the violent, cruel and rapacious qualities of the romance novels, the sheiks of the *People* stories had a charming manner appropriate to the commercial social space of the hotel dance-floor. Ibn Ben Ali, the 'Prince of the Desert',

> 'had no lack of women patrons . . . He held them spell-bound with his tales of the desert that was supposed to have been the home of his fathers for scores of generations, and when he dropped into love-making in supposed Arabic his admirers were thrilled more than ever.[26]

To readers, the figure of the desert sheik promised an imaginary world of sexual pleasure, exoticism and wealth. His unmasking as a woman added a further transgressive layer of same-sex desire to this highly charged fantasy. 'The revelation I am able to make today', announced the Paris correspondent of the *People* in 1933, 'that the handsome sheik Ali Ben Azrael was really a girl, will come as a shock to "his" host of women admirers who fought for his favours and showered presents on "him".'[27] A convention of the desert novel sheik is that he too is passing. E. M. Hull's original sheik is revealed to be the son of a Scottish earl and a Spanish princess, and later formula novels followed this turn in the plot.[28] Similarly the sheiks in the gigolo stories turn out to be of upper-class European stock. Ali Ben Azrael was 'a young Parisienne belonging to the French equivalent of . . . the Bright Young People', her French origin meaning she still retained the flavour of the Latin lover.[29]

The Latin lover, the idea already inherent in the term gigolo, was, like the sheik, gaining in popularity after the First World War, becoming a common hero of romantic fiction. His 'Mediterranean' characteristics, his passionate and fiery temperament as well as his good looks, and the tempting possibilities of 'abroad', gave him the sexual edge over northern European heroes. These stories traded in complex and contradictory markers of race and masculinity. The foreign man might be figured as a macho brute, thrilling and dominating European womanhood, but also as effeminate and androgynous. In the gigolo stories he did, after all, make a living by being a charming partner on the dance floor, far removed from manly physical labour, and in contemporary fiction as well as in the press stories he was also often mixed up with the interwar hero as 'boy', as younger and of lower status than the heroine.[30] Cultural historians have explained the appearance of these exotic romantic heroes as a response to the damage done to young British manhood on the wartime battlefields. Wounded in spirit as well as in body, no longer tough and heroic, they were superseded by these virile racial others. The diminished and domesticated image of British masculinity between the wars – the reliable clerk in his cardigan, the foppish upper-class chap – could not compete.[31]

The Latin gigolo encompassed all these personae. He was the well-dressed, smooth-talking lounge lizard – 'such a nice boy' – while he also demonstrated a wilder and dangerously attractive sexuality as an 'apache'. This slang term, meaning a Parisian 'tough' or hooligan, had entered both French and English at the turn of the century.[32] It was further popularised in both languages through the violent and titillating apache dance devised in Paris cabaret in 1909, exciting audiences across Europe and North America in the following years. In its original version by the French music hall star Mistinguett at the Moulin Rouge, the dance theatricalised a fight between a woman of the streets and her apache, or pimp (though the latter connotation did not remain in the English usage).[33] Newspaper readers were familiar with the resonant term. A fashion report of 1925, for example, dramatised the challenge of new masculine styles for women. 'There is a new battle of male v. female going on in Paris . . . But do not imagine any pitched battle between Gigolettes and Apaches, or secret skirmishes between mocking midinettes and boulevard beaux.'[34] So when it appeared in the gigolo stories, the description added further eroticism. '[M]asquerad[ing] as a gigolo or dancing partner and a typical Apache' an English girl had convincingly moved around Montmartre and Montparnasse during 1933, according to the *People*. The term 'Apache' evoked the sexual excitement attached to lower-class foreign gangsters, with added same-sex titillation. As well as living off the women who patronised the Montmartre bars as a gigolo, this particular cross-dresser was also accompanied for a while by her own girlfriend, 'as the typical "petite amie" of the Apache'.[35]

Unlike the lingering attention paid to the broad shoulders and athletic build of the romantic fiction hero or the British cross-dressing woman, the physical appearance of the sheik or Latin gigolo was not described in any detail, beyond presenting them as handsome. Their sexual appeal was already established as stock hero types, and it was developed further in the press stories by descriptions of their facility in love-making and the extraordinary response to them by women. '[H]e not only recited charming love poems to them, but actually composed them to order and recited them impromptu into the ears of his charmed companions.'[36] It was usually rich middle-aged women who used the services of a paid dancing partner, but the sexual attractiveness of several gigolos was underscored by their popularity with younger women. Among Gerald Bruce's conquests 'was an English girl of nineteen and another was a woman who has certainly passed forty-five. They figured in scenes more than once because each resented the interest of the other in the gay and graceful Gerald.'[37] The powerful sexual desire unleashed in their strings of women patrons was demonstrated by their lavish gifts (often the subject of later police investigations), and the jealousy exhibited as the women fought (sometimes literally) over the gigolo's favours. 'As much as a hundred pounds was paid as gratuity to [the sheik Ali Ben Azrael] for an evening as cavalier, and costly jewellery was given "him" openly by admiring women . . . Infatuated women worshippers wrote "him" long and passionate love letters.'[38]

The use of the term 'gigolo' is also pertinent to the portrayal of licentiousness in these stories. The newspaper was concerned to explain the word simply as 'professional dancing partner', or 'danceur mondain' (society dancer),[39] but it also had wider connotations of 'kept' man, especially a younger man supported by an older woman in return for sex. Reversing conventional heterosexual prostitution, here the independent desiring woman enjoys romance and sexual favours in a commercial transaction. While there are several marriage proposals and engagements between the gigolos and the wealthy women,[40] it is the divorce petitions involving the sheik Ali Ben Azrael and Juan the Basque which are really important for suggesting not only illicit but also transgressive sex. '[T]he open manner in which an American woman well-known in Paris society went about with the "Sheik" led to trouble with her husband and the filing of a divorce suit in which the "gigolo" was cited.'[41] Divorce cases were a staple feature of the Sunday newspapers in this period, and the use of the terminology of the divorce courts signalled sexual wrong-doing in a manner both salacious and coy. In these cases it was revealed that the adulterous sex actually occurred in a same-sex liaison, which was easier to suggest as part of continental immorality than in the stories set on British soil. The extraordinary 'Dual Divorce Dupes' case involved an American couple and the cross-dressed Spanish dancer Juan or Juanita who was cited as co-respondent for both parties. Court enquiries 'resulted in the disclosure that the "co-respondent" and "the woman in the case" are the same person'. Indeed the term 'co-respondent' (which implied that adulterous sex had actually taken place) was used several times in the article.[42] Juan's changing gender but continuous work role as dance partner to both husband and wife enabled her to disrupt heterosexuality both figuratively and literally.

These gigolo stories engage with the fantasies of female sexual desire developing in other sites of popular culture in this period to evoke a much more suggestive sense of sexual immorality than the cross-dressing stories set in Britain in the same period, which are rather restrained by comparison. They expand the cross-dressing genre by portraying a broader range of desirable masculinities – lower-class French gangster types, British aristocrats, the exotic and passionate Arab sheik and the charming Latin lover. This is lust, not respectable courtship, on the part of the wealthy society women spending time in these louche French resorts. Their liaisons involve paid-for sex, adultery, cross-racial desire, and also, it is revealed, same-sex eroticism.

The sting in the tale: morality and the gigolo

How can we account for the appearance of this burst of stories at this particular time, given that the gigolo was already established as a feature of the more disreputable end of upper-class society from the 1920s and that the 'Sheik' had already excited popular culture for almost a decade?[43] What social or moral concerns were addressed by introducing women's desire and the attractions of cross-racial sexuality in this sub-cycle of cross-dressing stories? There is plenty of evidence to suggest that these gigolo stories (and probably the French domestic stories discussed earlier) were largely works of fiction, pointing not only to the popularity of these themes but also to a significant cultural function. They were not anchored in reports of particular court cases at named and dated judicial proceedings as passing women stories normally were, but were merely 'reports of the Paris police'. Unlike the classic British cross-dressing stories, no pictures of the individuals involved were published. While reports of 'real' men–women were picked up by other Sunday and daily papers, sometimes with interviews with the different protagonists, these gigolo stories only appeared in the *People*. No cases of cross-dressing gigolos apparently occurred before 1930 or after 1933, the constrained timeframe perhaps indicating the work of a particular reporter. And the stories repeat and rework not only particular character types – the wealthy English or American woman, the Latin, Arab or upper-class gigolo – but also the very narrow range of plot elements discussed above. The fictional nature of these stories suggests active management of the genre as a controlled way of both sensationalising and dealing with new sexual anxieties.

Rather than playing out respectable courtship as the British passing women did, the cross-dressing gigolos exploited their patrons – they were sexy but dangerous men. In Cannes, one of the two cross-dressing gigolos got engaged to a young American widow but took the jewels of the intended bride, hence the headline 'Done by Dunne Girls'.[44] The unnamed society women were always thoroughly 'duped' by the gigolo – romantically betrayed, financially exploited and sexually and socially humiliated – but were too ashamed to pursue the matter: 'This girl has refused to prosecute because of her desire to avoid publicity.'[45]

The gigolos on the other hand are tricksters in every way. The fictionalised format and particular themes of this cycle of stories enables the passing woman to flourish especially powerfully in her activities as boundary-crosser and moralist. The gigolos are swindlers and confidence tricksters in their criminal deceptions. They are cheats and chancers in romance. They cross multiple fixed boundaries in pretending to be someone they are not – class, race, nationality as well as gender – and are much more accomplished than the British gender-crosser who remains in her class of origin. Despite their dubious and criminal activities they disappear or escape censure and turn the tables on their victims. The links made in many stories to theatrical performance also allow them to escape both the consequences of criminal behaviour and imputations of same-sex immorality. It was Hilda Batty-Langley's success

> in amateur theatricals as a male impersonator that inspired her with the idea of darkening her skin and trying her luck as imitator of the supposed Sheiks who are in such demand among a certain class of women visitors to French and North African holiday resorts.[46]

The stories, then, explore the question of what would happen if the sheik or Latin lover from the popular romance were to appear in reality. Positioned halfway between fiction, stage and screen on one side and everyday life on the other, they work more profoundly in the world of fantasy than the domestic British cross-dressing narrative which was entangled in neighbourhood, workplace and courtroom. In doing so, they point to the moral lessons to be drawn from these escapades, each chiming with concerns continually paraded in the popular press.

In the first place they reveal moral corruption among the elite, a perennial theme for the popular press, and in particular the true colours of pleasure-seeking upper-class women, who are depicted as uncontrolled, abandoning their duty to preserve sexual and racial purity. The 'victims' of these stories – the wealthy women who have their property swindled – were from an international English and American set, already represented as a class of women prone to 'decadence'.[47] Almost all the gigolos were convincingly claiming elite lineage of some kind, while actually coming from a range of backgrounds, from West Country parlourmaid to Parisian 'smart set'. This allows the press to emphasise the fascinating details of upper-class life while at the same time condemning its useless and frivolous aspects: the world of 'exclusive hotels', 'the fashionable "dancings" of Paris, Nice and the North African seaboard', haunts of 'middle-aged women with leisure and lucre at their command'.[48]

This is a gendered attack on class privilege which also serves to condemn women's active sexual desire. The 'maudlin middle-aged ladies' who are ridiculed for brazenly exercising their sexual desires are described in scathing tones as besotted, ageing and self-deluding. They were 'the sentimental type of women who haunt such resorts in order to enjoy the luxury of being flattered by the Adonis-like creatures who are generally summed-up in the term "gigolo"'.[49] They are the butt of the trick which has been played and are opened to scorn as silly society women. This is an attack on the female search for romance, but also on their assumption of the masculine prerogative of paying for erotic pleasure. Women's sexuality is figured in these stories as passionate, active and violent, reversing the usual gendered model of heterosexuality and enabling the press to describe it entertainingly while at the same time deprecating it. As the story of one gigolo unfolded, his lovers' undisciplined behaviour descended to that of street-walkers in their violent desire for his sexual attention:

> One night one of his rejected 'flames' turned up and began a savage attack on her successor. The pair picked up knives from the tables and engaged in a duel at close quarters. When separated they resumed the battle with plates, wine bottles and such other missiles as came to hand, and in the end both were arrested. On another occasion a middle-aged English Society woman who had fallen for the young Adonis had the contents of a soup tureen thrown at her because she had dared to give expression to her triumph over her predecessor.[50]

This suggests anxiety about female sexual subjectivity in the modern world. Marie Stopes' well-publicised work on marital pleasure and birth control between the wars meant that women's sexual desires both inside and outside marriage now had to be acknowledged and reckoned with.[51]

The twist in the tale of the English girl who masqueraded as an 'apache' in a Montmartre night-club was that she was from the same class as her victims. She told police that some of her clients 'were women well known to her socially at home. She declares that none of these indiscreet women ever suspected that they were dealing with one of their own sex who had met them frequently in London night-clubs and other resorts.'[52] This threatens fast women with the warning that their actions are being watched and noted, potentially to surface in the popular scandal sheets. It also cautions against the social and sexual dangers of night-clubs. We have seen in Chapters 2 and 3 that the press represented decadent lesbian desire as located within the dissolute upper class and the bohemian world of the theatre and the arts. Female desire was unbounded in the milieu of the gigolo where it could easily overflow into further categories of sexual deviance – same-sex relationships and cross-racial desire.

Of these dangers, the one more explicitly made through the voice of the trickster gigolo is the condemnation of cross-racial sexual desire. Playfully gender- and race-crossing as a sheik, the gigolo enables readers to witness the true breakdown of civilised values that would occur if miscegenation were permitted. The physical fighting between women is important here. Ali Ben Azrael, the sheik who provoked a divorce suit, was '[s]o convincing . . . that friends quarrelled over "him", and in one instance mother and daughter came to blows on the dance floor because of their rivalry'.[53] Here sexual competition and jealousy corrupt family relationships as society women abandon their controlled western behaviour and descend to 'primitive' violence in their passion. In their response to these indeterminately raced and gendered figures, they betray their superior racial status as well as their gender and class position. Since in this story, 'an American woman well-known in Paris society' went around with the sheik in an 'open manner', the newspaper may have been taking an indirect pot-shot at the heiress Nancy Cunard, whose racial mixing and anti-racist politics had been attacked in the popular press, hinting at her sexual relationships with black women as well as men.[54] Directly accusing society women of interracial relationships was likely to land newspaper proprietors in court for libel, as they found in the early 1930s. In 1932 the *People* had been forced to apologise in court to Lady Mountbatten, whom they had accused of having a scandalous 'association with a coloured man'.[55] The gigolo 'sheik' stories appear in the years immediately afterwards, and were a safer way of making such allegations than through the gossip columns.

In the 'Sheik was a She' story of summer 1932, the cross-dressing Hilda Batty-Langley makes the moral censure explicit. She 'treats the whole thing as a joke' – she is a trickster after all – 'and declares she did it solely to show up the folly of her own sex, who are content to pamper and pet low-class natives who call themselves princes'.[56] Potentially still figured as exotic herself, by virtue of her French nationality and Paris home, Batty-Langley in fact stands for the defence of pure European womanhood against interracial immorality.[57] There are many different and contrary layers of moral condemnation centred in the trickster gigolo. She plays a conservative role in warning about female desire and sexual deviance, while also embodying it. She attacks the laxity of upper-class women and particularly condemns mixed-race relationships, but also wags a finger at the louche ways of the French. Continental location works both ways – it adds sexual suggestiveness and affords an opportunity for moral superiority.

Cosmopolitanism at home

In the late 1930s the sexualised cross-dresser fleetingly makes an appearance in the unreliably English metropolis, central London. The emergence of fears about female sexuality and the integrity of national identity led to new ways of figuring illicit desires, not only 'abroad' but also at home, in the unstable centre of empire. London was seen as the decadent foreign body within the nation, and it was in the cosmopolitan spaces of the capital that the cross-dressing woman began to acquire recognisable sexual codes.

The interwar period saw a range of anxieties about nation and empire explored in popular culture. The British empire was still powerful and dominant, but facing demands for autonomy and independence from its colonies and dominions. Following First World War mobilisation and labour needs there was a larger black population within Britain itself, especially in London and the ports. Colonial challenge was also felt at home, witnessed in racial unrest in 1919–20 in port cities: attacks on black seamen justified by white men in terms of their sexual as well as economic fears. The interwar period saw the growth of significant black anti-colonial organisations based in London. State legislation constructed a narrowing definition of Britishness, in which women's bodies played an increasingly important role in maintaining eugenic quality – policing the borders of nationality through marriage, while symbolically representing the purity of the nation.[58] Women's role in delineating national identity was crucial as mothers but at the same time insecure as citizens.

There were contradictory discourses and representations of race and sexuality at this time. Racial superiority was taken for granted in the imperial world-view, promoted by the authorities' responses to miscegenation and racial unrest, and established in legislation by the state.[59] Ordinary people undoubtedly shared in these ideologies while also being fascinated by racial difference, an attraction exploited in popular culture and entertainment.[60] Lucy Bland and Mica Nava have developed important analyses of the balance between the denigration of and attraction to the 'other' in their reading of race, gender and sexuality in interwar popular culture. Bland shows how antipathy to miscegenation and orientalist perceptions of Arab men as sexually perverse led to the acquittal of a white woman for the murder of her Egyptian husband in 1923 in the face of the evidence.[61] The sexual dangers of racial mixing 'also connoted the political dangers of challenge to white hegemony' in the post-First World War period, amplified by uncertainty about women's increasing agency following wartime changes in gender roles.[62] While Bland draws attention to the underlying attraction of the exotic in mass literature, Mica Nava makes a more emphatic reading of the importance of utopian and radical visions of modernity in popular culture. She argues that cosmopolitanism – other places, peoples and cultures – was seen and consumed as alluring and erotic in this period, especially by women. We have seen how new forms of masculinity were sexualised through race and orientalism and became attractive to women readers of romance. In advertising, consumer culture and the arts, Nava argues that women were particularly open to reading racial otherness as symbolising modernity and escape from domesticity; it represented an 'else-where' of the imagination associated with freedom and pleasure.[63]

The popular press certainly milked all these angles to draw in readers, whipping up indignation about racial mixing and miscegenation, while working with the widespread fascination with racial difference. The Sunday newspapers had for years been full of stories of black boxers and musicians, but there was an increasing obsession between the wars with the nature of cosmopolitanism and its perceived threats, played out in stories of unwise interracial marriages and the exotic East End.[64] If not in connection with sport and entertainment, then black, Asian and Arab men appeared in the newspapers in relation to drug-dealing, prostitution and the 'white slave trade', exploiting ignorant young white women of all classes.[65] An 'Outbreak of Sexual Dementia' was how one clergyman described the enthusiasm of white girls for 'coloured men' in the Liverpool, Cardiff and London docks. These girls belonged to the better class: 'They were not driven there by poverty, but by wantonness.'[66] In opium dens women could combine all kinds of lurid worst fates at the hands of Chinese gangsters.[67] At best they might contract ill-advised marriages with Lascar sailors who did not speak English.[68] The *People* linked interracial sex, 'lax morality and sordid passion' together with the 'smear' (homosexuality) in a 1924 editorial to warn that the lowering of moral standards was the 'visible sign of the inward and spiritual degeneration of a race'.[69]

Race and gender-crossing on stage

The seductive Arab sheik who turns out to be of European stock was a new hero of interwar romance fiction. Racial crossing was already well established in popular theatre and was joined by new variants of exotic othering in popular culture in this period. Blackface minstrelsy was an extremely successful genre within and outside the music hall in Victorian England, and continued to be a common staple into the late twentieth century. Michael Pickering argues that its success was due to a number of factors. It provided comedy through caricaturing and stereotyping black people, creating a black 'other' who inverted the 'civilised' work ethic of the white bourgeoisie and unleashed their repressed human desires for pleasure. Sentimentalism, nostalgia and comedy could be enjoyed in songs of happy plantation life, and these styles worked to domesticate and defuse the threat perceived to be embodied in other racial groups and classes.[70]

Since minstrelsy was established in the nineteenth century as a highly respectable form of family entertainment, it used all the stock caricatures of black people *except* those of promiscuity and aggressive sexual drive.[71] Simon Featherstone, however, argues that George Chirgwin's minstrel act in the late nineteenth century did work with the sexual meanings attributed to black masculinity, carrying a coded sexual charge and the threat of miscegenation.[72] We have already seen how blackface racial stereotypes contributed to the humorous reporting of a black American passing woman, Paul Downing, arrested in London in 1905. The newspapers made play of Downing's religious mania and her preaching to the chickens, which recalled comic stereotypes about the black man's love of food, especially chicken.[73] Pickering describes a turn-of-the-century minstrel 'stump speech' involving a sketch based on the black man as chicken-thief.[74] One of the newspapers also introduced a gratuitous part of the tale in which Downing is sacked for sexually pursuing the servant girls.[75] In the press, then, as well as on stage, the double passing of race and gender-crossing carried a sexual resonance. Traditional blackface minstrelsy continued to be a ubiquitous form in British variety after the First World War, providing comic characters and sentimentalism both in revue and at seaside concert parties.[76] Pickering speculates that the genre lost its force during the twentieth century due to the commercial development of variety, but there is a very limited amount of research on this period and the fate of older forms as more polished productions became commercially dominant.[77]

Yet, from the turn of the century, white entertainment began to be influenced by new black styles – more 'authentic' African and African-American influences as opposed to the synthetic fantasy of minstrel shows. Primitivism, the exotic and the influence of black art forms were all central to the development of avant-garde modernism higher up the cultural scale. But they also profoundly affected popular culture and were seen as part of interwar modernity. Jazz and ragtime became enormously fashionable dance music, though derided by middlebrow commentators as 'primitive'.[78] Mica Nava argues that the huge popular success of the singer Paul Robeson in Britain was based on his appeal as a black American, the nation which was the locus of modernity.[79] In considering entertainment built on fascination with the exotic other, is there a shift in the nature of its address from respectable and amusing to more dangerous and desirable between the wars?

In its inversion of power and social relationships, the blacking-up of white men as minstrels parallels theatrical gender-crossing. Both forms created a temporary fantasy world which was licensed to mock and critique dominant cultural assumptions about the essential difference of gender and race. Both reinforced some assumptions about social hierarchies while undermining others, through the use of humour, eroticism and projected fantasy. Historians of minstrelsy maintain that it was almost exclusively performed by men in its various professional manifestations.[80] Yet we can find a number of women who included blackface male impersonation as part of their variety acts. We can only speculate on the effects produced when women performed in blackface. Race and gender-crossing in combination may have intensified their sexual appeal. Just as possible, the plantation song might have gained added comedy or sentimentalism in their hands. Bessie Wentworth, who died in 1901, was the best known of the women who performed minstrel male impersonation, but the genre continued to flourish after the First World War.[81] The *News of the World* pictured May Henderson in blackface in 1920. 'With her face blackened, eyes rolling, her step-dancing, and quick wits' she enjoyed success as the 'Dusky Comedy Queen' from the 1900s until her retirement in 1932.[82] In 1925 it was announced that Ella Shields, who had previously included blackface plantation songs as part of her act, had developed a new Spanish lover number suggesting that these male impersonators were adapting their performance to appeal to current interests.[83]

Some traditions of race- and gender-crossing, as we have seen, were well established. Like the idea of French erotic naughtiness, the blackface male impersonator dates from the nineteenth century. The sheik and the gigolo figures rest upon these existing tropes, but as part of interwar modernity are more overtly sexualised, both as potent masculinities and as suggesting socially disapproved-of sexual behaviour. While they were, at one level, dealing with political and eugenic fears about miscegenation and women's sexuality, these figures from popular entertainment were about much more than that. They also lent exotic glamour to what was supposedly illicit, playing with the fascination for interracial romance and same-sex eroticism.

Cross-dressing and the urban underworld

While the sexualisation of the cross-dressing woman and her only half-hidden performance of same-sex desire was established in the early 1930s as decidedly outside British culture, she did not remain abroad on the 'naughty Continong'. Like the working out of imperial conflicts, exploration of the meanings of women's gender-crossing came back home, and in the late 1930s the sexual mannish woman began to appear – at this point fleetingly – within the cosmopolitan capital.

London's vibrant central districts were spaces perceived as not truly British, polluted by other ethnic groups, sexual licentiousness and by the social mixing of classes, races, respectability and criminality. Those communities seen as most foreign included the Jewish 'ghettos' of Whitechapel and Stepney, and the Chinese area of Limehouse, near the docks. The connection between these areas and crime was made in the popular press through general 'exposés' and by the sensationalist representation of particular court cases, such as the suicide of Freda Kempton from an overdose of cocaine in 1922, following her association with the Chinese man Brilliant Chang.[84] Week after week during February and March 1923, for example, the *People* ran regular articles on crime in cosmopolitan London, beginning with 'Unmasking the Underworld' in which it revealed the perils of night-clubs, dope traffickers, 'body worship' and abortion.[85] The paper progressed to 'Down East' with London's Orientals and the menacing 'Lure of London' to young girls.[86] West End night-club life, which ranged from smart venues to shabby, illegal dens, was described as a particular arena of decadence, where drugs might be found, excessive alcohol consumed and racial mixing occur. The black proprietor of a club off the Tottenham Court Road was fined in 1923 for allowing dancing and out-of-hours drinking. This 'Black Men and White Women's Haunt' was condemned as harbouring 'persons of notorious character, bullies, [and] cocaine traffickers'.[87] Miscegenation fears and anxieties about the moral corruption of the nation, as witnessed in its capital, were prevalent during the years of social readjustment following the First World War, but these topics continued to be preoccupations in popular culture throughout the interwar period. The 1929 film *Piccadilly* sensationally depicted a sleazy Limehouse club where Chinese, black and white people danced together. Foreign depravity was literally imported in a 1937 story about a dance hostess who had cocaine and hashish sent over from Paris.[88] While the *News of the World* was also interested in juicy exotic stories, the *People* was particularly obsessed. This subject matter gave the paper opportunities for its moralising brand of journalism, but the fascination with racial mixing also made the newspaper appear more modern in the interwar years.

Various kinds of social integration and boundary-breaking caused alarm. Aristocrats and the wealthy might meet chorus girls and film stars, or seek more edgy fun by slumming it in after-hours drinking clubs.[89] These were the play-grounds of the wealthy 'fast set', already associated in the press with both hetero-sexual and homosexual decadence, the theatre and gender-crossing parties.[90] And it was from central London venues that a string of police raids on drag balls and queer clubs was reported from the early 1930s, associating male-to-female gender-crossing with the shameless display of the queer male community.[91]

Mannish lesbians made one or two appearances in popular press depictions of decadent London clubs in the late 1930s, following police raids on male homo-sexual meeting places. In the trial (of 100 defendants) following the Caravan Club raid in 1934, where it was alleged that men 'danced together in an indecent manner' and 'talked in effeminate voices', it was also reported that 'some of the women sat on men's knees and embraced each other. One of the women smoked a pipe.'[92] After the raid on Billie's Club in Soho, it was suggested that both men and women were implicated in this alarming vice. The venue was described as 'a meeting place for a type of moral pervert who seemed to delight in imitating persons of the opposite sex'.[93] These mentions are so brief as to hardly constitute a clear representation of the mannish lesbian – that does not happen until the late 1940s – and they are firmly situated in cosmopolitan clubland, far from the suburban respectability of the standard cross-dressing woman. The use of the 'Eton crop' as a referent for female homosexuality in the late 1930s, discussed in the Harrogate wedding case of 1937 in Chapter 3, also began to feature in these stories. In a report on low-life London night-clubs published in the *People* in 1939, under the sub-heading 'Rouged Men', a journalist wrote:

> I could take you to three different dens almost next door to one another in the same alley that should be closed immediately. One caters for blond and rouged young men *and Eton-cropped women*; the second for coloured men and women of low repute; and the third for a gang of criminals with convictions ranging from blackmail to drug peddling.[94]

Lesbian styles were cautiously beginning to be identified by the press, but at the same time were also disowned as part of Englishness by their connections with criminality, racial impurity and the cosmopolitan West End.

This potent mixture of outsider associations provided the context for the 1937 story of Elsie Carey, a notorious cross-dressing criminal gang-leader with a black girlfriend. Carey was sentenced to imprisonment for shop-breaking, reported in the *News of the World* under the headline: 'Eton-Cropped Woman Crook Led Bandit Gang'. Her masculinity was emphasised in the opening paragraph of the article, which read: 'Without flinching, an Eton-cropped woman of 28, who always dressed as a man, and who ruled men twice her age, and hypnotised them with her daring, walked from the dock . . . to start a sentence of four years' penal servitude.'[95] Carey was depicted as a powerful modern woman and as a modern criminal – she used a motorcar in her gang's smash-and-grab raids, a new form of crime glamorised in contemporary gangster films.[96] Carey wore men's clothes habitually, not only for raids, but did not pass as a man to her friends and associates.

> Residents in the neighbourhood of Carleton-road [north London] never dreamt that the 'man' in a sports car, often accompanied by a coloured girl, was in reality a dangerous criminal . . . As sentence was passed on Carey a woman cried 'Oh, oh!' and rushed from the court.[97]

The fact that Carey was a successful (even notorious) criminal, and that her companion was a black woman, linked her, in the discourses of the popular press, with the underworld of the inner city and its associated sexual decadence.[98]

Conclusion

Women's gender-crossing was a well-established British theatrical and cultural tradition. In its more reputable aspects, highlighting ideals of masculine respectability and patriotism, it formed part of the imaginative community of nation. This framing of cross-dressing stories continued into the 1930s for most domestic British reports, as we saw in Chapter 3, but at the same time foreign stories began to appear which associated cross-dressing more strongly with sexual immorality, including sex between women. French female husband narratives begin to suggest that the attractive passing woman might spell sexual danger. They also afford an opportunity for ridiculing the French through their bureaucracy, seen as an unappealing feature of modernity. It is the set of gigolo stories in the *People* which fully exploit the sexual coding of foreign terrain by linking the passing woman with sexual impropriety, upper-class decadence and often with a racialised masculinity. Exoticism, race and class work together in these accounts to produce an image of sexualised cross-dressing outside Englishness.

The cross-dressing gigolo – the chancer trickster figure – reveals the shameful consequences of cross-racial desire and censures the conduct of the spoiled rich women. But the gigolo does not escape entirely unscathed as a character. Her own involvement in continental immorality (both heterosexual and potentially homosexual) adds an element of sexual ambiguity which could not be so strongly implied in the stories set firmly on domestic soil in British towns and cities. It is not the case that cross-dressing or mannish women begin to be explained as lesbians from the late 1930s. The process was considerably more uneven and complex. But the foreign stories did mark a change, and another means to render sexuality and same-sex desire as a possibility within women's gender-crossing. What is new in the 1920s and 1930s is the way that the Latin, Arab or black man is positioned as an object of sexual fantasy for white women. Extended to cross-dressing there is no mistaking the way this sexualises the genre.

The meanings provided from other forms of popular culture – the Latin hero of the romance novel, the sexual innuendo around the French in music hall song, the potent combination of race and gender-crossing – shows that the gradual movement towards connecting the cross-dressing woman with same-sex desire in the popular press depended upon existing cultural associations between sexuality, decadence and exotic foreigners. It was enhanced and developed by the continual commercial updating of popular entertainment, the intensified eroticisation of racial otherness, the coding of unspeakable desires as not British. The sexualising of the gender-crossing woman in popular culture relied on these themes in mass entertainment. It was these strands of modernity which made her a sexual actor, not medicine or sexual science.

5   The 1930s 'sex change' story
Medical technology and physical transformation

In 1932 the *News of the World* reported a different kind of gender-crossing story, an 'Amazing Change of Sex' in which a teenage girl from Sussex, apparently with medical intervention, had become a boy. The parents hoped to change her name from Margery to Maurice. "'I cannot think of my baby as a boy even now," the child's mother confessed.'[1] This was not an isolated example. Other reports, such as that of Zdenka Koubka in 1936, suggested that it was possible to choose to change sex.

> Mr Zdenka Koubka, the 24-year-old Czecho-Slovakian 'woman' athlete who last year underwent a surgical operation to change her sex, to-day left New York for Europe for another operation . . . 'I want to be a man,' declared Koubka. 'I have always had more inclination to be a man than a woman. I am going to have the [second] operation, if necessary, because I am marrying a girl law student in Prague in 1937.[2]

The popular discourse of sex change is often dated to the male-to-female transition of Christine Jorgensen in 1952 and believed to have mainly involved men changing to women. Yet much earlier than this, in the interwar British popular press, the capacity to change sex was presented as the property of female bodies which could become male. These sex change stories were strongly framed by the idea of modern medical advances, and it is with these accounts rather than in the cross-dressing reports that we first see the influence of medical and scientific ideas in explanations of gender-crossing.

While there were occasional earlier stories of people who changed physical sex, it was in the mid-1920s that the language of 'sex change' began to be used in newspaper headlines to describe both spontaneous and medically assisted changes of sex.[3] Sex change really came into its own as a theme in the 1930s when there was a noticeable and sustained increase in the number of stories published in the *People* and the *News of the World*. From 1932, two or three reports were published in most years; in 1936 five stories appeared. They had their own distinct format and were treated by both papers as entirely unrelated to cross-dressing stories until after the Second World War.[4] Of the 21 accounts of sex change appearing in the 1930s, most were female-to-male transformations. Thirteen told of young women becoming male and only three described male-to-female transitions. Two further stories were of women who had begun to change into men, but who had received medical treatment which reversed this change of sex and restored them to femininity. Two other stories were represented as borderline cases where the individual's 'true' sex could not be determined, and the final report was of hormone treatment for feminine men. Eleven reports were from Britain and 10 were foreign, the latter from all over Europe, but particularly Eastern Europe: Bulgaria, Poland, Czechoslovakia and Hungary. Sex change added to the rich mixture and extraordinary range of gender-crossing stories in this decade.

Although it was not immediately apparent from the sensational style of the reports, most of these stories involved forms of intersexuality or hermaphrodism, both terms which were used in the medical literature of the time. Many of the cases where young women apparently changed sex into young men at puberty were situations in which sex had been wrongly assigned at birth. Advances in surgical techniques, the development of endocrinology (the study of sex hormones), and new treatments of adrenal tumours causing 'virilism' in women, lay behind some of the sex change stories.[5]

The relationship between advances in medical science, popular knowledge and individuals' own sense of cross-gender identification is particularly contested in historical accounts of the development of transsexual identity in the twentieth century. Bernice Hausman argues that the availability of technology was crucial. She suggests that 'the emergence of transsexuality in the mid-twentieth century depended on developments in endocrinology and plastic surgery as technological and discursive practices'.[6] In contrast, Joanne Meyerowitz, in her study of the United States, stresses the agency of those people who identified themselves as belonging to the other sex. Inspired by reports of overseas sex change in the American tabloid press, which, as in Britain, appeared as early as the 1930s, a growing transsexual community lobbied for treatment in concert with sympathetic doctors, and succeeded in creating transsexual identity in medical and popular discourse in the 1950s and 1960s.[7]

The first section of this chapter explores how the Sunday newspapers promoted the idea that modern medicine and surgery now had the power to effect miraculous transformations from one sex to the other. While sensationalised as curious medical case histories, people who changed sex were also humanised through interviews with them and their families. The second half of the chapter suggests that the continuing inheritance of the 'hermaphrodite' in the fairground sideshow was an important backdrop to the newspaper representations. Older notions about physical gender-crossing and hermaphrodism, formed as they were through showmanship and spectacle, enabled the press to conceptualise and present sex change in the way that it did in the 1930s. The receptiveness to a populist medical discourse couched in terms of entertainment and the out-of-the-ordinary was part of leisure culture, whether in a Sunday newspaper or on a seaside holiday. I argue that in order to make sense to readers, the scientific explanations of modernity and the technological solutions to these anomalies of the sexed body depended upon, rather than superseded, the established spectacle of fantastic gender-changing bodies.

Sex change and modern medicine in the Sunday press

The prominent British sex change stories were reported in some detail, including interviews with the individuals concerned and people who knew them, and often photographs. They were presented as human-interest stories, the transition from one sex to the other described as 'extraordinary', sometimes 'bewildering'. After a number of stories had appeared and the notion of sex change had become more familiar, the press found further ways to dramatise them. The *News of the World* had an unusual scoop in 1939: 'Two Sisters Are Brothers Now' was the headline flagging the story of the Ferrow sisters who were both turning into boys in a double change of sex.[8] Like cross-dressing, sex change was found in everyday life, in small towns and among ordinary families. Though they shared some similarities, the sex change stories were not just a variant of the cross-dressing genre but had distinct features of their own. One difference was the medicalisation of these stories, both in terms of the significant role of doctors within them, and the mode and style in which they were reported. A second distinction was in the nature of the transformation. Rather than the external social appearance of clothing, smoking or posture, or performance of masculine skills and character (though these are important), the sex change stories pivot on the challenge of the unstable sexed body as both the cause of the problem and the means by which the transition from one sex to the other is made.

Sex change stories typically contained much more detail about the background of the gender-crosser, including their upbringing and their gendered behaviour as a child. Such narratives recounted the discovery of usually unspecified symptoms, often at puberty. There followed a visit to the specialist, the advice to have an operation and, finally, the transformation. This is a medical case history approach, and almost all British female-to-male sex change reports involved medical procedures of some kind. Readers were gradually introduced to the idea of specialist doctors, particular hospitals and the concept of advanced research and pathbreaking new operations, which could apparently produce or complete sex change. While medical advances in hormones were sometimes mentioned, it was modern surgery that was highlighted as key to the new technical possibility of changing sex.

One of the earliest reports signalling sex change as an extraordinary medical innovation came in 1932 and was headlined: 'Girl Becomes A Boy: Amazing Change of Sex at 14: Hospital Research Leads to Big Discovery'. In fact the story conflated two separate issues: spontaneous change of sex, and recent medical research to treat virilism (the development of male physical characteristics in women). Margery, 'a Sussex girl of 14 [who] has suddenly changed her sex', was introduced alongside the results of 'long and careful research work in Charing Cross Hospital [which] has resulted in a new discovery which may throw a new light on the determination of sex'. The mother described how her daughter's voice broke a few months ago while she was attending a girls' school. 'The discovery came as a shock to us. Margery's voice became very gruff, and she hated speaking to anyone . . . she never spoke unless she could help it.' All the specialists consulted agreed that she was a boy, and the newspaper interviewed one 'medical expert' who tried to account for these physical changes. He explained that there had been instances where normal girls had suddenly developed masculine characteristics, and there were other cases where it was almost impossible to determine sex at birth. 'One has to wait until the child grows up.' He described how the activities of the suprarenal and pituitary glands could cause opposite sex characteristics in an apparently normal body. However, the simplified rendition of this explanation suggested a continuum of causation, and by implication treatment for 'sex change', as the headline announced.[9]

This kind of narrative produced a shift in the relationships between the key characters. With doctors presented as heroes of the plot, the gender-crosser takes the position of being rescued or saved. The human-interest thread lay in the presentation of people who changed sex as individuals whose lives could be normalised by modern surgery. One consequence is that there is less humour (though there is still some) in the sex change genre. And the protagonists – the women who have changed into men – are attributed far less agency than women cross-dressers. They were by no means tricksters, although they were usually presented as assertively beginning a new life. Their condition was pathologised; changing sex could produce shame and shock for them and their families, only remedied by modern medical prowess.

Mary or Mark Weston, whose sex change was recorded in 1936 as '"Girl" Athlete's New Life After Change of Sex' (see Figure 7), experienced a protracted transition. The *News of the World* described how Weston – an internationally successful athlete – began to have doubts about her sex in 1928 while competing in the Olympic Games. 'I did not have the nerve to see a doctor, but I realised that something was happening to me, and that I could go on no longer as a woman.' She eventually consulted a specialist and was advised 'that it would be to my advantage to undergo an operation'. She then underwent two operations at the Charing Cross Hospital performed by Mr Lennox Broster, whose work to both prevent or enable transition to the opposite sex had previously been described in the press. The second operation was described as 'a very unusual one' – typically vague but portentous, implying a major medical achievement.[10]

Reference was often made to the 'growing number' of cases of sex change, building up a tradition and lending weight to the idea that 'sex change' was becoming an established medical procedure. This process began as early as 1932, when a '17-Year-Old Indian Student Has A Surprise', finding himself changing into a girl. Little detail was given and most of the article retold the recent story of Margery and another girl-to-boy story. It also assured readers that: 'Medical records contain numerous such cases of sex change and of indeterminate sex.'[11] The Mary Weston report continued this tradition by reference to previous cases, listing six recent sex changes, four of them British, as well as the parallel story of a

"GIRL" ATHLETE'S NEW LIFE AFTER CHANGE OF SEX

Amazing Result of Two Operations

(From Our Own Correspondent)

THIS is the amazing story of a well-known "woman" athlete, winner of international honours, who after 30 years as a woman has now become a man.

Up to two months ago "she" was wearing silk stockings and skirts. To-day, following two operations, "she" is wearing men's clothing. "She" has been medically certified to be of the male sex, and is faced with the problem of starting life all over again.

The athlete whose sex has changed in this extraordinary fashion is Mary Edith Louise Weston, of Oreston, near Plymouth, who in 1924 won the British women's championship for putting the shot, retained the title for six years, and in 1927 won the British women's championship for throwing the javelin.

"Mary" Weston—now Mark Weston—recently returned home after seven weeks

Many complicated problems are facing him. All his friendships, for instance, are now on a different footing. For years, as Mary Weston, he was very friendly with a particular girl. "We are still firm friends," he explained, "and shall continue to be so."

At Charing Cross Hospital the second operation on Mr. Weston was described as "a very unusual one."

Mr. Lennox Ross Broster, who signed

A photograph of Mark Weston as a woman.

MARK WESTON, formerly Mary Edith Louise Weston, out for a walk with a girl friend.

Figure 7 Mark/Mary Weston. *News of the World*, 31 May 1936, p. 3. Reproduced with the permission of the British Library.

Czechoslovakian athlete and a 'Danish artist's change of sex from male to female' in 1931.[12]

Medical science was the vector through which sex transformation was enabled and legitimised. The hospitals and surgeons involved were frequently named, including the London Hospital, and Dr Lennox Broster at the Charing Cross Hospital, which was established as a leading player in the advancement of science from the story of Margery in 1932. The Weston report went on to 'explain' the extraordinary research done at the hospital. 'Many remarkable sex operations have been carried out at Charing Cross Hospital, including it was recently stated, no fewer than 25 on women who were changing into men.' Dr Broster 'has shown that in many cases the change can be reversed by removing one of the adrenal glands on the kidney'.[13] This discussion has the effect of muddying the waters in the case of Weston, begging the question of why she was not restored to woman-hood, but the overall impression is that of rapid scientific advance. The implication is that doctors have the power to change people's sex in either direction.

These discourses of science and medicine – the discussion of adrenal glands, of Weston's second 'very unusual' operation – through which sex change comes to be understood in the popular press, are discourses of modernity. The research done by these surgeons is represented as being at the cutting edge of contemporary scientific discovery; it promises to unravel the mysteries and secrets of sex. Other stories underlined the power of science. The *People* reported in 1938 that 'Science Solves Sex Problem'. This riddle was about sex determination of babies: 'Boys Or Girls At Will! But Doctors Dare Not Use This Secret' (because parental preference would produce too many boys and an imbalance in the population). The rhetoric was typically overblown: the injection was simple and harmless, tests had shown that its success was practically guaranteed, yet it was, and would remain, a secret.[14]

The subjects of these reports, the people who have had their sex changed, are presented as the beneficiaries of modern medical technology. 'One of the greatest riddles of the human body has been solved by a London doctor. He has discovered the secret of the intermediate sex, and . . . perfected a surgical cure for women who are changing into men.' In melodramatic style, it was reported that a woman with masculine physical features had been cured by 'this latest miracle of modern surgery'.

> A 'man–woman' was admitted. Her body had grown heavy and masculine. A beard covered her face. It was a case which would have been considered incurable. The doctor performed three operations and the woman was completely cured . . . she left the hospital . . . absolutely normal.[15]

Doctors were generally represented as bringing positive solutions to otherwise confused and tragic lives. Dr Broster was described as 'the famous surgeon, who has brought new hope and happiness into the baffled lives of many men and women who were desirous of changing their sex', a comment which further implied that sex change was available on demand.[16]

These gender-crossers demonstrated far less individual agency in the process than the classic cross-dresser, the free-spirited trickster who made her own life choices. Sex-changing women presented their desires in terms of medical problems and confusions and had to negotiate medical professionals who offered access to the appropriate surgical solution. But despite the undoubted inflating of the doctor's role, a sense of who had the power to determine sex change was not fixed in these stories but floated around the various interested parties: primarily 'nature', the doctor or the gender-crosser. What did the language of 'sex change' reveal? Did someone's sex change in a spontaneous transformation, or was a sex change carried out, and at whose volition? Mary/Mark Weston himself had some, albeit limited, agency in the process, describing his understanding of his sex change in physiological terms – something (unspecified) was happening to his body. Weston eventually consulted a doctor – an expert who confirmed his understanding of himself, advising an operation. The balance of power in the naming process appears to lie first with Weston, but the verification and validation depended on the power of the medical profession. Indeed, Mark Weston was given a certificate by Dr Broster: '"She" has been medically certified to be of the male sex.' His sex was legitimated by experts, not himself.[17]

Fixing gender and sexuality

Like the cross-dressing stories, these medical narratives derive some amusement from the transition to a new life as one of the opposite sex. While masculinity is shown as something which has to be learned by these newly formed young men, gender fluidity tends to be closed down as a possibility in contrast to the cross-dressing stories, which demonstrate the everyday performance of gender. Instead of gender being something which can be played with, there is considerable emphasis on the way innate psychology demonstrates the true sex of the individual. Mark Weston, described by the *News of the World* 'with one hand in the pocket of his grey flannel trousers, and the other holding a cigarette', explained how during his seven-week hospital stay he was in the men's ward. He spent time

> meeting with different men, talking and joking with them, and now the change from 'Miss' to 'Mr' seems quite natural. I always had a deep voice and dark skin. I used to shave and use powder, but never lip-stick. Of course I used to wear women's clothing, silk stockings, etc.

This highlights the incongruous aspects of Weston's changeover, and the reader was also treated to before and after photographs.[18]

Most stories dwelt on the way the gender-crosser felt so much more at home in his new sex/gender, emphasising the notion that true sex will show itself. Madeleine/Mark Woods' account was typical of how the newspapers filled in a little more psychological depth. Asked how he felt about the news that he was really a man he replied:

> I scarcely know . . . You see, for years I had never felt about life in general just as other women felt. Always, boys and men had been my companions. While other girls would be playing 'rounders' or hop-scotch, I'd be playing cowboys and Indians . . . And when other women were thinking of marriage, I'd be thinking of getting a job. I was brought up as a girl, but I felt I wanted to be a boy . . . when the prison doctor told me the truth . . . I felt rather glad than sorry.

Woods rather spoiled this picture of complete sex/gender congruence, however, when he told the reporter he would be starting life afresh in the West Country where he hoped to run 'a little home-made cake business'.[19] The family of Doris/Donald Purcell re-read her tomboyish ways as revealing her true gender. He himself declared, 'I have always wanted to do a man's work . . . and when I leave hospital I hope to obtain a job as a chauffeur – to start with at least.' A sister said that if Doris now became her sixth brother, 'well, good luck to her' and described Doris's boyishness at length:

> Doris was always a tomboy and my brothers called her Donald. She always wanted to do a man's work and for some time was a chauffeuse. She knew all about motors and engineering, and was never happier than when tinkering with engines. She has had five motor-cars at various times.

Although Doris normally wore women's clothes – 'mainly costumes'[20] – 'she was happiest when she was wearing men's overalls, or, at week-ends, when she wore plus fours for cycling. Pretty frocks made no appeal to her . . . She never used paint or powder, and she smoked like a man.' The newspaper already read masculinity into Doris/Donald's appearance: 'with her fair, cropped hair brushed straight back, and her open boyish face, [s/he] looked a picture of health and fitness'.[21]

Unlike the cross-dressers, none of the 'sex change' women already had a partner and same-sex love does not appear as a theme. Once the sex/gender problem had been treated, however, the press was keen to find girlfriends for these newly identified men. The psychological and physical 'truth' of correct sex assignment was thus demonstrated by heterosexual desire in these patients. Mark Weston was pictured with a woman friend. 'All his friendships', the paper noted, 'are now on a different footing. For years, as Mary Weston, he was very friendly with a particular girl. "We are still firm friends," he explained, "and shall continue to be so."'[22] In the 1938 case of Doris who became Donald Purcell, the paper developed a story that he might marry his friend Charlotte far beyond the actual evidence. It engineered a meeting between them while he was still in hospital, and constructed its report around this 'Drama Of Girls' Surprise Meeting'. 'Strange though it seems, they may never meet again as girls . . . [Donald's] surprise and delight [at the visit] were revealed in the slow smile which crept over her boyish-looking face.' Donald Purcell's mother also described and sanctioned 'the great attraction' between the two: 'Devotion like theirs is bound to continue.'[23] The existence of a girlfriend serves to naturalise the change of sex – now that the inner and outer selves are correctly aligned, this is normal heterosexual affection which proves Donald's masculinity and provides a frisson of romantic interest.

If appropriate gender role behaviour and heterosexuality were both key tests of true sex, any outcome other than successful sex change could be problematic. A half-comic, half-tragic case reported in 1936 was told as if the man could request sex change at will: 'Tired of being a man, Bosilko Stoyanoff, the twenty-two-year-old Bulgarian bank clerk who changed his sex, wants to become a girl again.' At 16 a doctor noticed her male characteristics and performed an operation. 'Basilka became Bosilko, grew a beard and became a husky footballer.' But his beard disappeared and he began to turn into a girl again. 'The real turning point came when "he" fell in love with a young man.' He was reported to be suing the first doctor, whom he alleged made a mistake.[24] The European stories were more likely than the British ones to be treated as comic or have melodramatic outcomes.

The language of tragedy was often used. Doctors were battling on the edge of scientific knowledge to help people whose gender confusion would otherwise render them miserable, it was reported. The importance of knowing and demonstrating an appropriate and stable sex/gender identity was emphasised by the descriptions of the shame which followed any deviation from the norm. Both Ferrow sisters of Great Yarmouth began to change from girls into boys. 'At 13 each developed a deep voice and became more and more masculine. Majorie left school and for a year and a half kept in the house reading and painting, bewildered at what was happening to her.' There had 'been gossip for years' according to one neighbour, but a local benefactress enabled them 'to escape to Maidstone', where they 'both studied as boys at a local art school', and later provided for their medical treatment.[25]

The tragedy of intersexuality was emphasised by one of the few cases reported without a happy ending provided by medical science. The problems faced by Hannah/Gene Joynt were described at length over two pages (including the front page) of the *People* in 1938: 'Tragic Misfit in Life: Man–Woman Reveals "Her" Sufferings'. She was 'driven to despair after five years of mental torture in a world of curious glances and pointing fingers'. The problem of her sex 'has baffled more than 50 of the most eminent doctors and scientists in Europe'. Joynt's 'bitterly unhappy existence' was due to the attitudes of others towards her and her own lack of clarity about her indeterminate gender, feeling both masculine and feminine inside herself. 'Her family could not understand her difficulties and, for a long time, she dared not show her face in the neighbourhood', only slipping out after dark. When she moved to her aunt's and 'changed to pretty frocks and lipstick, to try life as a normal girl' she was even more unhappy. 'Unless science can help her – and doctors are once again studying the facts of the case – she seems doomed to be happy neither as man nor woman.'[26]

Joynt had a greater sensitivity about and consciousness of her borderline gender than people in earlier press reports of mistaken gender. When 20-year-old Dora Lewis was arrested in 1917 on suspicion of being a man evading military service, she apparently had few doubts she was a girl, despite her need to shave. An army sergeant 'noticed that her build was somewhat masculine and that while her hair was long and arranged like a woman's she had traces of a slight growth of hair on the upper lip and her face bore evidence of shaving'. A police doctor pronounced her to be a man. Shocked and surprised at the news, Dora explained she had been brought up as a girl, despite 'certain masculine peculiarities [which] had frequently aroused the curiosity of neighbours'. The mistake was partly accounted for by her having left her mother's care at six months old.[27] This explanation was also put forward by Mark/Madeleine Woods who explained that his confusion over his sex was due to lack of advice at puberty. 'Of course . . . I should have known long ago that I was not as other women were; but my mother died when I was young, and I had no other women relatives to advise me.'[28] The greater self-awareness and unhappiness in the later story of Hannah Joynt reflected the modern development of self-identity, the conscious internalisation of a stable gender identity as crucial to one's sense of self. While young women throughout the period were encouraged to groom their bodies and present themselves as appropriately feminine – removing superfluous hair for example – this requirement of awareness and appropriate maintenance of the gendered body strengthened between the wars.[29]

The notion that spontaneous or surgical sex change was possible played a role in the establishment and policing of gender boundaries at the wider social level as well as for individuals. A succession of almost identical stories in the 1920s advising that 'Bobs Cause Beards' used spurious scientific facts to warn young women to preserve their femininity. Cropping the hair would cause it to grow elsewhere on the face. An amusing tale, this also suggested unease about young women adopting masculine clothes, hairstyles and public freedoms in the years after the First World War.[30] Lightly clad to enjoy greater physical freedoms in sport and exercise, modern young women were expected to contain their energies within appropriate femininity. As the female body was increasingly sexualised in the press, it also became more open to the general scrutiny of others.[31] At times in the later 1930s the phenomenon of female-to-male sex change was linked to women athletes in particular. The *News of the World* reported in 1937 that 'Another distinguished woman athlete, Sofia Smetkovna, 23, woman javelin-throwing champion of Poland, is to undergo an operation to change her sex', and reminded readers of the cases the previous year of Miss Zdenka Koubkova of Czechoslovakia and Mary Weston.[32] This might suggest there was something innately masculine about elite sportswomen. Yet the popular press was full of pictures of women enjoying sport – it was a means of showing their shapely bodies, drawing attention to their odd masculine clothing (such as trousers for tennis or cricket), while proclaiming modernity in gender relations in these new opportunities for women. This sex change story was counter-balanced by another on the same page about a fashion competition for the best tennis frocks. In the accompanying photograph the athletic-looking tennis player demonstrates an appropriate feminine regard for becoming sportswear. In some respects these interwar stories continue the late nineteenth-century reprimands to sporty young women that they might lose their womanhood and fertility, but are recast with an updated scientific context to reflect modern gender concerns.

From the late 1920s and into the 1930s, the 'sex change' story appeared more and more frequently in the British Sunday press. Moving from one sex to the other was presented as a spontaneous transition or, increasingly, as achieved by the powers of modern medicine. While not an everyday occurrence, it was sufficiently common to have a recurring formulaic treatment of its own. These stories emphasised that individuals needed to know to which sex they truly belonged, and that this was a function of both the physical body and their psychology. Any malfunctioning of their bodies or glands could now be tackled by medical science, which had the power to maintain or reverse sex characteristics at will. Since most sex changes reported were of young women who became men, femininity was apparently less secure and more malleable than masculinity.

Popular narratives of hermaphrodism

The popularisation of scientific advances was important to the popular press – it was part of the drive to appear modern and appealing, and sell newspapers. The discourses of scientific advance, of adrenal glands and operations in the press stories of sex change are discourses of technology and modernity. Entertaining and intriguing in their own way, they appear to be from a new, more rational world of expert knowledge, leaving behind superstition and puzzling phenomena.[33] I have also suggested that they presented the beginnings of a new way of understanding gender – in which the sense of inner gender stability and the importance of self-policing of the body begin to appear. So far, so Foucauldian. However, we will see that the sex change stories, like the cross-dressing reports, had antecedents within entertainment and existing forms of popular knowledge. The concept of the 'hermaphrodite' – indeterminate gender displayed in the physical body – was maintained in popular culture by anatomical museums and freak shows, commercialised attractions in large cities and at the seaside. The term 'hermaphrodite' never appeared in the press stories, but it was found in the medical literature, in arenas such as fairground sideshows and in people's everyday speech.[34]

Did medical science, with its apparently far-reaching modern techniques, take over from the existing popular cultural idea of the weird and wondrous hermaphrodite as a way of comprehending the problem of confused or changing physical sex? At first sight, these might seem to be two very different structures of understanding. Yet commercial entertainment presented the body, its functions, diseases and unusual forms as both scientific enlightenment and as a titillating spectacle. This merging of high and low approaches continued to be vital in popular forms of medico-sexual knowledge in the mid-twentieth century. The remainder of this chapter will suggest that the modern medical narrative of 'sex change' overlapped with the older framing of freakish monstrosity as entertainment, education and magic and, indeed, relied upon this form of address to make sense to readers as both an enjoyable story and a novel possibility.

Freaks and fairgrounds

The exhibition of freaks in sideshows, which were commercial attractions in large cities, fairgrounds and at the seaside, mobilised shock-horror and fascinated responses to physical abjection. Common types of freaks who drew the crowds included giants and midgets, people with missing limbs, Siamese twins, extremely fat women, bearded women, dog-faced men and so on. The most popular exhibits in this world of extremes were freaks with extraordinary talents, who could do normal things despite their disabilities, using their feet as hands to sew or play musical instruments.[35] The kinds of freaks who presented indeterminate gender in the physical body and can be mapped on to the sex change stories include man–woman hermaphrodites and bearded ladies. Historians suggest that freak shows marketed disability in a palatable way by arousing feelings of fascination, horror and *Schadenfreude*. Ann Featherstone describes how the showman sold the exhibit by telling the person's tale – their life history and the medically fabulous explanations for their oddity. In their size, hairiness or features, these individuals were presented as grotesque, but had a connecting humanity to the viewer, who was encouraged to touch them, speak to them and buy postcards commemorating their visit.[36] Tom Norman, the most successful showman of the late nineteenth century and manager of the Elephant Man, exhibited his acts, including a midget troupe and Leonine the Lion-Faced Lady, until the First World War.[37] While there were changes in fashion, freak shows continued to command audiences throughout the first half of the twentieth century.[38]

Freaks might be exhibited by itinerant showmen on market days and in 'penny gaffs' in the back streets of large cities, and were an essential component of travelling fairs.[39] These kinds of shows increasingly shifted to become part of summer entertainment at the developing working-class seaside resorts such as New Brighton, Southend-on-Sea and Blackpool. Waxworks shows, phrenologists and exhibitions of all sorts expanded in seaside towns in the late nineteenth century and became more risqué in nature. By the interwar years, the large-scale permanent fairgrounds of the bigger resorts dwarfed the seasonal fairs of inland towns.[40] We know most about the holiday resort of Blackpool, the largest in the country and the destination for the factory workers of Lancashire, as a consequence of the ethnographic research carried out by Mass Observation from the late 1930s. The middle-class assumptions of the investigators tend to colour the data they collected, but this is an extremely useful picture of the recreations and complex attitudes of these working-class holiday-makers.[41]

Freak shows were enormously popular, especially those featuring spectacular women.[42] The holidaying public actively sought out these and similar sideshows. In a survey carried out at Blackpool by Mass Observation, by far the largest group of people said the sideshows were their favourite draw.[43] One promoter told investigators that 'The sillier the thing, the more it gets the people . . . If the thing is educational, they're not interested. They want the *curious* and the sensational.' He maintained that half the people did not go on the beach at all, but patronised the fairground and promenade, moving around paying for shows.[44] At Blackpool there was a competing mixture of attractions, from fairgrounds to donkey rides. 'The pie stalls are frequent links in the chains of slot machines, fortune telling booths, monstrosities, autophotos and Walkie-snaps.'[45] Seaside holidays were also an opportunity to indulge an obsession with health and well-being. The origins of seaside holidays lie in the curative and rejuvenating qualities of fresh air and sea-bathing, originally for the rich and for invalids, but also taken on fully by twentieth-century working-class crowds, who went to lectures on health, consumed quack medicines and faith healing, praised the quality of the sea air (less so the sewage-polluted seawater), and enjoyed jokes about health at seaside music halls and on postcards.[46]

Populist science and medicine – the latest technological marvels and patent cures – were intimately bound up with the traditions of showmanship, the fairground and holiday entertainment. The popularity of quack medicines among all classes continued well into the twentieth century and vast fortunes were made from selling remedies which promised to cure disease.[47] Performing quack doctors worked the fairgrounds and seaside throughout the period. Sequah the Medicine Man drew great crowds at Kirkcaldy Fair demonstrating his cure for rheumatism and selling the liniment for a shilling a bottle.[48] One of the best known was the charlatan Walford Bodie, who from the 1890s to the 1930s performed a stage show in which he defied death in an electric chair, demonstrated hypnotism and 'Bloodless Surgery' (manipulation) and cured cripples on stage.[49] Mass Observers were amazed at the holiday obsession with health and disease that they found at Blackpool. Alongside the freak shows and museum of anatomy, large numbers of phrenologists, quack doctors, patent cures and medical exhibitions (including 'sickening prints of skin diseases') were found in working-class resorts.[50] The highly popular fortune-telling services used scientific or medical-sounding terms to promote the services they offered, including pathognomy, astrology and graphology, among other 'ologies'.[51]

Medical and educational justifications were also used to sell sexuality at the seaside and fairground. Patent medicine stalls at these locations promised a more anonymous type of consultation (like mail order) for anxieties and fears on matters of sexual health, including venereal disease, fertility and birth control, than was otherwise available at home. Sex education materials and pornography might also be obtained here or in back-street shops.[52] Museums of anatomy (there was a well-established one at Blackpool, discussed below), which showed models of the human body and explained the organs and mechanism of human reproduction, as well as pathological oddities, were commercial sexualised attractions, but justified their respectability by reference to their educative function in explaining scientific processes and giving medical information. *Tableaux vivants* (also known as *poses plastiques*), very popular at fairgrounds as well as at music halls, were justified as artistic and therefore as a higher class of entertainment. While they may have purported to be representations of classic works of art, in fact they displayed the nude female body (covered by a body stocking) as a type of peep show, no doubt promising a way into greater sexual knowledge for adolescents and titillation for adults.[53]

As well as appealing to curiosity and pleasure in the grotesque, freak shows also provided sexual titillation. The *News of the World* reported on the strange romantic attraction of those featured – that every year hundreds of spectators fall in love with them, 'leave home and hopelessly follow Bearded Ladies, Midgets, and Armless Wonders'. Some sexual fetishisation of these gender-crossers is suggested: 'For one man who has left home for a pretty tight-rope walker, it is said that 10 leave home for a bearded lady.' A 'lion-man' was pursued for years by women of all classes. 'Even wealthy and titled women would descend heavily veiled from their carriages and go secretly to his tent.'[54] This echoes the pot-shots at oversexed upper-class women discussed in the gigolo stories. It was said that any type of woman freak would see tickets sold, but fat ladies were the most sexualised of freaks, often infantilised as schoolgirls. Other fetishised sideshows included tattooed women and other exotic presentations.[55] Not surprisingly, there were perennial anxieties about the corrupting influence and moral dangers of seaside shows and fairgrounds similar to those expressed around the reporting of sex and divorce in the popular press and the effects of modern cinema.[56]

The whole ambience of seaside resorts such as Blackpool was remarkably similar to that of the Sunday newspapers in the desires and fantasies they worked upon to sell spectacle. The entertainment offered by both was based on sensation, sex and the pleasure of enjoying disasters and other people's misfortunes, while providing escapism through music and laughter. The popular press constantly reported medical oddities (such as the Woman Who Shrank into a Child) and mysterious means of accessing the future, in parallel with the magical promise and dreadful attractions of the fairground.[57] Waxwork shows, like the popular press, recreated notorious murders. The Blackpool Chamber of Horrors showed various tortures from around the world, and in the late 1930s included the library of Dr Buck Ruxton who was executed in 1936 for the murder of his wife, a gruesome story followed in the newspapers. Ruxton was both 'oriental' (he was from India) and a medical man – as Mass Observation observed, these themes together attracted the crowds like no other sideshow. Exoticism ran as a thread across the press, variety theatre, and seaside shows.[58]

The mixture of tradition and modernity found in seaside resorts and fairgrounds mirrored that of the Sunday press. They each suspended the everyday world and played on the boundaries of work and recreation, respectability and excess. Funfairs and showmen seized on new technological developments which could enhance their attractions and advertising techniques. They were the most prominent early sites for the new cinematograph shows, and between the wars, speed and flight became key features of new funfair rides and shows such as the daredevil motorcyclists on the Wall of Death. Seaside resorts were key sites for the modernist architecture of lidos and hotels, and for the increasing display of the body – seen as part of the modern expression of gender relations and exploited by the interwar press in photographs of bathing beauties.[59] Advertisements claimed the latest attraction or novelty, while well-established elements remained dependably constant – donkey rides, fish and chips, sideshows, health cures and fortune-telling.

The man–woman and the bearded lady

The showing of gender-crossing freaks also demonstrated this movement between older and modern forms of explanation, the context of science and medicine, and the titillation of sexuality. There was a continuum of interpretations presented by and about the gender-crossing freak, ranging from magical belief in the possibilities of nature to sceptical enjoyment of a theatrical performance, which suggests some common characteristics with the medical model presented by the Sunday press in the 1930s. It is difficult to estimate how frequently man–woman or hermaphrodite sideshows were presented, although they were certainly shown in Blackpool and elsewhere in the north of England.[60] Hairy-faced women were common in the nineteenth century and bearded ladies had a great vogue in the early twentieth century.[61] The 'educative' presentation of sideshows, waxworks and anatomy museums was to interpret physical gender-crossing as 'real' freaks of nature – unusual natural phenomena turned into entertainment. The bearded lady or lion-face woman might be the woman who by the 1930s would be medically diagnosed as suffering from virilism. The hermaphrodite in the museum of anatomy or sideshow could parallel the intersexed 'man–woman' from the medical literature or popular press story who has a puzzling physical sex.

The Museum of Curiosities was a successful draw for at least a century. First based in Liverpool it moved to Blackpool in the 1930s and was still going strong in the 1950s, showing a collection of several hundred models and diagrams. In this exhibition sexuality and horror were powerfully mixed, but presented as scientific education and curiosities. Straightforward reproductive and physical information was interspersed with moral warnings of the effects on the body of masturbation and venereal disease, the fearful outcomes of abnormal pregnancies and deliveries, and the occurrence of freaks of nature in which opposite sex functions were confused.[62] Using explicit, though Latin, terms for parts of the body (e.g. uterus, scrotum, clitoris), a number of models were shown of the male and female body including genital organs, the developing embryo, the structure of the breasts, and a whole variety of pathological variations – a forceps delivery, a Caesarean section, problems in childbirth, including displacement of the womb and advice on how to avoid it. The section of the exhibition devoted to the effects of syphilis on the human body included a model of the head, neck and breasts of a woman of 25 with syphilis showing ulceration over her whole body, flagged as being a recent case in Birkenhead.[63]

Focusing very much on the reproductive body and its maladies, among the main exhibits were the Caesarean birth and the pregnant man, presented as an 'Extraordinary Freak Of Nature Of A Man Being Discovered In The "Family Way"'. This is an interesting example of how the exhibition mixed colloquial and scientific language. The catalogue was at pains to verify the accuracy of this model, and quoted the explanations of several named doctors on the case.[64] There were three more models of hermaphrodites in the show. Two, from Dresden and Sheffield, had their external genitals described in detail, in ways which were broadly similar to the accounts of doctors writing in the medical press. 'He was devoid of a scrotum and a testicle was found on either side of the entrance enveloped with the external labiae. The clitoris was the size of the first joint of a finger; and the mouth of the vagina was very small.'[65]

Yet gender-crossing and other kinds of 'freaks' were also commonly constructed by showmen as illusions. Vanessa Toulmin describes how they exaggerated the age of midgets and the height of giants, while hairy-faced boys or women might in reality be animals. Horrifying acts such as the guillotine or headless wonders, or the Spider Girl, were created by mirrors.[66] The prosecution of fake 'half-man/half-woman' sideshows was occasionally reported in the popular press in the same period as the 'sex change' stories. The proprietor, door-keeper and performer of a 'man–woman' sideshow in an amusement arcade at Blackpool were each fined in 1930 for conspiracy and false pretences. They had exhibited a 25-year-old man as 'Phil-Phyllis' – 'half-man, half-woman, brother and sister in one body'. The court and readers of the Sunday press were told of the theatrical devices which he had used to achieve the illusion and draw the crowds in this 'Seaside Sham Show'.[67]

> His left side was covered in women's lingerie, from shoulder to knee. On his left foot was a sock and a woman's shoe. His right side, which purported to be that of a man, was bare over the right breast to the knee. On his right foot he wore a sock and a man's shoe. There was no hair on the left arm and left leg, and he was wearing a false breast on his left side.

'His body', reported the police superintendent, 'was that of an entirely normal male person.'[68]

Newspaper reportage here suggests that a more sceptical approach to the freak show tradition was in play by the 1930s. Earlier reports had paralleled the presentation of the sideshows. In 1917 a 'Bearded Opera Singer: Girl Wonder with a Bass Voice' was reported to be the principal attraction at a forthcoming fair in Breslau. 'Hedwig, the Bearded Girl', who was 14 years old, was pictured with her full moustache and six-inch-long beard. While her voice was that of a man, and she could sing 'all the best-known bass songs', her body 'has retained to the full its feminine contour'.[69] A more rationalistic approach to the fairground freak in the 1930s emphasised the boundary between the freak as illusion and the medicalised stories of sex change. The *News of the World* in 1932 revealed the deliberate creation of freaks in 'Freaks Made to Order', generating synthetic outrage that the public was being tricked.[70] It described in detail the construction of a man–woman.

> It is always a man who is turned into a man–woman. The one side is pink and white and plump and powdered, with waved hair and jewelled hand. The other is left masculine, wiry, strong, muscled, and cropped headed. The softness and whiteness of the 'female' side, which is so puzzling, needs long months of massage, shaving, injections of paraffin under the skin to make it rise gracefully where it is meant to rise; make-up on one half of the face; one jewelled earring, one high-heeled shoe – and behold the man–woman.[71]

This presented an alternative, indeed a modern, rationalist discourse – that such freaks were constructed by human ingenuity or cruelty, unless they were medically certified by doctors as changes of sex.

But any distinction between constructed freaks and 'real' medical problems of scientific interest was immaterial in terms of their entertainment value to both newspaper readers and fairground crowds alike, and probably evoked a range of responses. Mass Observation documented the mixture of scepticism and gullibility among audiences, eavesdropping in 1937 at the Headless Woman booth in Blackpool. This girl was advertised as 'Baffling SCIENTISTS & DOCTORS the HEADLESS GIRL'.[72] A 'professor' showed the crowd how the girl breathed and was fed. Among the onlookers, a man said jokingly: 'I bet she would show [her head], if you offered her a drink.' One woman said 'I don't think it's right to show such things', but her husband said in reassurance, 'Oh, she's a contortionist.'[73]

People's responses to the varied packaging of physical gender-crossing suggest they may have made little distinction between hermaphrodism, the man–woman and sex change. The Colonel Barker case possibly encouraged renewed interest in exhibiting 'man–woman' sideshows in the early 1930s and she herself made a living as an exhibit entitled 'Strange Honeymoon' on the Blackpool seafront in 1937, alongside the 'museum of anatomy' with its hermaphrodites discussed above and comedian George Formby's sex change jokes at the Palace Theatre.[74] In this sideshow Barker and her 'wife' were established on two beds, separated by a pedestrian crossing with a Belisha Beacon (a contemporary sex symbol), and the public was invited to decide whether Barker was really a man or a woman. Would she – could she – consummate the marriage? Barker's landlady, interviewed by Mass Observation, offered a range of interpretations.

> I think she's one of them women who like women you know what I mean . . . I don't know it's a mystery, he's a man and a woman . . . I can't tell what he is, I call him a Gene, Jack [her husband] calls him a Moxphrodite.[75]

A Scottish female husband case also demonstrated the currency of the half-and-half concept. 'Shortly after the marriage "his" 'wife' questioned "him" about "his" sex, and "he" declared that "he" was half-man and half-woman. This she believed.' The marriage continued for 15 years until doubts resurfaced in 1932.[76] While popular genres tended to present the performance of social masculinity by the cross-dressing woman as a separate phenomenon from the somatic manifestations of 'sex change' stories or hermaphroditic freak shows, the reactions to the spectacle of Colonel Barker shows that ordinary people seemed to have access to a complex grid of meanings and could fuse both science and 'traditional' beliefs.

Conclusion

Sex change was reported sensationally in the popular press as a new scientific feature of modernity. These stories show that new discourses from science and medicine do appear in the popular press before the Second World War to explain gender-crossing, but only in relation to 'change of sex' and not as a means of understanding cross-dressing or desire between women. Like the adventures of British cross-dressers the sex change phenomenon was set within everyday life and found, however astonishingly, among ordinary folk and otherwise unremarkable families. There are significant contrasts, however, between how these different kinds of gender-crossing women were figured. Cross-dressing women were active agents, and part of a long-understood tradition, a tradition which flowers further in the 1930s as we have seen in the last two chapters. They were admired for their skills, and explained through familiar rationalisations. They created humour, and as tricksters were in charge of the jokes and often of the whole story. Hermaphrodites and 'sex change' men–women, who crossed gender physically, were understood through the existing concept of the 'freak' as physically malformed as well as marvellous. They traditionally elicited curiosity, but it was that of the gawping audience at the exhibit – they are most definitely objects of the gaze. Now that 'sex change' cases start to appear regularly in the press and are interpreted medically from the late 1920s onwards, they are also humanised (to a greater extent perhaps than on the sideshows) and presented to elicit sympathy as well as, still, a touch of horror and awe. But they are made objects of medical science, and while they are given a voice which many of them use to assert their cross-gender desires, they are only partially agents in the process.

Over this decade and in the longer term, however, these stories create within popular culture the idea that sex change is now obtainable through the advances of medical science.[77] The transmutation of physical sex through the newest scientific innovations was broadcast as 'fact' in the press from the 1920s, long before the medical possibility existed. The newspapers themselves in the 1930s begin to construct a parallel tradition to that of cross-dressing. The existing masquerade narrative was about dissembling, about performance and humour and, increasingly, a frisson of risqué sexuality which before the Second World War was neither stated directly nor pathologised. The new technological, modern concept of changing sex was anchored in the physical body. British readers heard about sex change much sooner and more clearly than they heard about lesbianism.

The sex change stories are represented in the press as primarily about gender; they are not about either heterosexual or same-sex desire. Sexuality and sexual allure form one of the ingredients in the fairground freak show (if not necessarily the most dominant), but this does not translate into the newspaper stories. Most do not introduce a partner into the narrative until after physical gender-crossing is already underway, and this serves as proof of true sex and heterosexual normality. They therefore suggest another potential way of understanding the mannish woman – as having a pathological physical problem around gender identity. If we see sex change stories in the context of concerns expressed about male effeminacy and masculine women, they work to establish a notion of 'correct' heterosexual and gender identity, now in a modern scientific form and rooted in the body. It appears to be the female body which is more changeable and malleable. Liminal and not fixed, it needs individual attention and work to maintain appropriate gender. In the cross-dressing stories gender is a performance, though it has to conform to particular parameters of respectable class and gender to be applauded. Sex change introduces an alternative idea – that gendered behaviour is directly related to the sexed body, and is normally felt as part of a person's sense of self.

It was not only scientific legitimacy and medical 'progress' that contributed to the idea of sex change, but also the established idea of hermaphrodism which related to a hinterland of popular performance in the fairground in the same way as the cross-dressing figure did to the music hall. I have suggested that the scientific and the theatrical were complementary and overlapping frameworks of under-standing, not oppositional approaches to sex change. Medical procedures, theatre and fairground were hardly poles apart in their promise of magical transforma-tions of sex and gender. The elements of fantasy, secret knowledge and the manip-ulation of belief were part of medical professionalism as well as of popular performance. Doctors themselves did not resist using the language of transforma-tion and magic to explain their scientific breakthroughs and cures. The specialist Dr A. P. Cawadias spoke of the 'almost magical results of hormone therapy' in a lecture on hermaphrodism.[78] Mass Observation commented on the pleasures and meanings created in Blackpool: 'For most people there is, in fact, no hiatus between the miraculous and the scientific; electricity and television are their mira-cles.'[79] We have seen how many of the freak shows were presented using scientific jargon and paraphernalia. Malformed or hairy children were explained as the result of a fright in pregnancy – a very old belief. The Headless Woman had wires and pipes bubbling into test tubes to supposedly keep her alive. Modern medicine promised something exceedingly similar to the astonishing spectacle and fabulous cure. The alchemy of physical gender transformation could be understood and represented in both arenas. Though it was framed in the shiny modern context of synthetic hormones and operating theatres, the promised unravelling of the secrets of sex and the body and the capacity to change them at will had much in common with older forms of medical magic.

Scientific and medical accounts were not relayed in the press as sober, positivist discourses and they did not displace the worlds of fantasy and entertainment as ways of explaining gender-crossing women. Rather, they developed out of these traditional understandings and indeed were reliant upon them. Not only were there plenty of 'traditional' ways of knowing found in the 'modern' mass media and entertainment, but the framework for presenting modern developments depended upon familiar ways of reading unstable bodies as freakish, entertaining and magical. New scientific and medical procedures which promised to manage and solve these puzzles of nature, transforming women into men and vice versa, were no less magical and fantastic. Scientific modernity had not lost the gloss of enchantment.[80]

Part III

Gender and sexual identities since the 1940s

6 'Perverted passions'

Sexual knowledge and popular culture, 1940–60

The classic trickster cross-dressing story dramatically declined as a popular genre during the 1940s and 1950s. This chapter shows that as pathologising medical discourses of lesbianism and sex change are more clearly recognised in culture, and gender-crossing decreases on stage and in film, it becomes increasingly difficult for the press stories of passing women to retain their tone and formula as familiar entertainment.

These two decades were a period of immense social change. As the Second World War placed new demands on men and women, there was considerable emphasis on maintaining the markers of gender difference, from the use of lipstick to the stress on the temporary nature of women's new workplace roles.[1] While women in uniform became commonplace, and pictures of them were often published in the press, they were treated as more familiar and unexceptional than in the First World War. Sue Bruley observes that '[i]n contrast to earlier wars . . . sexuality became much more overt'.[2] Wartime mobility and call-up, especially of younger women and men, led to increased opportunities for sexual affairs and the spreading of sexual knowledge.[3] Concern about the low birthrate and the social disruption of wartime generated an enthusiasm for rebuilding the family and domesticity in the years immediately following the war, while the welfare state settlement entrenched a conservative view of woman's place as primarily housewife and mother. Modern social and medical expertise would aid family life, promote proper childrearing practices, and identify and contain any threats to domestic stability through the social services and courts. Marriage became immensely popular and the birthrate took off, and while rationing continued into the 1950s, economic growth and full employment soon led to rising living standards, increasing affluence and consumerism for most classes of people. Yet the 1950s was a period of moral panics around various threats of sexual disruption, amid fears that sexual pleasure could not be contained within the moral parameters of stable marriages.[4] These anxieties focused mainly on young people's heterosexual promiscuity and their subversive sub-cultures, and from 1953, following some prominent cases, also on the perceived threat of male homosexuality, which now began to be reported across the press in generally hostile and sensationalist terms.[5] Seen from the perspective of the popular press, the 1950s appears to be a time of immensely conservative ideologies, with much more limited room for diversity within gender roles or ambiguous expressions of sexuality than had been the case in the 1930s. Normative ideals of femininity were ubiquitous and attempts to step outside of them were pathologised. There was a greater willingness to identify sexual deviance and express abhorrence of it within press reporting. The cross-dressing story rapidly fell victim to all these cultural changes.

Some classic elements, including humour, remain in wartime reports, but from the late 1940s and as the 1950s progressed, cross-dressing stories mainly lost their light-hearted presentation and were often associated with the pathologising discourses of sexual deviance – homosexuality and transsexuality. The three strands of stories – cross-dressing, lesbianism and sex change – frequently merged, and the gender-crossing woman was, for the first time, explicitly named as a lesbian or transsexual. The classic cross-dressing genre breaks down and declines as these newly recognised categories of sexual and gender deviance come into play.

All kinds of gender-crossing stories were reported far less frequently in the 1940s and 50s than they were earlier in the century. While there were a number of interesting female husband stories, cross-dressing was generally very thin on the ground, with 24 cases in the two decades. There were 11 reports concerning female-to-male sex change, and virtually no reviews or discussions of male impersonation in entertainment after the early 1940s. Narrative styles changed and the diversity and richness of cross-dressing stories of the 1930s vanished.

The cross-dressing story loses its most entertaining classic features after the mid-1940s, when it is linked explicitly with lesbianism in a female marriage case of 1946. As lesbianism emerges as a clearer theme than it had been in the prewar period, it is associated with psychiatric disturbance, crime, violence and the negative features of mannishness. The cross-dressing tradition becomes increasingly corrupted by association with deviance, and a 1954 case suggests that the assertive choices of the trickster cross-dresser can now best be understood in terms of a sex change discourse. There is no longer a broader tradition of male impersonation in entertainment through which to understand cross-dressing, as even in pantomime it is seen as increasingly odd and unappealing in the 1950s.

A turning point for cross-dressing

Very quickly after the Second World War the cross-dressing story became associated with sex between women, at least for the *News of the World*. This initially arose from a major wedding story in 1946 – which contained many classic elements alongside a modern account of perversion – and was then cemented by references to 'intimacy' in subsequent stories.

The fall-off in cross-dressing reports can be partly accounted for by the severe newsprint rationing from 1939, which gradually eased in the 1950s (and finally ended in 1958). Some daily newspapers had only four pages during the war years, though the *People* published six to eight pages and the *News of the World* managed at least eight. There were also some changes in newspaper priorities during the war

years, as propaganda, war news and information competed for space with entertainment and features.[6] Rationing temporarily halted the trend towards an ever-
greater proportion of human-interest stories in the popular press as a whole – the
1940s was an 'atypical decade of newsprint-rationed high-mindedness'.[7] The
sensationalism of the *News of the World* continues almost unchanged from the 1910s
and 1920s, however. Throughout the 1940s it reported bigamy cases, the shooting
of young women by their boyfriends, underage sex (as 'offences against a 14-year-
old girl' for example), gang rape ('criminal assault' by a group of youths), the
sending of obscene letters and so on. It did also reflect contemporary social
concerns; in 1945 it asked what married women thought about family size and in
1949 reported on sex education in London schools. In the mid-1950s the paper
increasingly emphasised scandalous sexual crime: child abuse, peeping toms,
pornography cases, male homosexual blackmail and underage girls 'in moral
danger', though there were fewer reports of prosecutions for illegal abortion than
there had been between the wars. The *People*, in contrast, distanced itself from sex
scandals for much of the 1940s and early 1950s. It was always more inclined to
avoid such a high proportion of the darker crime stories beloved by the *News of the
World* in preference for more whimsical or heart-warming lightweight news, and
in this period concentrated on sport, spiritualism, health and royalty. By the
mid-1950s it became more sleazy, relishing sex change stories and persecuting
male homosexuality, like the rest of the popular press.

As suggested above, these newspapers continued to use coded allusions and
established vague phrases to discuss sex crime. The consistency of these phrases
and the context – torn clothing of the girl, for example – spelled out the actual
nature of the 'grave offence' to most adult readers. These vocabularies expanded
in the postwar period to encompass a wider range of offences, and became somewhat less circuitous. Some newspaper accounts began using simplistic versions of
psychiatric vocabularies to describe sexual categories, but the *News of the World* and
the *People* rarely used the terms lesbian or homosexual, even after the media witch-
hunt against male homosexuality in the mid-1950s.[8] For sex between women,
constructs such as 'forms of perversion' between women, or 'unnatural passions'
were the phrases used.

In the Second World War there were no reports of passing women trying to
join the men's services.[9] The few wartime stories of cross-dressing kept to the
classic tradition. The 1942 'Wedding Puzzle' of a year-long marriage between a
35-year-old husband, revealed to be a woman working in engineering and a
30-year old bride, a motor driver on war work, 'recall[s] the masquerade of
'Colonel Barker'' said the *People*.[10] The *News of the World* promised that the 'extraordinary investigation' would produce 'a sensational story of the devotion of one
woman to another'.[11] The vicar who had married them at the village church in
Stoke Poges had been fooled, as had the husband's mother-in-law, who had lived
with the couple in Hendon for the past three or four months. 'I noticed that he
never shaved and that he never seemed to be in need of a shave', she said.[12] The
war supplied new mechanisms for disclosure. Plain-clothes police had stopped the
husband in the black-out and discovered in his suitcase 'a number of women's

articles of a personal nature unlikely to be carried by a man'. Accompanying him home, the police were almost convinced by the corroboration of his wife, but then checked his identity card which 'bore a woman's Christian name and also indicated that the owner was a female', leading to his arrest.[13]

Recalling the French stories about identity papers of the 1930s, we can see modern state bureaucracy and controls intruding into British life. In this wartime context, identity cards hinder the agency of the cross-dresser who cannot any longer either ridicule or circumvent them. This also 'proved her undoing' in the case of Michael Johnson, 'The Baker's "Man"', when she needed to change the address on her registration card. At the national registration office in Leeds, 'wearing a trilby hat and a mackintosh, a clerk noticed that the name on her card had been altered from Muriel to "Michael"'.[14] Muriel Johnson had a traditional explanation for her 'extraordinary masquerade', admitting that 'she posed as a man so that she could earn £5 10s a week instead of £2 10s a week as a baker'. Asked by the magistrate how she had managed to conceal her sex, 'Muriel, who smiled, replied: "I really don't know."' She had passed successfully for some time in London and Leeds, and as in the earlier stories the men whom she worked with were convinced of her gender. The foreman told the paper: 'I thought she was a man. She looked like one and she worked like one . . . We called her "Ginger". She used to swagger out like a man, too.' Johnson had joined the ATS since her arrest and was pictured in uniform.[15]

A Warwickshire wedding

It was another country wedding, this one in 1946, which explicitly introduced sex between women and the idea of 'perversion' into the cross-dressing narrative, although the first of the two reports on the case was full of humorous and entertaining elements. Despite newsprint rationing, the *News of the World* devoted a good deal of space to it. In November 1946 Ellen (or Allan) Young, aged 26, was prosecuted for making false declarations for the purpose of procuring a marriage, and also for forging an identity card, following her wedding to Irene Palmer, also 26, at Baddesley Clinton Catholic Church in Warwickshire just a few weeks earlier (see Figure 8).

As recounted in the courtroom and then in the *News of the World* the story had various twists and turns. Ellen Young is represented as a bit of a trickster and some familiar jokes appear, as she fooled her girlfriend, her girlfriend's family and some young men into accepting her masculinity. Young began to wear men's clothes for convenience when she worked at a factory in Guildford during the war. She found that when she dressed as a man, girls took notice of her, and she thought it was 'a lark' to pretend to make dates with them – though she said it never went further than a joke until she met Irene Palmer. The two young women met at Christmas 1945 on Waterloo Station, when Irene accepted an invitation to the pictures and made friends with her. Irene Palmer assumed Young was a man and the relationship flourished. Ellen Young wrote over 50 passionate letters to Palmer, two of which were read out in court and excerpted in the *News of the World*, and got a

WOMAN SAID TO HAVE WOOED AND MARRIED FORMER A.T.S. GIRL

Bench Told Warning Letters Were Disregarded

SCORES of women, many of whom had brought their knitting, packets of sandwiches and flasks of tea, crowded the courtroom in the town hall at Coleshill, Warwickshire, to hear unfolded what the prosecution described as "an amazing and extraordinary story."

The principals in the case were a 26-year-old Surrey factory girl and a former A.T.S. private, referred to as "a simple village girl" from Chadwick End, Warwickshire.

The former, Ellen May Young, of Oakdene-road, Peasmarsh, near Guildford, was alleged, while posing as an ex-R.A.F. pilot, to have gone through a marriage ceremony at Baddesley Clinton Roman Catholic Church with Miss Irene Mary Palmer, also aged 26, who resides with her parents at Chadwick End.

Ellen Young, who was dressed in a brown tweed jacket and pin-striped grey trousers, and wore a collar and tie, was committed for trial at Warwick Assizes on charges alleging that:

On Aug. 12 she made and signed a false declaration for the purpose of procuring a marriage; and

On Sept. 7 she made a statement, false as to details required by law, for the purpose of insertion in the marriage register.

Mr. C. C. Ladds, prosecuting, stated that "warning" letters were sent to Miss Palmer by a Guildford girl friend of Ellen

told Irene I was a girl. I took it for granted she would find out, but she has never questioned me about it since the marriage.

Since I met Irene I obtained employment as a man at Birmingham, and I have never been challenged about my sex while working.

Outlining the circumstance which led up to taking the alleged statement, Mr. Ladds said that Miss Palmer's story and Ellen Young's description of how they met agreed.

PASSIONATE LETTERS

"While they were apart," Mr. Ladds observed, "the defendant wrote passionate letters to Miss Palmer. There were more than 50 altogether, but two I will read are typical. In one, Ellen Young wrote:

My dearest Irene.—I miss you, Irene, darling, very much. I love you, dearest, very sincerely, and I'm not kidding.

God bless and keep you for me safe for ever. With all my love to the sweetest girl in the world. My love is yours, and yours alone, darling sweetheart.

The other letter ran:

My dearest Irene.—Please try and understand how I feel. My heart is yours, darling, but it has just got to be. Don't you think it is hurting

Ellen May Young photographed in male attire at her home.

I would commit suicide. That seems the best way out of it."

Miss Irene Palmer went into the witness-box. She described steps she took to find out the truth about Ellen Young after she and her mother had received letters.

"I believed Young's story," Miss

In this picture, taken when she was out for a walk, Ellen May Young is seen in women's clothing.

Figure 8 Ellen/Allan Young. *News of the World*, 3 November 1946, p. 3.
Reproduced with the permission of the British Library.
© NI Syndication Limited. Reproduced with permission.

factory job in Birmingham, as a man, in order to be nearer her. In summer 1946 Young 'more or less jokingly' proposed, was accepted and the marriage was arranged. The engagement and Warwickshire wedding were presented as a comedy of compounding errors. Young was received at Irene Palmer's home as a man, her proposal of marriage was accepted – and she found she was in too deep. Getting cold feet, Young tried to retrieve the situation and various letters whizzed back and forth. She pretended she had fathered a child by another young woman, whom she persuaded to write to Palmer. Then Young's mother wrote to the bride's parents to tell them it was her daughter Ellen not a son named Allan who was engaged to Irene. Not surprisingly Irene was upset and confused, and Ellen Young decided to renegotiate these stories and reassure her. 'I could see that I was hurting her feelings, and I told her I was a man and that the arrangement would stand.' The wedding went ahead, the couple had a week's honeymoon and a brief period of married life before the police investigated.

Young represented her story as an accident of deception which ran out of control. She tried to maintain her pose as an ex-RAF pilot by finding some young servicemen to be her best man and guard of honour. In the week before the wedding two of these young men had shared beds with Young, without being aware she was a woman.[16] Evidence about this episode, given by one of them, provoked loud laughter in court from 'a number of women in the public seats' – clearly at the expense of the young men rather than Young. The *News of the World* reported that '[s]cores of women, many of whom had brought their knitting, packets of sandwiches and flasks of tea crowded the courtroom', and were rebuked by the clerk and chairman more than once: 'If you think this is amusing, you had better go somewhere else for your amusement.' The crowd also enjoyed Irene Palmer's evidence. Her protestations of innocence evoke those of Holton's wife in the 1929 story. Irene said she was in love with Allan Young and after the wedding: 'So far as I knew I lived with the defendant as man and wife.' Young promised her a baby. 'Young always made a point of undressing in the dark, but at no time had I any reason to think that the defendant was other than a man.'[17]

Unlike most earlier stories of female marriage, the bride appears to have been completely deceived. Indeed in reporting on the second part of the trial, when the defence case was presented, the *News of the World* emphasised their contrasting sexual experience. Irene Palmer was described as 'a simple village girl' 'who had had very little to do with the opposite sex', and was deceived by the more sexually experienced Young, who, it now transpired, had been introduced to lesbian sex while serving a prison sentence: 'certain incidents took place in Holloway prison'. The tone of this second report, and the explicit references to sex between women make a considerable contrast with the first story. It was Ellen Young's own defence counsel who cited her same-sex experience, in trying to make a case that Young should not be seen as fully responsible for her actions. He 'said the case was difficult because it arose out of something deep in Miss Young's nature'. Her hair was cut short at age 14 for an operation and she'd never worn it long since. 'She had been greatly affected by the fact that a soldier of whom she was fond disappeared at Singapore.'[18] After this she had begun to steal and had four previous convictions. Her lawyer explained: 'When she was serving a sentence in Holloway prison she was brought into contact with a form of perversion through an older woman', and asked Ellen Young's mother '"Do you realise your daughter is not quite normal?" "Yes, sir," replied Mrs Young.'[19]

Two-thirds of the newspaper's story was taken up by an interview with Ellen Young, who expanded on many of these difficult issues in more detail, clearly framed to gain the reader's sympathy alongside their prurient interest in her wrong-doing. She blamed the war and her Holloway experience for 'my downfall'. Recounting a tomboy childhood and pride in her sporting achievements, she continued to play football with men in her factory's team. She described how she 'fell in love with a young soldier' and was broken-hearted when his letters ceased. 'Then came a War Office message that he had been captured by the Japanese.' After a couple of court appearances for theft she was sent to Holloway for six months. 'My companions there were women of every class. Vice was the usual topic of conversation of many of them. I was young and some of them set out to corrupt me. Several times I was threatened with a "beating up".' When the war had ended her boyfriend was still missing, she 'lost heart in things' and began to dress in men's clothes.[20]

There are several types of explanation here, both of why Young was passing as a man and of her lesbian sexuality. One was essentialism – something deep in her nature, expressed perhaps in her tomboy youth and the shearing of her hair in adolescence. There was the traumatic crushing of legitimate romantic hope focused on her soldier boyfriend which disrupted the usual path of femininity. There are also older notions of homosexual contagion woven into the story. The motif of the older predatory lesbian who seduced young girls had been appearing since the time of the First World War in middlebrow literature and journalism – though not until now in these Sunday newspapers.[21] Young had been seduced in Holloway prison by an older woman, and in turn had taken advantage of Palmer. The vice was contagious. All of this added up to a quasi-medical perspective as 'not normal'. Yet while her sexual behaviour is represented as perverted, the complex causative factors in this case – biological, psychological and circumstantial – mean she could be seen as a victim, albeit a pathologised one, as well as a perpetrator.[22] Even when her behaviour was sexualised and labelled deviant, the female husband could still be viewed with some sympathy by the press, an approach apparent in one or two later postwar stories too.

The *News of the World* gave Young plenty of space to put her side of the story. She was clearly redeemed by her heterosexual past. Having a boyfriend killed in the war counted as heavy freight in 1946. Like the women in the 1937 Harrogate wedding case, Young is also positioned as sufficiently young and penitent to straighten out in the future; her youthful sexuality is not seen as fixed. Although she says she dressed as a man and dated girls 'for a lark', Ellen Young does not assert herself as a trickster and backtracks rapidly. She was pleased to be drawing a man's wages, but professes amazement that with her soprano voice and feminine ways she was so successful in passing as a man. Young told the readers of the *News of the World* that she was 'thoroughly ashamed of the whole episode in my life which has just ended'. She had been brought up in a happy home by affectionate parents in Surrey, and after serving her nine-month sentence she was going to return there and try to make it up to them. 'I have always longed for a similar home of my own.'[23] Young is now pictured 'smartly dressed' in women's clothes, in contrast to the first report which depicted her in trousers, collar and tie. This capitulation to normative femininity is a marked shift from the buoyant cross-dressing jokers of the classic stories.

The shadow of lesbianism

The *News of the World* had now found a language to describe working-class lesbianism – one presumably comprehensible to its readers – and decided to use it. These formulations are 'certain incidents', 'a form of perversion', vice, corruption, 'not quite normal'.[24] It had earlier reported the phrase 'certain associations between the two women' in a case in 1942 in which Jacqueline Aspland had attacked her married lover and tried to cut her throat with a razor blade when the woman's husband was due to return from the army.[25] The proximity of cross-dressing stories alongside other reports of sexual wrong-doing now made a different kind of sense to readers. Next to Ellen Young's story was a case of a man sending obscene letters to a woman neighbour; below it a scoutmaster was sentenced for 10 years for 'offences concerning boys'.[26] Not all the popular press took this new line, however, tweaking and censoring the Ellen Young story for their different readerships. The *Daily Herald* published a much shorter report (like the other dailies) but was more sexually explicit. Describing her prison contact with older 'perverted women', it explained: 'From them she learned to deceive the girl she "married," and maintain the pretence of being a man during a week's honeymoon and a further week during which they lived as man and wife.'[27] The *Daily Mirror* emphasised her criminal history, her prison contact 'with a form of perversion with women' and an earlier period of 'psychological treatment' in hospital.[28] There was absolutely no mention of the sexual aspects in the *Daily Express* report, which simply described Young's appearance as a man and the loss of her boy in the war, and the *People* declined to report the story at all.[29]

While this story remained, in many ways, in the rumbustious tradition of the cross-dressing genre, it also marked a turning point in the tone of reporting. Subsequent stories were reported in fairly flat, straightforward language; the incitement to astonishment and curiosity and the terminology of the amazing masquerade largely disappears. The continuing reports still invite the reader to be entertained, but more often by the peculiar or criminal aspects.[30] The medium-length reports of the late 1940s and early 1950s use a variety of codes to raise the question of whether sex between women was a factor in the case. Explanatory paradigms for the cross-dressed woman's behaviour were also in the process of change, from socio-economic motives to increasing focus on individual psycholog-ical explanations. The questions shifted towards: did she have a tomboy child-hood, did she always want to wear men's clothes, was there a personal or romantic tragedy involved? Joanna Grant, a 26-year-old mill-worker from Elgin in Scotland, had been dressing as a man (though not completely passing) for some years and was engaged to another girl. She was charged with altering her identity card to her male name. Her solicitor explained that she came from a very large family and had always associated with her brothers rather than her sisters. Discharged from the ATS after a year (on medical grounds) she 'constantly went about dressed as a man'. She met an older man who proposed marriage but 'At the last minute he let her down.' Her lawyer told the court: 'It appeared that she contracted a genuine affection for her girl workmate at Stanley . . . She assures me that *never at any time was there any suggestion of intimacy between them*, but only a deep and genuine feeling of affection.'[31] Like Ellen Young she had had a disappointment in heterosexual love, her same-sex love was thwarted and she undertook not to dress as a man in future.

The story of Pearl Brown and Margaret Haworth mobilised several codes for sex between women. 'Teaming up on release from prison, the two girls went to Blackburn, where, covered with confetti, they posed as a honeymoon couple.' Brown was described as 'Eton-cropped' and the pair were also charged with defrauding 'a Mayfair hotel, where they lived in a double room for nearly a week'.[32] And when Muriel Johnson, the baker, turned up again in 1951, still determined to live as a man, it was because she had tried to join the Territorial Amy 'while masquerading as a man, [and had] attended drill parades and rifle practice'. She had been engaged to two young women, who had complained to the police, and was now described as having 'become a menace' because of 'her associations with other women'.[33]

How can we explain this postwar shift towards seeing cross-dressing as potentially connected to sex between women, and the greater willingness to report it as such? As shown in Chapters 3 and 4, codes such as 'Eton-cropped' and 'going too far' had begun to signal a link from the end of the 1930s. Various social changes during the war itself had led to increased sexual knowledge and a desire for greater frankness about sexual matters. Young women in particular were more likely to leave home and acquire knowledge from their peers in factories and the forces, though this does not seem to have been the case for Irene Palmer (Ellen Young's wife) who preserved her ignorance despite having served in the ATS.[34] Sex reformers' campaigns for the greater spread of straightforward sexual information were facilitated by the need to contain VD (venereal disease, i.e. sexually transmitted diseases) and more positively by the social consensus of building a new healthy Britain after the war. The wartime drive against VD prompted the *Daily Mirror* to be less evasive about sexual topics, and its lead was subsequently followed by other newspapers.[35]

At the same time, the sight of women wearing trousers and other masculine clothing such as jackets and overalls was becoming unexceptional. Women had worn such clothing in the First World War, of course, and it had excited much comment. Between the wars trousers had become acceptable for women's sportswear, but were still remarked upon as an inappropriate feminine fashion in other contexts.[36] The Second World War changed this for good, and while feminine frocks remained popular as utility wear and were revived in the postwar New Look, it was no longer possible to conceive of women wearing men's clothing and being mistaken for men as automatically astonishing or entertaining – though they might be deemed unfeminine or even, in the 1950s, sexually dubious. The crossdressing story, as a tale of magical masquerade, was running out of time. Ellen Young, under a sub-head 'Slacks were the Fashion', described how she came to wear trousers habitually. 'Because women were doing men's work in the factories it became the fashion to wear slacks at the plant and smart trousers and tweed jackets off duty.'[37] A working-class lesbian sub-culture was beginning to grow in cities such as London and Manchester in the postwar years. While still limited to a few pubs and clubs, this community gradually became more socially visible, especially through the figure of the butch lesbian as this sexual self-fashioning became culturally recognisable.[38] Lesbian desire as a motive for gender-crossing was increasingly likely to be identified and understood as such in the new psychologisation of offending which spread rapidly in the postwar criminal justice system. The professionalisation of probation officers and social workers introduced greater probing of the background and psychology of those brought before the courts, informed by both functionalist and Freudian perspectives of the society and the individual. This was also fanned by a widespread social anxiety about the family after the war which led to debates on how to deal with youth delinquency, strengthen marriage and encourage motherhood.

The pathologising of lesbianism

The more explicit naming of sex between women in the press was accompanied by a heavy pathologising of this 'perversion'. An increasing number of stories appeared in the 1950s, especially in the *News of the World*, and while the women involved were not always 'mannish', the confluence of these themes in the late 1940s meant the cross-dressing story was textually associated with these negative and stigmatising discourses. We have seen in Chapters 2 and 3 that before the Second World War, the figure of the lesbian which emerged in these Sunday newspapers was only faintly drawn, but was given shape by reference to upper-class decadence, male homosexuality and her power to break up marriages. Her favourite location was in the bohemian milieux of the modern city, where in the late 1930s she was occasionally joined by the Eton-cropped mannish lesbian. This powerful (if undeveloped or 'twilight') idea of the lesbian as seductive wife-stealer, glamorous gangster or arty Bright Young Thing was neutralised remarkably quickly in the 1940s. Although lesbianism was reported more clearly after the Second World War – in divorce and assault cases, for example – it was increasingly associated with a semi-psychiatric discourse of neurotic and uncontrolled emotion, criminal violence and even murder. It might be found anywhere, in mundane working-class districts and potentially in the ordinary middle-class family. The varied anti-social expressions of lesbian desire were increasingly mediated by professional agencies within the criminal justice system and welfare state. These themes produced a tone of distaste and repugnance for sex between women in the press reports.

Criminal reports involving relationships between women represented the lesbian as an unbalanced and marginal individual. Excessive sexual jealousy prompted criminal violence by a wife's girlfriend in a couple of 1940s cases. The vocabulary of 'certain associations' used in the 1942 Aspland report was mentioned earlier.[39] In another jealousy case involving an army husband in 1949, Margaret Snelgrove tried to hit Captain Hill with a metal bar outside his home, but the attack was foiled. She also had a sheath knife strapped to her wrist. Her probation officer said that she 'was an unhappy woman who had formed a strong attachment for Capt. Hill's wife'. The magistrates remanded her to 'a home' for 21 days to be examined by a psychiatrist.[40] From 1949, and the Snelgrove case, we can trace the psychiatrisation of the lesbian by the courts and its translation into the popular press. After this date medical evidence is often called in criminal cases involving lesbians or cross-dressers, although not always followed up or reported upon in detail by the press. Since doctors' pronouncements were fairly specific (usually to establish the biological sex of the defendant or whether she was insane) and only elaborated in the murder trials, it was the descriptions given by the other professional actors in the criminal justice drama, the police, probation officers and lawyers, which were most frequent and consistent in building up a picture of emotional excess or unbalanced personality. These comments reflect the infiltration of a psychiatric discourse of criminal behaviour into the courts. Developed between the wars in relation to particular groups such as juvenile offenders and male homosexuals, it now reached across all types of crime as new powers were given to the courts.[41] The reports of these professionals were phrased mainly in non-technical language – the lesbian had had a poor upbringing and was neurotic, over-emotional, unhappy and out of control, and thus prone to violence. Many of the ideas they presented fit a loose Freudian typology (as Chris Waters has argued for gay men's treatment by forensic medicine) rather than a sexological model of innate homosexuality.[42] The defendant was seen as an immature woman stuck in a phase of adolescent crushes, unable to control her emotions effectively.

The hopeless and socially unacknowledged nature of love between women was part of this theme. The story of a schoolgirl who had drowned herself after writing a dozen affectionate letters to her teacher was headlined 'Tragedy of the Girl with "Disorderly Emotions"' and given an extended psychiatric analysis in the coroner's court. The pathologist confirmed that 'hero worship and over-affection for older women' was 'quite a natural manifestation of a girl of that age' but was here 'manifested to an excessive degree'. The girl's teacher had found the letters 'very distasteful': 'I completely ignored them.' The middle-class worry about same-sex adolescent attachment and homosexuality was now voiced in the mass-circulation press.[43] Unrequited or unhealthy love between women was hinted at in several suicide cases of the early 1950s. (The *News of the World* enthusiastically reported suicides right through this period.) A lonely single woman, a shoe-shop owner in Fulham, had gassed herself after a misunderstanding with a married woman neighbour of whom she was fond. She 'was shy and reserved with men, but very attached to his wife' reported the husband.[44] Later the same year readers could hear of a 40-year-old receptionist who had attempted suicide after becoming, in the probation officer's words, 'infatuated with a woman of undesirable character who mixed with a very fast set in Chelsea'. The receptionist wanted to return to her former 'decent, wholesome life'. 'Her life had been practically ruined by a woman and she had felt there was not much to live for. "This woman knocked me about," she added. "My mouth is bruised and my face swollen."'[45]

But what was lesbianism? The popular media implied it had to have a pathological edge. Divorce court stories suggested it was more than a physically close loving friendship. The issue of the alienation of a wife's affection by another woman was now dealt with more openly than it had been before the war. Lesbianism was not a legitimate grounds for divorce (the 1951–6 Royal Commission on Marriage and Divorce considered whether it should become one[46]), but it might be cited as mental cruelty. Judges were reluctant to agree with husbands that the close female friendships of which they complained should be seen as a matrimonial offence. A clergyman alleged to the divorce court in 1954 that his wife and her friend

> had been seen hand in hand; they called each other 'darling'; they kissed on the lips; they spent a number of holidays together; they were constantly alone

in the wife's room and on two or three occasions they occupied the same bed.[47]

However, the judge found that their friendship was extremely close but not close enough to entitle Mr Davis to a reasonable belief that the association was 'improper'. In a 1959 case, a court heard how a couple came to what the judge described as 'a peculiar arrangement' before marrying, by which a woman friend of the wife would live with them and sleep with the wife. In adjudicating a maintenance order in the wife's favour, the judge declared: 'It is fair to the wife and Miss Barker [her friend] to emphasise that there was never any suggestion that there was any kind of Lesbian relationship between them, either physical or emotional.'[48] This was the first time the term 'lesbian' was used in these two newspapers in the period. These and other 1950s divorce court cases bore some marked similarities to those of prewar years – the exclusion of the husband from the marital bed, the preference of the wife for her woman friend and sometimes a refusal to have sex with her husband.[49] Only after the Second World War were these relationships between women explicitly scrutinised for sexual deviance. But the female friendships were normalised, absolved of lesbianism and the threat to the domestic circle dismissed. Of course these divorce judgements reflect a judicial desire not to soften the legal grounds for divorce, but they discursively serve to suggest that the marital bond was impervious to lesbian challenge and also that 'real' lesbianism must be characterised by additional grossly anti-social and pathological traits.

Despite continuing repressive censorship (even, in the early 1950s, the prosecution of saucy postcards as well as erotic literature and pornography), ideas about lesbianism were increasingly accessible in other texts. Radclyffe Hall's novel *The Well of Loneliness* was reissued in 1949 without hindrance. American pulp fiction brought images of predatory sex between women in institutions such as prisons and schools.[50] Female homoeroticism in postwar cinema no longer took playful forms but, as in the press, was more openly referenced as sexual deviance in some, generally minor, movies (despite the Hays Code being still in force) and associated with prisons, violence and psychiatric maladjustment.[51] The burgeoning literature of sex education in the postwar period was part of a new welfare state and reforming ethos to promote healthy bodies and families, to replace shame about sexuality with (generally normative) information. It included some reference to lesbianism, as 'He-Women' in Eustace Chesser's 1942 *Love Without Fear*, and as a pathology of motherhood avoidance in his *Sexual Behaviour. Normal and Abnormal* (1949).[52] Although seen as a reformist liberal doctor, Chesser described the lesbian temperament as jealous and sado-masochistic, quoting some lurid case histories, while studies such as Frank Caprio's *Female Homosexuality*, published in Britain in 1957, continued to represent lesbianism as a psychiatric problem.[53]

Murderous lesbians

The excessive nature of the lesbian's emotions and her lack of self-control was emphasised in the postwar popular imagination by the reporting in the British press of a succession of *three* murders by lesbians (all of other women) within six years. Carried out by very different types of women, in diverse settings, they brought into play the themes linked to lesbianism discussed above. The first of these is particularly important in linking cross-dressing with mannishness, lesbian desire and an inexplicable murderous impulse.

In 1948 Margaret Allen, an unemployed working-class woman of 41, for no apparent motive, battered to death a neighbour, 68-year-old Mrs Chadwick, in Rawtenstall, a small town in Lancashire (see Figure 9). In its report of the trial, the *News of the World* focused on Allen's mannish appearance and habits, her sexual desire for her friend Annie Cook, and her violent emotional temperament indicated by an earlier threat of suicide.[54] Allen had begun dressing as a man 12 years earlier, and preferred to be known as Bill, but her neighbours and acquaintances all knew her to be a woman. 'She always had her hair cut short, wore men's shirts, ties and trousers, and at times worked as a labourer.' Headlined 'Murderess Dressed as a Man for 13 Years', the paper described her lack of interest in feminine duties and skills, but noted that she could mend boots and carry out repairs with the efficiency of a man. 'If ever she lost her temper she fought like a man – with her fists.' The only real friendship Allen had since her mother had died was with Mrs Annie Cook. She told the court that Allen had once claimed to have had her sex changed. When Mrs Cook had told Margaret Allen to 'pull herself together', about six months previously, Allen became angry and accused her of trying to break up their friendship. 'She rushed to a gas jet, put a tube in her mouth and turned the gas on.' Annie Cook was also asked about Allen's sexual propositioning. 'Did you go to Blackpool together last Whitsun for your holidays? – Yes. Did Margaret Allen register herself as Mr Allen? – Yes. Did she suggest that something should happen while you were there? – Yes. And of course you refused at once? – Yes.' Allen's same-sex desires are emphasised here, while Annie Cook is given an opportunity to deny that the relationship was sexual. Although a medical defence was attempted, this was rejected by the prison doctor who reported that Allen 'behaved normally' while awaiting trial.[55]

Sentenced to death on 8 December 1948, Margaret Allen was executed just one month later, the first woman to be hanged since 1936. An attempt by Annie Cook and others to petition for her reprieve was unsuccessful, despite the contemporary debate over the death penalty. Other mass-circulation newspapers did not report the trial, but did follow the story of her hanging, promoting a similar emphasis on Allen's mannish habits. The *Daily Express* front-page story was headlined: 'Pint for Woman Who Dies at Dawn', described her masculine clothing and told how she spent her last night writing a letter to Annie Cook, asking her to stand vigil at the spot where they always used to meet. 'As she wrote she drank a pint of beer and smoked a cigarette.' It was also reported that she would have to wear women's clothes for the execution.[56] This murder trial unequivocally linked wearing men's clothes with female homosexuality and suggests that the concept of the butch mannish lesbian was already current in popular perception.

In the other two murders there was no evidence of masculine appearance but instability and excessive feminine emotion characterise the lesbian. The widely

MURDERESS DRESSED AS MAN FOR 13 YEARS

Twentieth Child in a Family Of Twenty-Two

"News of the World" Reporter

FOR 13 years a 41-year-old Lancashire spinster, found guilty at Manchester Assizes of murdering a neighbour, aged 68, had dressed like a man. She always had her hair cut short, wore men's shirts, collars, ties and trousers, and at times worked as a labourer.

The woman, **Margaret Allen, of Bacup-road, Rawtenstall, Lancs,** showed no sign of emotion when Mr. Justice Sellers sentenced her to death for what her counsel had described as "a senseless, unjustified and purposeless crime."

The victim, Mrs. Nancy Ellen Chadwick, of Hardman-avenue, Rawtenstall, was, according to the prosecution, murdered in Miss Allen's house on Aug. 28.

Her body was apparently dragged into a coal cellar, where it remained until just before 4 o'clock the following morning. Later it was discovered in the roadway by a bus driver.

During the trial brief glimpses were given into the strange life of Margaret Allen, the 20th child in

MARGARET ALLEN, on the right, with MRS. ANNIE COOK, who was called as a witness at the trial.

Figure 9 Margaret Allen. *News of the World*, 12 December 1948, p. 3.
Reproduced with the permission of the British Library.
© NI Syndication Limited. Reproduced with permission.

reported trial of Bertha Scorse for murder in 1952 had the most extensive array of doctors in court: two called by the defence to argue that she was guilty but insane, and one by the prosecution. Scorse had formed an 'unnatural attachment' with a married woman whom she had met in a sanatorium while they were both being treated for TB, but fatally stabbed her when she later ended their relationship. The medical defence arguments pathologised lesbianism as likely to lead to insanity and violence. Dr Roy Neville Craig (a specialist in mental diseases) diagnosed Scorse as a psychopath with strong anti-social traits. She suffered from 'a gross perversion which was an extremely powerful driving force'. In his account her murderous violence was a consequence of her insanity which was elided with her perverted same-sex passion. Dr Matheson, principal medical officer at Brixton prison, for the prosecution, considered that 'perverted emotion . . . might lead to loss of self-control' but 'did not think that lack of self-control amounted to insanity'. The case was depicted by both sides as a crime of 'perverted passion . . . the result of thwarted love and jealousy', and the jury agreed with the prosecution that Scorse was responsible for her actions, taking only one hour and six minutes to find her guilty.[57] Still ill with tuberculosis, Scorse was sentenced to death as she lay on a stretcher in the dock, an image which provoked a sensational tone in the popular press.

A more sophisticated psychiatric analysis emerged in relation to lesbian love between teenagers, following the conviction of Juliet Hulme, 15, and Pauline Parker, 16, for killing Parker's mother in a park in Christchurch, New Zealand, because they feared she would break up their relationship. Reporting of the 1954 trial was typically sensationalist and moralistic. It was alleged that the girls 'indulged in wild orgies which left them ecstatic but exhausted', and Pauline's diary was described as 'a mirror of evil'.[58] Subsequently the *People* published an article by a psychiatrist purporting to answer parents' concerns about 'unnatural friendships between young people' entitled 'Love off the rails'.[59] He described the teenage murderers as 'those two pathetic girls' and 'morbid neurotics' and merged essentialist, Freudian and Kinseyesque models to explain the development of female sexuality. He reassured readers that 'there isn't really much cause for alarm' since only one in 200 adult women 'has these tendencies in a practical sense' (though the figure was one in 30 for men). '[T]he homosexual stage . . . is a perfectly normal one' in a child's development, and when adolescence arrives the sex instinct should be transferred to the opposite sex. When menstruation begins, 'her maternal feelings start and she begins to look around for a mate'. However, very few of us are perfectly normal, the Harley Street psychiatrist warned: 'there are many women with a homosexual background . . . [who] marry, but their real love life is spent over the teacups with their girl friends'. This was a scare story comparable to Leonora Eyles' warnings about female decadence in 1924, but the homosexual danger here is located specifically in adolescent development and the domestic circle. Lesbian tendencies were described as amenable to medical treatment and particularly to the wise guidance of parents who were allocated heavy responsibility in the matter. The author recommended that the best way of ensuring children grew up normally was to give them a happy home: 'the future sex life of Tommy and Effie is in your hands – to make happy or horrible as you will it'.[60]

Not all the lesbians appearing in the popular press were mannish by any means, but many of them were, and after the Ellen Young cross-dressing case in 1946 and the Margaret Allen murder trial of 1948, subsequent gender-crossing of all kinds was tainted with homosexuality, or what was more commonly referred to as perverted or unnatural relationships between women. From the 1940s the lesbian becomes increasingly visible but pathologised by a variety of textual associations with criminal violence, uncontrolled emotion and psychiatric comment. She is seen as a danger to herself or to specific others through domestic crimes of violence. Unlike the homosexual man in this period, she is not represented as a general threat lurking in a public space or challenging modern marriage and the family in any wholesale way. Female homosexuality is now seen as an identity category but as a deeply unappealing and socially excluded one.

Respectable gender-crossing: the Catford wedding

Cross-gender identification and the desire to change sex is explored for the first time as a rationale for cross-dressing in one or two 1950s stories. A 1954 Catford wedding case is perhaps the last great story in the cross-dressing tradition in terms of its treatment by the press, its entertainment values, and the protagonist's trickster qualities. In December 1954, Vincent or Violet Jones (26) and Jean Lee (21) were each fined £25 at the local magistrates' court for making a false statement to obtain a marriage certificate, three months after their church wedding in Catford, an ordinary working-class district of south London (see Figure 10). They had met as women four years earlier, both working at the local telephone exchange, and had fallen in love. Elements of traditional humour were revived in this report, such as deceiving the priest. Vincent Jones had obtained an employment card stating him to be male but the vicar told her she could not marry as a man unless her sex was altered completely. However, a few months later the new vicar assumed she was a man when they went along to put up the banns.

What marked this story as peculiarly of the 1950s was not only the white wedding dress and elaborate wedding cake, but the competing interpretations of their behaviour put forward by the couple themselves, the presiding magistrate, the medical doctors cited in the case and the popular press. Vincent Jones' solicitor claimed that: 'It seemed ridiculous for her to be a female.' She had been to the hospital two years after meeting Jean Lee to try to get her sex changed but was told she had the normal feminine attributes. When interviewed by police, Jones said: 'I am a man but if you mean physically I still possess female organs. There is more to marriage than the physical side. I have been to doctors to alter my sex completely but I was sick of waiting.' Her lawyer said she had suffered from this disorder since childhood. Jones was built as a man and believed she was one. She 'had written to Denmark where there was a case of a woman doctor who changed her sex after an operation in Switzerland and later married her housekeeper'. However, a medical report to the court said she had a delusion about being a man. The magistrate refused to accept Jones' assertion of her innate male gender and her medicalised justification of what would later come to be labelled transsexual identity, appeared to blame the parents of both young women for allowing them to pursue their way of life and condemned both for their immoral sexual desires: 'The fact remains that you made a grave false statement to cover your unnatural passions with a false air of respectability.'[61] That is, he positioned the couple as sexual perverts, refusing to accept their own version of their relationship as perfectly proper, based on their

WOMEN WHO 'WED' EACH OTHER ARE FINED

TWO women were fined £25 each yesterday for making a false statement to obtain a marriage certificate.

They were alleged to have gone through a form of marriage together at St. Luke's Church, Downham, on September 25.

Violet Ellen Katherine Jones, 26, and Joan Mary Lee, 21, of Ardgowan-road, Catford, pleaded guilty to the summonses at Greenwich magistrate's court. Jones appeared in court in man's clothes.

'Called Vincent'

Mr. E. G. MacDermott, prosecuting, said that Jones gave the name Vincent Eric Kenneth Jones at the church and described herself as a bachelor.

Mr. MacDermott went on: "The couple first met about 1950, when they were employed at the South-Eastern telephone headquarters as tracers.

"In 1952, after consultation with Lee, Jones went to see a doctor and spent about four weeks under observation in the Maudsley Hospital but was not given any treatment. When she left she wore man's clothes and last February or March she went to see a Mr. Rowe, the clergyman at St Luke's.

"She was dressed as a man but explained to him that, though she was a woman, she felt more a man than a woman.

"She was friendly with Lee and was seeking to get her sex changed, she said.

She wanted to marry her. "Mr. Rowe told her she could not go through a form of marriage without revealing the true circumstances."

On August 3, after Mr. Rowe had left that church,

A 'grave false statement'

Mr. MacDermott said, Jones obtained an application form to put up the banns.

No mention was made about the sexual matters.

The banns were duly called, and Jones, dressed

she suffered from this disorder."

"She was finally taken to doctors. Some were sympathetic. Others simply suggested it was 'too bad' and told her she must wait and see. She felt like a man."

The "wedding" picture of Violet Ellen Jones (left) and Joan Mary Lee taken outside St. Luke's Church, Downham, London.

Figure 10 Violet/Vincent Jones. *Daily Mirror*, 14 December 1954, p. 6.
Reproduced with the permission of the British Library.
© Mirrorpix. Reproduced with permission.

belief that Vince was a man. In the Mary/Mark Weston case of 1936 and other similar stories of sex change discussed in Chapter 5, we saw how the suggestion of a girlfriend normalised the sex change. In the Vincent Jones story, the plea for a sex change normalises same-sex desire – for Jones himself, for his family and indeed for the press, though not for the magistrate.

The press did not pursue the angle of 'unnatural passions' and instead took on Jones' own account of an innate masculine self.[62] All of the newspaper reports were reasonably sympathetic to the Catford couple, apparently accepting that they were honest in their attempt to pursue marriage as the morally appropriate answer. The *Daily Herald*, which did not report the magistrate's comments, was especially understanding, publishing Jones' own account after the trial, described as 'this touching story of her life'.[63] Female husbands could enlist more public sympathy if they were seen as having gender dysphoria rather than lesbian desire, it seemed, since this resolved the mismatch between sex, gender and sexuality in a culturally acceptable way.[64] In the Catford story the sexual aspect of their relationship was barely mentioned in the press, except to deny its importance – love was asserted as the basis for marriage. In accepting Jones' claim to be a man, the press could represent this as a love story, with the two partners thwarted in their understandable and conventional desire for marriage. In its endorsement of this respectable behaviour it also parallels the journalistic framing of earlier stories in which cross-dressing women were applauded for their performance of honourable masculinity.

In the *Daily Herald* story in particular, Jones took a heroic trickster position and was represented as courageous and gallant in maintaining his love for Joan despite these setbacks. 'We both love each other and when everything is put right we intend to get remarried. We shall have a public ceremony. We have nothing to be ashamed of.' They planned to save from their wages 'so I can go abroad for treatment. Then I shall apply for an alteration of my birth certificate.' Meanwhile they would continue to live together in furnished rooms in Catford and according to the report were welcomed back to their usual old-time dancing lesson as Mr and Mrs Jones.[65] In asserting his agency and seeking sex change, Vince demonstrated a trickster sense of surviving and besting the petty barriers of everyday life. He retained the trickster's protection and humour, despite the magistrate's sullying interpretation of it as an unnatural relationship, and (unlike Ellen Young) did not pedal back into femininity and recant his actions.

The idea of a cross-dressing tradition, which was frequently reiterated in stories before the Second World War, is not mentioned after 1942. The reference made by Jones to a previous example in Denmark was not an appeal to tradition but to a more recent knowledge of sex change. For the United States, Joanne Meyerowitz has traced the emergence of a small but growing community of transsexuals who, inspired by reports of sex change in both the tabloid and sex reform press, demanded sex change treatment and helped create transsexual identity in the postwar years.[66] Vince Jones was not part of such a network or community, but clearly felt he shared the experience of the Danish woman and made his claim to this identity as a direct result of reading about the possibility of sex change in the mass-circulation press.

Sex change, gender and desire: moral readings

What did 'sex change' mean in the 1950s? Were these stories still represented as a new sensation as they had been in the 1930s? There were fewer major female-to-male sex change stories than there had been in the 1930s. The Weston case was reprised in 1942 – it turned out that Mark's sister Hilda/Harry had also had a sex change but had been found hanged while depressed.[67] The genre got going again in the 1950s, with four British stories and a number of foreign reports, mostly Italian. While the number of female-to-male stories was roughly the same as the reports of male-to-female cases (in the 1930s there had been very few male-to-female cases), the press was now far more interested in the latter after the initial story of Christine Jorgensen in 1952.[68] It was the men who changed into women who received whole-page treatments, sometimes extended over several weeks with lengthy interviews.[69]

Some of the cases of women changing sex also made the front page, especially of the *People*. Sex change stories had taken the mantle as the only truly astonishing gender transformations – for example, from young Italian peasant girl to married man with pretty wife.[70] Doctors were less in evidence than in the 1930s stories, and the former claims of amazing scientific breakthrough were considerably dampened. If details were reported at all, and some stories were quite limited, they give the impression of spontaneous changes occurring. While featured stories were flagged up as having particularly interesting twists, they also took place in mundane postwar circumstances. Darryll Marsh, aged 22, who as Joy Clark had married at 16 and had two children, living in a prefab on a Dover housing estate, received front-page billing by the *People* as the first mother who had changed sex. He told the paper how his body was becoming more muscular and masculine, and the paper vaguely reported that s/he might have operations to fully become a man.[71] Other sex changes seem to have involved older women, two of whom had served with distinction in the women's military corps. In two of the Italian cases, both involving sisters who were facing or had achieved a change of sex to become male, the medical labelling vied with a different construction of events by the individual concerned. Vittorio Alvaro presented himself as having been a girl who always had boys' interests. Since he felt like a boy he made considerable efforts to reach out of his peasant background and seek assistance from doctors. The doctor quoted said Vittorio and his sister were hermaphrodites, but since Vittorio was predominantly male he had decided to change him into a boy.[72] The term pseudo-hermaphrodite was also used in a 1960 case of some other Italian sisters and explained as meaning that they outwardly appeared to be female but were biologically male.[73]

These stories suggested more potentially conflicting interpretations than had been the case in the 1930s. Most of these 'sex changes' were presented as triggered by physical changes experienced in the body, associated with an inborn condition. Yet one or two of the young men involved described actively searching for a sex change since they felt male, a realisation which was also associated with an interest in girls at adolescence. Male-to-female sex change was also questioned at times. One headline sensationally asserted that Roberta Cowell was not a 'real' woman because she could never become a mother, a classically 1950s definition of womanhood.[74] But despite the now more cautious claims of doctors, the idea of 'sex change' was commonplace. Intersexuality and sex change were also discussed in popular books on sexuality. In his 1948 book *Everyday Sex Problems*, the sex reformer Norman Haire tried to disabuse people of the idea that sex change was available on request. Following newspaper stories, 'several readers have written to me asking if it is possible that human beings can change their sex. The answer is no – definitely no.'[75] He explained that the press reports concerned individuals who were partial hermaphrodites.[76] Together with Vincent Jones' story, this suggests there was a widespread popular understanding that sex change was indeed possible, fostered by the British press since the 1930s.

While sex change was treated sensationally by the popular press, Jones' story shows that it was a much less stigmatised motivation for gender-crossing and basis on which to explain same-sex love than lesbianism. Familiar to the wider public, sex change was presented as a more morally approvable choice, an involuntary and therefore legitimate medical condition which was amenable to surgery. The alternative cultural reading of lesbianism was much more heavily pathologised as lack of self-control, unnatural or immoral perversion, as we have seen. This was reinforced by the treatment of male homosexuality in the tabloid press after 1953, as it began to be reported far more widely than before and in the most damning (if still euphemistic) terms. Chris Waters argues that popular journalism was resistant to the modern interpretations of psychoanalysis and psychiatry, preferring the language of 'moral condemnation'. Terms such as 'degenerate' or 'perverted' were used to describe criminal cases of male homosexuality.[77] Bernice Hausman notes that most transsexuals from the 1950s to the 1970s insisted on their distinctiveness from homosexuality: theirs was a pathology of gender identity which could be medically corrected, not an immoral sexual deviance.[78]

There had been several instances in the earlier stories when cross-dressing women had reportedly told the women they were courting that they were really male, after initially meeting them as women. Joan Coning had told her girlfriend she was really a man, following which they began a sexual relationship and got married in 1937.[79] After the war, however, this aspect of the masquerade was more frequently represented in the language of sex change. Annie Cook said that Margaret Allen 'once told her she had had an operation which had turned her into a man'.[80] The cross-dressed John Amsden, in a 1960 theft case described by the press as 'a riddle', told the police that though technically a woman, he considered himself a man and had changed his Christian name by deed poll.[81] Two 16-year-old factory girls who tried to run away from Newcastle to Jersey in 1959, one dressed as a boy, told the juvenile court they were in love with each other, but by this period there was no cultural knowledge of a tradition of cross-dressing for them to draw on. One of the girls said they had bought a wedding ring and an engagement ring with money they stole: '— is my boyfriend. We are in love.'[82] Interviewed in 1956 by the *Empire News*, Colonel Barker refused to retell her life story using modern categories – she said her cross-dressing was neither perversion, a complex, nor any kind of physical sex change – as James Vernon observes.[83] But the notion of the masquerade no longer referred to a known formula of entertainment and tricksterish humour.

If affiliation with the sex change narrative was one possible postwar version of the cross-dressing story, then another outcome of gender-crossing was to repudiate the behaviour, perhaps with a semi-psychological explanation, and find the true path back to femininity and possibly marriage. This resolution was suggested in Ellen Young's account and was developed in a late 1950s cross-dressing story, a rather unpleasant tale of jealous violence. The acid-throwing story of Joyce Irons was run by the *News of the World* in considerable detail, though not by the *People*. It was headlined as a 'Fantastic Masquerade' – the language of the cross-dressing tradition was not entirely dead – but the judge's 'searing comments' were also prominently reported. After passing as a man, at least to some of her friends, 32-year-old Irons got engaged to a young woman, Patricia Jenkins, who later broke off the relationship and found a new boyfriend. A few months later while feeling depressed, Irons paid a lad of 13 to throw acid in Jenkins' face outside the block of flats where she lived in Islington. She was jailed for three years. The police 'were satisfied that there was nothing improper in her association with the girl', though Irons' mannish appearance, jealous violence and the age gap between them fitted the contemporary press and media codes of lesbianism.[84] In an interview with the *News of the World* Irons described the courtship as a series of accidents, as Jenkins mistook her for a man. Irons said she started wearing slacks in the Blitz for practical reasons. 'In every other way I was a perfectly normal girl. I had been kissed by men and did not find it unpleasant.' She had been unofficially engaged to a soldier, who was unhappily killed during the war. 'Otherwise we would have been married . . . [and] today I would be just another London housewife.' Bitterly regretting her incitement to violence, Irons says she has since met a man and hopes that after her prison term she will eventually settle down with him. 'And Now I'm a Woman in Love.' She is photographed looking attractive in women's clothes, next to a 'before' photograph looking extremely butch, frowning with a cigarette in her mouth.[85] This narrative of fantastic masquerade, like that of Ellen Young, was resolved by the transition back to conventional womanhood. It had ceased to be possible to play on the boundaries of gender.

Male impersonation on stage and screen

At the same time as cross-dressing was losing its vitality as a genre in the press, and its humour was becoming muted or non-existent, it no longer had a relationship to male impersonation as formal entertainment which was also in decline. Whether in pantomime, variety theatre or film, male impersonators just did not feature in these Sunday newspapers after the early 1940s.[86] This means that 'real' female husbands cease to be intelligible as a traditional genre and as an amusing and established part of working-class culture in the way that they were earlier.

While variety was much less important now than cinema, it remained significant. In their 1949–50 survey of leisure, Rowntree and Lavers noted: 'The popularity at the present time of variety of the music-hall type is astonishing', with one or more theatres in large towns. Some American stars had huge success on stage, generating 24-hour queues for tickets in the postwar years.[87] In the bleak postwar climate there was a real sense of nostalgia around the music hall and it was reprised in film as well as on stage, now framed as representing a 'carefree past', when people 'seemed to laugh so much more easily'.[88] A *People* interview with the elderly Vesta Tilley in 1946, positioned next to a government notice about fuel rationing, described her as 'a gracious, fascinating, lovable link with the romantic past'.[89] Male impersonation on stage persisted but was fast becoming an archaic form. Between 1948 and 1950, the *Thanks for the Memory* show made the most of this nostalgia as veterans of the variety stage, including Ella Shields and Hetty King, toured the country and played at the Royal Variety Show in 1948.[90]

But male impersonation could not be viewed in the old way as amusing entertainment for very long after the Second World War. Since young women wearing trousers had become commonplace it was no longer an automatically extraordinary and entertaining sight. Men in skirts, in contrast, remained astonishing and slightly shocking, and female impersonation continued to be part of British popular theatre and postwar comedy film.[91] The perplexing nature of male impersonation in the 1950s was made explicit in some commentary, and in the obituaries of Ella Shields and Vesta Tilley who both died in 1952. The *Times* obituary of Vesta Tilley stressed her patriotic portrayals of military men and the respectability of her performance.

> Vesta Tilley on the stage was the most dapper little man and the dandiest 'fellah turned sixteen' that could be imagined. And this 'Idol of the Girls' had a way with them so free of offence that to some of her admirers the song 'Following in Father's footsteps, Following the dear old Dad,' seemed a shade too coarse for her, while in any other hands it might have seemed insipid.[92]

The progressively more incomprehensible meanings of female gender-crossing were apparent in an obituary of Ella Shields in which the paper had to explain to readers that male impersonation had been acceptable light entertainment in the past, but had now 'faded out'. (In fact Shields was still performing at the age of 72 and had died soon after collapsing on stage at a Morecambe holiday camp.[93]) Ranking her with Vesta Tilley and Hetty King as the greatest male impersonators of the age, the journalist explained:

> There was nothing grotesque, nothing in the least embarrassing about the way these women strutted the stage in glove-tight uniforms and immaculate evening dress. They were never aggressively mannish. Like the best Principal Boys they brought a feminine charm to their masculine dash.[94]

Male impersonation on stage now had to be distinguished from what might be perceived as grossly unfeminine and sexually loaded. In fact even the principal boy form of gender-crossing had had its vitality undercut by the need to stay firmly on the feminine side of androgyny. Commenting on a big decline in the popularity of pantomime, especially in the West End, the *Observer* noted 'a special parting shove for the Principal Boy [as a] hangover from the tinsel-and-tights heyday'. It had to explain how to read one of the most popular principal boys, Dorothy Ward, who appeared almost annually between 1906 and 1957, often opposite her husband Shaun Glenville as Dame. Her act was described as being very different from male impersonation.

It is true that she has the strut and swagger of an Edwardian cavalry office. When to emphasise some observation . . . she swings one shapely leg forward and thumps a well-kept fist into the opposite palm, she is imitating some lost vision of man . . . [She presents] us with an attractive woman's version of how a man behaves in romantic circumstances.[95]

Even Dorothy Ward complained in 1952 that the role had dwindled and become less hearty. 'Principal boy parts are smaller than they used to be. Songs used to be more boisterous. Principal boys slapped their thighs as they punched their songs over. Now they take a musical comedy approach. Costumes are softer and prettier.'[96] Indeed as pantomime declined in the 1950s, principal boy roles were often taken by male actors.[97]

Women's gender-crossing continued in 1940s and 1950s cinema, however, where it had become an established, if minor, theme. A number of Hollywood films spanning a variety of genres, including musicals, Westerns and drama, featured stars in cross-dressing roles. Some had the theatre world as the frame within the frame, including Judy Garland as Sarah Bernhardt in one of her *travesti* roles in *Babes on Broadway* (1941) and Betty Grable singing 'Burlington Bertie' in the musical *Mother Wore Tights* (1947).[98] A couple of Second World War-related thrillers featured women disguised as young men as part of the dramatic action.[99] Like the historical dramas starring women dressed as men (Merle Oberon as George Sand in *A Song to Remember* (1945)[100]), Westerns were a genre presenting an imaginary time and place where women's cross-dressing was already established as part of the mythology. Marlene Dietrich's only postwar 'trouser role' was in a Western. If we take individual stars as symbolising particular versions of desirable femininity in specific historical periods, then Doris Day's image as the 1950s pin-up was far removed from the sexually exotic and ambiguous former leading women Dietrich and Garbo. A wholesome girl-next-door, she was an unquestionably heterosexual and vivacious ideal woman. She played a glorious and irrepressible tomboy (if also a bit of a buffoon) in the musical comedy *Calamity Jane* (1953), where she was eventually partially subdued by romantic love and adopted frocks and tidy hair, if not full 1950s femininity.[101] But by the late 1950s male impersonation had almost disappeared from the screen. It had even been lost as a memory of music hall on the popular stage, and with it had gone the potential for a theatrical cross-reading of the passing woman story.

Conclusions

What do we find when we look back over the stories of women's gender-crossing which are the focus of this book? How does the genre develop from the 1900s to the 1950s, from jaunty and passionate Adelaide Dallamore (the plumber's mate from 1912), via the 'perplexing' 1929 story of William Holton who claimed to have fathered a child (and Colonel Barker, of course, in the same year), to the 1954 report of Vincent Jones, in which 'perverted passions' compete with 'sex change' as an explanation? The British cross-dressing story shows that we must

rethink the chronologising of lesbianism and transgender as modern sexual identities in twentieth-century mass culture. It was not until the late 1940s that the
popular press acknowledged female homosexuality as a specific practice, located it
among working-class communities and reported it as one reading of the passing
woman. The continuing power and familiarity of theatrical gender play within
popular entertainment allowed women's cross-dressing to be framed as a thrilling
and humorous masquerade throughout the first half of the twentieth century.

British popular culture was distinctive in its highly developed and complex
deployment of codes, euphemism and ambiguity to refer to sexual matters, in relation to heterosexuality as well as more forbidden knowledges. Censorship and
prudery about sexuality were well entrenched in British culture, but so too were
inventive and playful ways of circumventing this taboo. From the beginning of the
century to the 1940s, the stories of passing women dance captivatingly and
successfully on 'the fine line between virtue and transgression, orderly and disorderly homoeroticism'.[102] The newspaper accounts of women's cross-dressing were,
on the face of it, addressed to a naïve reader and presented as an artless, amusing
tale. William Holton's marriage and paternity could be read as absurd, innocuous
or a mystery. Yet, as we have seen, the woman masquerader was analogous to the
male impersonator of variety, not only in her skills of mimicry but also in her para-
sexual appeal. Knowing humour drew on familiar jokes about heterosexual courtship or fooling authority figures. Often dapper and handsome, charming and with
a passionate attachment to a woman partner, the passing woman borrowed the
romanticised homoeroticism commonplace in popular culture, and signalled, if
only for a limited readership, a further range of 'twilight' sexual meanings. The
gender-crosser's trickster qualities offered many potential layers of meaning,
without owning any one of them as final.

Her familiarity as a character, firmly embedded in a recognisable working-class
environment, and everyday bantering among neighbours and workmates, also
gave narrative balance to the story. The genre was an important vehicle for
exploring the unstable nature of gender and the contemporary anxieties stirred up
by the suffrage struggle, the First World War and women's growing independence.
In successfully getting away with gender-crossing, the cross-dressing woman light-
heartedly demonstrated the real courage and capacities of women, and exposed
the fragility of social masculinity. Yet by celebrating her achievements and owning
her as part of a national tradition, the stories reiterated the ideals of respectable
British manliness.

These cross-dressing stories and theatrical performances were for decades a
powerful set of narratives – resonant, suggestive and flexible. The successive
reports of *The Well of Loneliness* and Colonel Barker trials in 1928 and 1929 did not
produce a new 'lesbian' interpretation for women's cross-dressing, or even for the
mannish woman in these newspapers. The idea of 'lesbianism' as a particular
sexual practice was muted in press reporting before the Second World War and
represented in highly class-specific terms. Associated with the excessive behaviour
of wealthy and bohemian women, it was an obscure form of sexual immorality,

found outside the experience of working-class life described in the cross-dressing stories.

The cross-dressing woman story was part of a long tradition, but it was not an unchanging or old-fashioned form which hung on, somehow unnoticed, into the mid-twentieth century. The genre constantly engaged with the themes of modernity. Indeed the euphemistic approach to sexuality produced huge creativity in the popular press as it sought to negotiate the growing knowledge of female homosexuality circulating in other literatures, such as middlebrow novels and medical writing, without directly naming it. The gender-crossing genre flourished in the 1930s as newspapers embellished and refined their codes. The more risqué implications were exported abroad in French female husband and gigolo stories, preserving the British cross-dressing woman and the national tradition for a little while longer. The trickster masquerader across the Channel borrows from modern narratives of desire as she becomes the new romantic hero, the exotic Latin lover, in this period. It is in these obsessions of modernity – Hollywood glamour, cross-racial desire, the erotic dangers of cosmopolitanism – not the discourses of science and medicine, where the more sexual possibilities of cross-dressing are explored.

Medical discourses are only significant in the emergence of the sex change story in the 1930s, presented as an achievement of twentieth-century technological advances in surgery and medicine. We have seen that the process of generating this new sexual category in mass culture depended on the continuing power of wonder and marvel as strong themes in popular culture, and the merging of these with modern scientific explanation as ways of knowing about sex and gender. Sex change was a magical transformation rather than a deviant sexual identity, especially before the Second World War. Wonderment, oddity and the irrational still featured strongly in modern popular culture and were recycled to weave new fantasies. Historians of sexuality have queried the nature of modernity by exploring the continuing purchase of alternative belief systems such as spirituality in forming ideas about sexuality well into the twentieth century, despite the increasing influence of sexual science.[103] The role of entertainment and the effects of humour also deserve attention from historians investigating modern cultures of eroticism and changing knowledges of sexuality.[104]

Disruption of the cross-dressing narrative only comes in the late 1940s, when passions between women are finally named as 'perverted' and the passing woman is irrevocably linked to the emergent idea of the mannish lesbian. The new willingness of some newspapers to report sexual topics more frankly during and after the Second World War is beginning to receive critical attention from historians.[105] Codes such as 'unhealthy friendship' to describe sexual relationships between young women, or the 'Eton-cropped' woman briefly glimpsed in shady nightclubs in the late 1930s, hint in passing at the growing recognition of lesbian sexuality. The period between the late 1930s and the early 1950s is the time when wider social acknowledgement of lesbianism began to circulate at all levels of culture, along with the seeding of sexual communities and networks. The reasons for this spreading of lesbian identity among middle- and working-class women in Britain, and its relationship to wartime conditions, deserves further investigation.[106] Comparative accounts, too, are needed. When we reperiodise the treatment of women's gender-crossing in the British popular press, noting the continuing celebration of the working-class masquerader until the 1940s, and the resistance to naming same-sex passion as lesbianism, we see a distinctive relationship between class, culture and the framing of sexual knowledge. The American press, in contrast, frequently associated mannish women with sexual deviance from the late nineteenth century, while there was much greater consciousness of lesbianism in Paris and Berlin where it was discussed more directly in interwar popular culture.

The diverse range of narrative styles for presenting women's gender-crossing and the desires contained within it narrows significantly in the 1950s. Before the Second World War the popular Sunday press separated the masquerading genre from reports of sex change and from any references to female homosexuality, but from the late 1940s this distinction began to collapse and the ideas of lesbianism and transsexuality became competing explanations for the cross-dressing woman. Some female husbands, such as those in the Warwickshire and Catford wedding stories, were now interpreted, at least for *News of the World* readers, as having 'perverted passions'. They were judged to be lesbians, and while younger women might be represented as having been led astray, they were still morally culpable and seen as psychologically deviant. However, if they claimed to be born in the wrong body and sought medical help, they might gain press sympathy through the modern discourse of sex change. The only other narrative outcome was repentance and a recasting of the self towards normative 1950s femininity.

Now that 'perversion' was more readily named across the popular press, the reporting of these stories shifted away from the values of the masquerading genre. But classic humorous elements still remained in the postwar stories. Two or three of the longer reports, including those of Ellen Young and Vincent Jones, were developed as human-interest stories with photographs, interviews and threads of comedy. These jokes might still have involved fooling the vicar – a stock comic figure retained on seaside postcards into the 1950s. The vicar was always gullible and sexually innocent enough to believe the gender-crossing story and marry two women, whether in the 1920s or the 1950s. Humour also continued to revolve around the deception of girlfriends in some stories, though this was harder to maintain in the more sexually knowing postwar context. The trickster gender-crosser was nevertheless losing her buoyant and fantastical qualities. She did not turn the tables, challenge her associates and the reader, or engage her capacity for powerful commentary in anything like the way she had done in the earlier cross-dressing formula stories. Now that the magic of the theatrical frame had faded, the wider force and multiple meanings of the gender-crossing woman were increasingly corralled into monochrome sexual identities.

By the 1950s, all these types of sexually deviant women – the cross-dresser, the female-to-male sex changer and finally the lesbian – could be found in ordinary working-class districts, according to newspaper reports. Gone were the glamorous gender-crossing parties of the Bright Young Things, the mysterious decadence of the Maud Allan trial, and the hints of same-sex practices in elite and cosmopolitan circles. Instead lesbians moved in and out of prison, stayed in cheap hotels, hung around army bases or married other women in dreary suburbs. The appearance of female homosexuality in these communities drew from the press a strong moral commentary alongside new psychological interpretations.

Newspaper interest in women's cross-dressing faded quickly in the 1950s. The Sunday papers, together with the rest of the popular press, were much more interested in reporting male homosexuality and sex change stories than they were in women's cross-dressing or sexual deviance as lesbians. As we have seen in this chapter, the *News of the World* published the parts of the courtroom commentaries which made reference to female 'perversion' in greater detail than most other papers. Lesbianism had become an occasional sensationalist topic in its sex and crime formula. The *People* enjoyed trumpeting about morality, and set itself up to educate readers on these new social issues, but it avoided reporting many of these cross-dressing or lesbian cases in the 1950s, or omitted the sexual details. It preferred sex change to 'perverted passions'.

Alongside their continuing humour and sensational tone, some postwar gender-crossing narratives inherited the comparative respectability of the masquerading woman. Framed as a physical rather than a psychiatric condition, a female husband claiming sex change might still avoid moral blame and assert respectable masculinity through the conventions of marriage, as had the cross-dressers of earlier decades. And although cross-dressing women were no longer celebrated for their daring achievements, the stories continued to show them actively constructing their lives around same-sex love and gender-crossing. In some instances, most notably in the story of Vincent Jones, we see the positive claiming of new sexual identities developing in the 1950s.

The rich sweep of newspaper cross-dressing stories discussed in this book reveals a distinct historical trajectory for the changing representation of sexual desires and gender identities in British popular culture. The magical properties of the gender-crossing woman – her astonishing transformation, her frisson of mystery, her homoerotic passions, her tricksterish powers, her lighthearted treatment of gender boundaries – are as much part of our contemporary sexual identities as the rationalist discourses of science and medicine.

Notes

Introduction: sex, scandal and the popular press

1 *News of the World* (hereafter *NoW*), 12 May 1929, p. 5.
2 For the most recent in-depth discussion see James Vernon's very useful article, J. Vernon, '"For Some Queer Reason": The Trials and Tribulations of Colonel Barker's Masquerade in Interwar Britain', *Signs*, 2000, vol. 26, no. 11, 37–62.
3 L. Doan, *Fashioning Sapphism: The Origins of a Modern English Lesbian Culture*, New York: Columbia University Press, 2001. M. Vicinus, *Intimate Friends: Women Who Loved Women, 1777–1928*, Chicago, IL: University of Chicago Press, 2004. For female masculinity see J. Halberstam, *Female Masculinity*, Durham, NC: Duke University Press, 1998.
4 R. Porter and L. Hall, *The Facts of Life. The Creation of Sexual Knowledge in Britain, 1650–1950*, New Haven, CT: Yale University Press, 1995. K. Fisher, *Birth Control, Sex and Marriage in Britain 1918–1960*, Oxford: Oxford University Press, 2006. L. M. Beier, '"We were Green as Grass": Learning about Sex and Reproduction in Three Working-class Lancashire Communities, 1900–970', *Social History of Medicine*, 2003, vol. 16, no. 3, 461–80. M. Sutton, *We Didn't Know Aught: Sexuality, Superstition and Death in Women's Lives in Lincolnshire during the 1930s, '40s and '50s*, Stamford, Lincs.: Paul Watkins, 1992.
5 L. Sigel, *Governing Pleasures: Pornography and Social Change in England, 1815–1914*, New Brunswick, NJ: Rutgers University Press, 2002, Chapter 4. H. G. Cocks, 'Saucy Stories: Pornography, Sexology and the Marketing of Sexual Knowledge in Britain, *c.* 1918–70', *Social History*, 2004, vol. 29, no. 4, 465–84. For a valuable analysis of the tension between sexual knowledge and ignorance and how it was gendered in relation to birth control in particular see Fisher, *Birth Control, Sex and Marriage in Britain*, and K. Fisher, '"She Was Quite Satisfied with the Arrangements I Made": Gender and Birth Control in Britain 1920–50', *Past and Present*, 2000, no. 169, 161–93.
6 For important recent studies of gay male sexuality and popular culture, see M. Houlbrook, *Queer London: Perils and Pleasures in the Sexual Metropolis, 1918–1957*, Chicago, IL: University of Chicago Press, 2005 and (for the nineteenth century), M. Cook, *London and the Culture of Homosexuality, 1885–1914*, Cambridge: Cambridge University Press, 2003. H. G. Cocks, *Nameless Offences: Homosexual Desire in the Nineteenth Century*, London: I. B. Tauris, 2003.
7 Historians have also challenged and refined this model. For a recent summary of the debates in the history of sexuality, see H. G. Cocks and M. Houlbrook (eds), *The Modern History of Sexuality*, Basingstoke: Palgrave Macmillan, 2006.
8 However, the appearance and development of sexological discourses on lesbianism and cross-dressing in the British professional medical literature remain almost completely unresearched for the period up to 1945.
9 L. Duggan, *Sapphic Slashers: Sex, Violence and American Modernity*, Durham, NC: Duke University Press, 2000.

10 L. Bland, 'Trial by Sexology?: Maud Allan, *Salome* and the "Cult of the Clitoris" Case', in L. Bland and L. Doan (eds), *Sexology in Culture: Labelling Bodies and Desires*, Cambridge: Polity Press, 1998. Also see Laura Doan's discussion of the anxieties expressed over the uniforms of women police officers at the end of the First World War in Doan, *Fashioning Sapphism*, Chapter 3.

11 For examples of the non-fiction, see A. Oram and A. Turnbull, *The Lesbian History Sourcebook: Love and Sex between Women in Britain from 1780 to 1970*, London: Routledge, 2001. For fiction see, for example, Doan, *Fashioning Sapphism*, Chapter 5.

12 Doan, *Fashioning Sapphism*.

13 J. Rose, *The Intellectual Life of the British Working Classes*, New Haven, CT: Yale University Press, 2002.

14 My survey began in 1910 in order to investigate cross-dressing and its representation in the years before the First World War. After 1960 the development of organised political groups concerned with the position of lesbians marks a new chapter of sexual modernity.

15 This figure counts each person or distinct story only once across the two Sunday newspapers. It includes all 'real life' reports of cross-dressing and sex change, and excludes male impersonation on stage. I also followed up the most prominent stories in the daily and local press.

16 For the women who were reported as changing sex I use their male name and pronouns post-transition. The terms lesbian and homosexual are rarely used in these newspapers until the 1950s – 'lesbian' not until 1959.

17 For eighteenth-century masquerade, see T. Castle, *Masquerade and Civilisation*, London: Methuen, 1986. For twentieth-century masquerade, see Vernon, '"For Some Queer Reason"', 46–7. Work on gender inversion which has used Bakhtin's concept of the carnivalesque includes N. Z. Davis, *Society and Culture in Early Modern France*, Cambridge: Polity Press, 1987, Chapter 5, and M. Garber, *Vested Interests: Cross Dressing and Cultural Anxiety*, New York: Routledge, 1992.

18 D. Dugaw, *Warrior Women and Popular Balladry, 1650–1850*, Chicago, IL: University of Chicago Press, 1996. For a more detailed discussion of the history of gender-crossing, see A. Oram, 'Cross-dressing and Transgender', in H. G. Cocks and M. Houlbrook (eds), *The Modern History of Sexuality*, Basingstoke: Palgrave Macmillan, 2006.

19 *NoW*, 26 June 1910, p. 6; 27 February 1927, p. 13.

20 For discussion of sexual modernity and modernity in general, see S. Alexander, 'The Mysteries and Secrets of Women's Bodies: Sexual Knowledge in the First Half of the Twentieth Century', in M. Nava and A. O'Shea (eds), *Modern Times: Reflections on a Century of English Modernity*, London: Routledge, 1996, p. 163. B. Conekin, F. Mort and C. Waters (eds), *Moments of Modernity: Reconstructing Britain 1945–1964*, London: Rivers Oram Press, 1999. B. Rieger and M. Daunton, 'Introduction', in M. Daunton and B. Rieger (eds), *Meanings of Modernity: Britain from the Late-Victorian Era to World War II*, Oxford: Berg, 2001.

21 M. Saler, 'Modernity and Enchantment: A Historiographical Review', *American Historical Review*, 2006, vol. 111, no. 3, 700.

22 A. Bingham, *Gender, Modernity and the Popular Press in Inter-War Britain*, Oxford: Clarendon Press, 2004. M. Conboy, *The Press and Popular Culture*, London: Sage, 2002, pp. 113–35. J. Curran and J. Seaton, *Power without Responsibility: The Press and Broadcasting in Britain*, London: Routledge, 1991, pp. 56–7, 66–8. M. Engel, *Tickle the Public: One Hundred Years of the Popular Press*, London: Victor Gollancz, 1996, p. 227. R. McKibbin, *Classes and Cultures. England 1918–1951*, Oxford: Oxford University Press, 1998, pp. 503–7.

23 Between 60 and 75 per cent of people in the south and the Midlands read the *News of the World* and/or the *People* in 1937. Engel, *Tickle the Public*, pp. 221, 228. Political and Economic Planning (PEP), *Report on the British Press*, London: PEP, 1938, pp. 84, 243, 247.

24 PEP, *Report on the British Press*, pp. 86, 235.
25 Mass Observation, *The Press and its Readers*, London: Art and Technics Ltd, 1949, pp. 28–30, 44–6, 108, 114.
26 C. Bainbridge and R. Stockdill, *The News of the World Story*, London: HarperCollins, 1993, pp. 90–3.
27 B. S. Rowntree and G. R. Lavers, *English Life and Leisure: A Social Study*, London: Longmans, Green and Co., 1951, pp. 290–1.
28 For theories of genre, see J. Cawelti, *Adventure, Mystery, and Romance: Formula Stories as Art and Popular Culture*, Chicago, IL: University of Chicago Press, 1976. J. Palmer, *Potboilers: Methods, Concepts and Case Studies in Popular Fiction*, London: Routledge, 1991. N. Lacey, *Narrative and Genre: Key Concepts in Media Studies*, Basingstoke: Palgrave, 2000.
29 Cross-dressing was not a crime in itself. The passing woman may have been arrested for fraud of some kind related to her disguise, but more often for an unrelated offence such as theft, and tried in a magistrate's court.
30 *NoW*, 20 January 1918, p. 1. *Sunday Pictorial*, 20 January 1918, p. 2.
31 *NoW*, 20 January 1918, p. 1.
32 W. J. Hynes and W. G. Doty (eds), *Mythical Trickster Figures: Contours, Contexts, and Criticisms*, Tuscaloosa, AL: University of Alabama Press, 1993. See also Chapter 1 discussion.
33 *Illustrated Police News*, 24 January 1918, p. 3. *Sunday Pictorial*, 20 January 1918, p. 2.
34 *Sunday Pictorial*, 27 January 1918, p. 2.
35 Police officer's comment to Lambeth court, *NoW*, 20 January 1918, p. 1.
36 Palmer, *Potboilers*, pp. 49–50, 113–14.
37 J. S. Bratton, 'Irrational Dress', in V. Gardner and S. Rutherford (eds), *The New Woman and her Sisters: Feminism and Theatre 1850–1914*, London: Harvester Wheatsheaf, 1992. L. Ferris, 'Introduction', in L. Ferris (ed.), *Crossing the Stage. Controversies on Cross-dressing*, London: Routledge, 1993, pp. 13–17.
38 Bratton, 'Irrational Dress'. P. Bailey, *Popular Culture and Performance in the Victorian City*, Cambridge: Cambridge University Press, 1998, pp. 120–1.
39 S. Maitland, *Vesta Tilley*, London: Virago, 1986, pp. 28, 69, 199–20. Bratton, 'Irrational Dress', pp. 86–9. L. Senelick, *The Changing Room: Sex, Drag and Theatre*, London: Routledge, 2000, pp. 332–7. For changes in music hall, see P. Bailey, 'Introduction: Making Sense of Music Hall', in P. Bailey (ed.), *Music Hall: The Business of Pleasure*, Milton Keynes: Open University Press, 1986.
40 R. Wilmut, *Kindly Leave the Stage! The Story of Variety 1919–1960*, London: Methuen, 1985.
41 D. Hoher, 'The Composition of Music Hall Audiences, 1850–1900', in Bailey, *Music Hall: The Business of Pleasure*. B. Dickinson, 'In the Audience', *Oral History Journal*, 1983, vol. 11, no. 1, 52–61.

1 Work and war: masculinity, gender relations and the passing woman

1 *NoW*, 7 April 1912, p. 9.
2 R. W. Connell, *Masculinities*, Cambridge: Polity Press, 1995, Chapters 2 and 3. S. Jackson and S. Scott, 'Putting the Body's Feet on the Ground: Towards a Sociological Reconceptualization of Gendered and Sexual Embodiment', in K. Backett-Milburn and L. McKie (eds), *Constructing Gendered Bodies*, Basingstoke: Palgrave, 2001.
3 *NoW*, 7 April 1912, p. 9.
4 *NoW*, 17 September 1905, p. 4.
5 *Daily Chronicle*, 14 September 1905, p. 4.
6 *NoW*, 18 May 1924, p. 9. Andrew Davies and Brad Beaven note the importance of clothing and appearance to young men throughout this period. A. Davies, *Leisure, Gender and Poverty: Working-Class Culture in Salford and Manchester, 1900–1939*, Buckingham: Open University Press, 1992, pp. 104–5. B. Beaven, *Leisure, Citizenship*

and Working-class Men in Britain, 1850–1945, Manchester: Manchester University Press, 2005, p. 171.

7   *Daily Chronicle*, 11 September 1905, p. 3.

8   R. Hudd with P. Hindin, *Roy Hudd's Cavalcade of Variety Acts*, London: Robson Books, 1997, p. 96. Vesta Tilley was similarly applauded for her accurate attention to detail. S. Maitland, *Vesta Tilley*, London: Virago, 1986, pp. 116, 122.

9   *NoW*, 8 June 1919, p. 6.

10 J. S. Bratton, 'Beating The Bounds: Gender Play and Role Reversal in the Edwardian Music Hall', in M. Booth and J. Caplan (eds), *The Edwardian Theatre: Essays on Performance and the Stage*, Cambridge: Cambridge University Press, 1996, pp. 98–100.

11 J. Butler, *Gender Trouble*, New York: Routledge, 1990, pp. 134–41. J. Butler, *Bodies that Matter*, New York: Routledge, 1993, pp. 125, 226–7.

12 *People*, 4 February 1923, p. 9.

13 *NoW*, 4 December 1910, p. 8.

14 *NoW*, 11 April 1926, p. 10.

15 *NoW*, 21 August 1910, p. 18.

16 On the function and effects of humour, see J. Palmer, *Taking Humour Seriously*, London: Routledge, 1994. C. Powell and G. Paton (eds), *Humour in Society: Resistance and Control*, Basingstoke: Macmillan, 1988. J. Bremmer and H. Roodenburg, 'Introduction: Humour and History', in J. Bremmer and H. Roodenburg (eds), *A Cultural History of Humour*, Cambridge: Polity Press, 1997, p. 2. S. Purdie, *Comedy: The Mastery of Discourse*, London: Harvester Wheatsheaf, 1993, especially Chapter 7.

17 *NoW*, 7 April 1912, p. 9.

18 For variations on this line see *Daily Mirror*, 17 May 1924, p. 3 (Ernest Wood); *People*, 10 March 1929, p. 1 (Colonel Barker).

19 *NoW*, 4 February 1923, p. 15.

20 For another example see Martha Hodson, discussed later in this chapter, pages 33–4.

21 *Star*, 11 September 1905, p. 2. Her previous name as a woman was established as Caroline Brogden.

22 See, for example, P. Honri, *Working the Halls*, London: Futura, 1974, p. 142. Doing illogical and bizarre things was both part of comedy and seen as a symptom of mental illness.

23 *Star*, 11 September 1905, p. 2.

24 M. Pickering, 'Mock Blacks and Racial Mockery: The "Nigger" Minstrel and British Imperialism', in J. S. Bratton, R. A. Cave, B. Gregory, H. J. Holder and M. Pickering (eds), *Acts of Supremacy: The British Empire and the Stage, 1790–1930*, Manchester: Manchester University Press, 1991, pp. 202–4 (see also below, Chapter 4, pp. 103–4).

25 A. Stott, *Comedy*, New York: Routledge, 2005, pp. 49–50.

26 W. J. Hynes and W. G. Doty, 'Introducing the Fascinating and Perplexing Trickster Figure', and W. J. Hynes, 'Inconclusive Conclusions: Tricksters – Metaplayers and Revealers', both chapters in W. J. Hynes and W. G. Doty (eds), *Mythical Trickster Figures: Contours, Contexts, and Criticisms*, Tuscaloosa, AL: University of Alabama Press, 1993. Stott, *Comedy*, pp. 51–5.

27 *Illustrated Police News* (hereafter *IPN*), 22 May 1924, p. 4.

28 *Wigan Observer and District Advertiser* (hereafter *Wigan Obs*), 20 May 1924, p. 2.

29 Ibid.

30 Ibid. Also see *Evening Standard*, 17 May 1924, p. 16.

31 *Wigan Obs*, 20 May, 1924, p. 2. *Evening Standard*, 17 May 1924, p. 16.

32 A number of historians have observed that middle- and ruling-class ideologies and experiences have dominated the history of masculinity, and there is a real neglect of twentieth-century working-class masculinities. R. Johnston and A. McIvor, 'Dangerous Work, Hard Men and Broken Bodies: Masculinity in the Clydeside Heavy Industries, *c.* 1930–70s', *Labour History Review*, 2004, vol. 69, no. 2, 135.

M. Francis, 'The Domestication of the Male? Recent Research on Nineteenth- and Twentieth-Century British Masculinity', *Historical Journal*, 2002, vol. 45, no. 3, 650. E. J. Yeo, 'Editorial: Taking it Like a Man', *Labour History Review*, 2004, vol. 69, no. 2, 129–30. Cross-dressing women can also contribute to the project of recovering working-class masculinities, by showing which attributes were necessary to convincingly pass as a man.

33 *IPN*, 22 May 1924, p. 4.

34 *NoW*, 18 May 1924, p. 9.

35 *NoW*, 7 April 1912, p. 9.

36 Ibid.

37 *NoW*, 4 February 1923, p. 15.

38 *People*, 4 February 1923, p. 9.

39 *Star*, 11 September 1905, p. 2.

40 Beaven, *Leisure, Citizenship and Working-class Men in Britain*, Chapter 2. Connell, *Masculinities*, p. 54. Johnston and McIvor, 'Dangerous Work, Hard Men and Broken Bodies', 141. Davies, *Leisure, Gender and Poverty*, Chapter 4. C. Langhamer, *Women's Leisure in England 1920–60*, Manchester: Manchester University Press, 2000, Chapter 3. Men took a portion of their wages for leisure as of right.

41 *NoW*, 4 February 1923, p. 15. Also see *West Ham and South Essex Mail*, 2 February 1923, p. 1.

42 For active heterosexuality as a requirement of hegemonic masculinity, see R. W. Connell, *The Men and the Boys*, Cambridge: Polity Press, 2000, pp. 83–4, 86, 102, 109.

43 *NoW*, 20 January 1918, p. 1.

44 *NoW*, 4 February 1923, p. 15. P. Bailey, *Popular Culture and Performance in the Victorian City*, Cambridge: Cambridge University Press, 1998, pp. 151–74. The wider range of meanings suggested by passing women's relationships with other women will be discussed in Chapter 2.

45 *Evening Standard*, 17 May 1924, p. 16.

46 *NoW*, 18 May 1924, p. 9; *Evening Standard*, 17 May 1924, p. 16; *Wigan Obs*, 20 May 1924, p. 2.

47 *NoW*, 18 May 1924, p. 9; *IPN*, 22 May 1924, p. 4.

48 For hegemonic concepts of manly character, see J. Tosh, 'Masculinities in an Industrializing Society: Britain, 1800–1914', *Journal of British Studies*, 2005, vol. 44, no. 2, 335. K. Boyd, *Manliness and the Boys' Story Paper in Britain: A Cultural History, 1855–1940*, Basingstoke: Palgrave Macmillan, 2003.

49 *Wigan Obs*, 20 May 1924, p. 2. For Ellen Capon, see Introduction.

50 M. P. Reeves, *Round about a Pound a Week*, London: Virago, 1979 (first published 1913).

51 *NoW*, 7 April 1912, p. 9.

52 Johnston and McIvor, 'Dangerous Work, Hard Men and Broken Bodies', 140. Tosh, 'Masculinities in an Industrializing Society', 341.

53 *NoW*, 26 June 1910, p. 6.

54 Ibid. Also see *People*, 26 June 1910, p. 17.

55 Bailey, *Popular Culture and Performance in the Victorian City*, pp. 119–21. L. Senelick, *The Changing Room: Sex, Drag and Theatre*, London: Routledge, 2000, p. 329.

56 J. S. Bratton, 'Irrational Dress', in V. Gardner and S. Rutherford (eds), *The New Woman and her Sisters: Feminism and Theatre 1850–1914*, London: Harvester Wheatsheaf, 1992, p. 89.

57 Bratton, 'Beating the Bounds', p. 109.

58 E. Aston, 'Male Impersonation in the Music Hall: The Case of Vesta Tilley', *New Theatre Quarterly*, 1988, vol. 4, no. 15, 247–57.

59 Bratton, 'Irrational Dress', pp. 85–8.

60 Bailey, *Popular Culture and Performance in the Victorian City*, pp. 120–1, and see pp. 119–23. Senelick, *The Changing Room*, p. 327. Maitland, *Vesta Tilley*, pp. 40, 116, 124. C. Breward, '"As I Walked along the Bois de Boulogne": Subversive Performances and

Masculine Pleasures in Fin-de-Siècle London', in R. Koshar (ed.), *Histories of Leisure*, Oxford: Berg, 2002, pp. 292–4.

61 Bailey, *Popular Culture and Performance in the Victorian City*, pp. 126–7. Aston, 'Male Impersonation in the Music Hall', pp. 254–5.

62 Although there is never any direct mention of the women's suffrage movement in cross-dressing stories.

63 *NoW*, 7 April 1912, p. 9.

64 *NoW*, 20 January 1918, p. 1.

65 *NoW*, 4 February 1923, p. 15.

66 *NoW*, 28 August 1910, p. 13; 4 September 1910, p. 13.

67 D. Dugaw, *Warrior Women and Popular Balladry, 1650–1850*, Chicago, IL: University of Chicago Press, 1996. J. Wheelwright, *Amazons and Military Maids*, London: Pandora Press, 1989.

68 P. Summerfield, 'Patriotism and Empire: Music Hall Entertainment 1870–1914', in J. M. MacKenzie (ed.), *Imperialism and Popular Culture*, Manchester: Manchester University Press, 1986, especially pp. 36–9. D. Russell, '"We Carved Our Way to Glory". The British Soldier in Music Hall Song and Sketch, c. 1880–1914', in J. M. MacKenzie (ed.), *Popular Imperialism and the Military 1850–1950*, Manchester: Manchester University Press, 1992.

69 Maitland, *Vesta Tilley*, pp. 117–19. Russell, '"We Carved Our Way to Glory"', p. 62. Aston, 'Male Impersonation in the Music Hall', pp. 253–4. Vesta Tilley's contribution to the war effort was emphasised in her farewell concert at the London Coliseum on her retirement in 1920. See *NoW*, 6 June 1920, p. 1.

70 *NoW*, 3 June 1917, p. 6.

71 See, for example, different types of soldier impersonations by Beatrice Lillie and Lee White in 1918, both in Beatrice Lillie file, the Mander and Mitchenson Theatre Collection, Jerwood Library of the Performing Arts, Trinity College of Music, Greenwich. George Robb argues that the troops had a much more jaundiced view of the war than civilians on the home front, and their own forms of humour to deal with it. G. Robb, *British Culture and the First World War*, Basingstoke: Palgrave, 2002, pp. 160–1, 178–84.

72 Ella Shields, 'I'm Cuthbert', written by Arthur Anderson, composed by Jas. W. Tate, London: Francis, Day and Hunter, 1917.

73 James Vernon mentions 'numerous cases', citing Julie Wheelwright's book. J. Vernon, '"For Some Queer Reason": The Trials and Tribulations of Colonel Barker's Masquerade in Interwar Britain', *Signs*, 2000, vol. 26, no. 11, 47. Wheelwright discusses Flora Sandes who fought with the Serbian army but was known to be a woman, and Dorothy Lawrence, a British woman journalist who, disguised as a man, spent a few days in the trenches. Wheelwright, *Amazons and Military Maids*, pp. 34–44, 66–7, 70–1, 79–81, 99–101, 148–52. There were, though, later interwar reports of French and Australian women who maintained they had indeed been frontline soldiers.

74 *NoW*, 25 April 1915, p. 5. Also see *People*, 25 April 1915, p. 14. After her discovery the woman was offered work in the shell-making department, work which was probably more dangerous, less healthy and lower paid.

75 *Hornsey Journal*, 18 August 1916, p. 3. See J. Bourke, *Dismembering the Male: Men's Bodies, Britain and the Great War*, London: Reaktion Books, 1996, p. 129, for mass inspections of naked troops in the First World War military.

76 *Hornsey Journal*, 18 August 1916, p. 3.

77 *NoW*, 20 August 1916, p. 7.

78 *Hornsey Journal*, 18 August 1916, p. 3.

79 *NoW*, 20 August 1916, p. 7.

80 G. Dawson, *Soldier Heroes: British Adventure, Empire and the Imagining of Masculinities*, London: Routledge, 1994, p. 1 and see pp. 1–4. M. Paris, 'The Youth of our Nation in Symbol: Making and Remaking the Masculine Ideal in the Era of the Two World

Wars', in H. Brocklehurst and R. Phillips (eds), *History, Nationhood and the Question of Britain*, Basingstoke: Palgrave Macmillan, 2004, pp. 289–90.

81 *NoW*, 3 January 1915, p. 3; 10 January 1915, p. 3. Reported variations of her name included Marina Hodson and Alice Hodgkinson.

82 *NoW*, 3 October 1915, p. 11. Also see the similar story of Mabel Joyce (aka Hilda Holland), *NoW*, 26 September 1915, p. 3.

83 Robb, *British Culture and the First World War*, pp. 38–47.

84 *Illustrated Sunday Herald*, 27 August 1916, p. 15. Berta Ruck, the author of this piece, was well known as the author of popular romance fiction, including wartime romances.

85 *NoW*, 30 April 1916, p. 7. This was almost certainly Constance Markiewicz, the first woman to be elected to the House of Commons. As a member of Sinn Fein, she declined to take her seat.

86 *NoW*, 2 April 1916, p. 6; *NoW*, 29 July 1917, p. 1. For the Russian Women's Battalion of Death see Wheelwright, *Amazons and Military Maids*, pp. 29–34, 73, 125–30.

87 S. K. Kent, *Making Peace: The Reconstruction of Gender in Interwar Britain*, Princeton, NJ: Princeton University Press, 1993.

88 A. Bingham, *Gender, Modernity and the Popular Press in Inter-War Britain*, Oxford: Clarendon Press, 2004.

89 *NoW*, 2 March 1919, p. 8.

90 *People*, 7 November 1926, p. 4. Davies also cross-dressed in other 1920s films. H. Dickens, *What a Drag*, London: Angus and Robertson, 1982, p. 30. And for other examples of feminine male impersonation see *People*, 8 November 1925, p. 3, depicting Phyllis Monkman: 'She's a Beau Belle!'

91 *NoW*, 10 April 1927, p. 12; 28 April 1929, p. 12. Dickens, *What a Drag*, pp. 30, 36, 66.

92 *NoW*, 21 May 1922, p. 12 for the revue, and p. 15 for the notice of the first woman barrister. This was three years after legislation was passed to admit women to the Bar.

93 Dickens, *What a Drag*, p. 24.

94 Ibid., p. 20. She also cross-dressed as a Paris pickpocket in *The Humming Bird* (1924).

95 R. Bell-Metereau, *Hollywood Androgyny*, New York: Columbia University Press, 1993, pp. 69, 80–1.

96 *NoW*, 27 May 1923, p. 11.

97 There were five in 1919–20, then a smattering of four further stories to 1928. And see Wheelwright, *Amazons and Military Maids*, pp. 155–7.

98 *NoW*, 28 September 1919, p. 5. A similar theme was found in film following the First World War. Dickens, *What a Drag*, p. 66.

99 *IPN*, 28 October 1920, p. 7.

100 *NoW*, 9 March 1919, p. 6. Also see other similar reports: *NoW*, 22 June 1919, p. 7; 23 January 1927, p. 4. These women were more middle-class than most cross-dressers.

101 For the debates over whether domesticity and ordinariness were incorporated into interwar masculinity and national identity see Francis, 'The Domestication of the Male?', pp. 643–8. J. Giles and T. Middleton (eds), *Writing Englishness 1900–1950*, London: Routledge, 1995. S. Rose, 'Temperate Heroes: Concepts of Masculinity in Second World War Britain', in S. Dudink, K. Hagemann and J. Tosh (eds), *Masculinities in Politics and War: Gendering Modern History*, Manchester: Manchester University Press, 2004.

102 *NoW*, 27 February 1927, p. 13.

2 Sexuality, love and marriage: the gender-crossing woman as female husband

1 Where the woman had passed for any length of time.

2 *NoW*, 7 April 1912, p. 9.

3 *NoW*, 23 January 1910, p. 5. *Wigan Obs*, 20 May 1924, p. 2.

4 *NoW*, 7 April 1912, p. 9.

5 Ibid.

6 *NoW*, 26 June 1910, p. 6. The notion of masculine honour was also used to account for Albert F's marriage of several years to another woman, and the relationship seen as evidence of her good character. *NoW*, 20 August 1916, p. 7. See above Chapter 1, pp. 32–3.

7 *NoW*, 26 June 1910, p. 6.

8 See A. Stott, *Comedy*, New York: Routledge, 2005, p. 43, for the reconciliation of socially forbidden love in comedy. D. Dugaw, *Warrior Women and Popular Balladry, 1650–1850*, Chicago, IL: University of Chicago Press, 1996, discusses the conventional heterosexual endings to eighteenth-century cross-dressing ballads.

9 M. Vicinus, *Intimate Friends: Women Who Loved Women, 1777–1928*, Chicago, IL: University of Chicago Press, 2004. S. Marcus, *Between Women: Friendship, Desire, and Marriage in Victorian England*, Princeton, NJ: Princeton University Press, 2007, pp. 20–1 and Chapter 5.

10 L. Bland, *Banishing the Beast: English Feminism and Sexual Morality 1885–1914*, London: Penguin, 1995, p. 117. T. Davis, *Actresses as Working Women: Their Social Identity in Victorian Culture*, London: Routledge, 1991, Chapters 3 and 5.

11 Bland, *Banishing the Beast*, pp. 95–6, 106–7.

12 M. Cook, *London and the Culture of Homosexuality, 1885–1914*, Cambridge: Cambridge University Press, 2003, pp. 26–9. M. Houlbrook, *Queer London: Perils and Pleasures in the Sexual Metropolis, 1918–1957*, Chicago, IL: University of Chicago Press, 2005, pp. 23, 56–7, 87. A. Sinfield, *Out on Stage: Lesbian and Gay Theatre in the Twentieth Century*, New Haven, CT: Yale University Press, 1999, pp. 1–13. See also pp. 56–8 in this chapter.

13 *NoW*, 8 March 1914, p. 4.

14 P. Bailey, *Popular Culture and Performance in the Victorian City*, Cambridge: Cambridge University Press, 1998, Chapter 6. J. Traies, 'Jones and the Working Girl: Class Marginality in Music-Hall Song 1860–1900', in J. S. Bratton (ed.), *Music Hall: Performance and Style*, Milton Keynes: Open University Press, 1986. S. Pennybacker, '"It Was Not What She Said But the Way in which She Said It": The London County Council and the Music Hall', in P. Bailey (ed.), *Music Hall: The Business of Pleasure*, Milton Keynes: Open University Press, 1986, especially pp. 128–37. P. Honri, *Working the Halls*, London: Futura, 1974, pp. 9–10, 89–91.

15 And see Lesley Hall's useful comments on the complexities of censorship and sexual innuendo in Britain in L. Hall, *Sex, Gender and Social Change in Britain since 1880*, Basingstoke: Macmillan, 2000, pp. 80–1.

16 Bailey, *Popular Culture and Performance in the Victorian City*, Chapter 7.

17 For debates about the changing nature of male impersonation, see E. Aston, 'Male Impersonation in the Music Hall: The Case of Vesta Tilley', *New Theatre Quarterly*, 1988, vol. 4, no. 15: 247–57. J. S. Bratton, 'Beating the Bounds: Gender Play and Role Reversal in the Edwardian Music Hall', in M. Booth and J. Caplan (eds), *The Edwardian Theatre: Essays on Performance and the Stage*, Cambridge: Cambridge University Press, 1996.

18 Bailey, *Popular Culture and Performance in the Victorian City*, pp. 116–18.

19 L. Senelick, *The Changing Room: Sex, Drag and Theatre*, London: Routledge, 2000, p. 332.

20 S. Maitland, *Vesta Tilley*, London: Virago, 1986, p. 114.

21 Ella Shields, 'In the Army (I Don't Admire the Girl in White)', written and composed by W. Hargreaves, London: B. Feldman and Co., 1910.

22 Ella Shields, 'The Lady Said, "Oui, Oui"', written and composed by William Hargreaves, London: B. Feldman and Co, 1911.

23 See C. MacInnes, *Sweet Saturday Night: Pop Song 1840–1920*, London: Panther, 1969, pp. 36–64. Traies, 'Jones and the Working Girl', pp. 44–5.

24 Vesta Tilley, 'When You're a Married Man', written and composed by E. W. Rogers, London: Francis, Day and Hunter, 1899.

25 *NoW*, 8 March 1914, p. 9.

26 *NoW*, 10 January 1915, p. 3. *Northern Evening Dispatch*, 9 January 1915, p. 3. (In these stories she is named Alice Hodgkinson.)

27 *Wigan Obs*, 20 May, 1924, p. 2. The bed-sharing joke appears into the 1950s. See also Chapter 6, pp. 135–6.

28 *IPN*, 22 May 1924, p. 4; *Daily News*, 17 May 1924, p. 5.

29 *NoW*, 18 May 1924, p. 9.

30 Ibid. Also see *IPN*, 22 May 1924, p. 4.

31 *Illustrated Sunday Herald*, 18 May 1924, p. 2; *Wigan Obs*, 20 May 1924, p. 2.

32 For comedy around courtship on the variety stage in this period, see R. Wilmut, *Kindly Leave the Stage! The Story of Variety 1919–1960*, London: Methuen, 1985, pp. 122–3, 142.

33 *NoW*, 7 April 1912, p. 9.

34 Ibid.

35 *Illustrated Sunday Herald*, 18 May 1924, p. 2. *Evening Standard*, 17 May 1924, p. 16.

36 T. Phillips, *The Postcard Century*, London: Thames and Hudson, 2000, p. 24, for an example of the last. On comic postcards generally, see G. Orwell, 'The Art of Donald McGill', first published 1941, reprinted in S. Orwell and I. Angus, *The Collected Essays, Journalism and Letters of George Orwell*, vol. 2, London: Secker and Warburg, 1968, pp. 155–65. For the euphemistic language of sexuality in this period, see K. Fisher, *Birth Control, Sex and Marriage in Britain 1918–1960*, Oxford: Oxford University Press, 2006.

37 S. Marcus, *Between Women*, p. 114.

38 A. Clark, 'Twilight Moments', *Journal of the History of Sexuality*, 2005, vol. 14, nos. 1–2, especially 140–1, 153, 155–6.

39 See, for example, J. Bourke, *Dismembering the Male: Men's Bodies, Britain and the Great War*, London: Reaktion Books, 1996, pp. 128–9. M. Houlbrook, 'Soldier Heroes and Rent Boys: Homosex, Masculinities, and Britishness in the Brigade of Guards, circa 1900–1960', *Journal of British Studies*, 2003, vol. 42, 351–8, 264–6.

40 Bourke, *Dismembering the Male*. A. Wollacott, '"Khaki Fever" and its Control: Gender, Class, Age and Sexual Morality on the British Homefront in the First World War', *Journal of Contemporary History*, 1994, vol. 29, 325–47. P. Summerfield, 'Patriotism and Empire: Music Hall Entertainment 1870–1914', in J. M. MacKenzie (ed.), *Imperialism and Popular Culture*, Manchester: Manchester University Press, 1986, p. 37.

41 Houlbrook, 'Soldier Heroes and Rent Boys', especially 364–7. F. Tamagne, *A History of Homosexuality in Europe: Berlin, London, Paris 1919–1939*, New York: Algora Publishing, 2004, p. 65.

42 J. Gould, 'Women's Military Services in First World War Britain', in M. R. Higgonet, J. Jenson, S. Michel and M. C. Weitz (eds), *Behind the Lines: Gender and the Two World Wars*, New Haven, CT: Yale University Press, 1987. S. Grayzel, *Women's Identities at War*, Chapel Hill, NC: University of North Carolina Press, 1999, pp. 198–202.

43 L. Doan, *Fashioning Sapphism: The Origins of a Modern English Lesbian Culture*, New York: Columbia University Press, 2001, p. 68.

44 This is explored in an unpublished paper by Krisztina Robert, 'Military Uniforms and Modern Femininities: Designing, Marketing and Embodying the Servicewoman in First World War Britain'.

45 Bratton, 'Beating the Bounds', p. 101.

46 *NoW*, 10 November 1912, p. 5.

47 Robert, 'Military Uniforms and Modern Femininities'.

48 *Bulletin* (Glasgow), 29 June 1915. Imperial War Museum cuttings collection, supplied by K. Robert.

49 *Daily Mail*, 7 August 1915. Imperial War Museum cuttings collection, supplied by K. Robert. I am grateful to Krisztina Robert for sharing her sources with me.

50 *NoW*, 8 August 1915, p. 11 (Hetty King); 3 June 1917, p. 6 (Ella Shields); 29 April 1917, p. 7 (Vesta Tilley).

51 *NoW*, 3 October 1915, p. 1.

52 Judging by the large number which are still extant in postcard collections and available from postcard dealers.
53 *NoW*, 14 January 1917, p. 1.
54 *NoW*, 10 November 1918, p. 2.
55 *IPN*, 5 August 1918, p. 4. *People*, 4 August 1918, p. 1.
56 *People*, 4 August 1918, p. 1.
57 *People*, 19 May 1918, p. 8.
58 K. Robert collection. WAACs were accused of sexual immorality and having a high pregnancy rate. Official investigation showed these rumours were without foundation. Grayzel, *Women's Identities at War*, p. 199.
59 P. Hammond, *French Undressing: Naughty Postcards From 1900 to 1920*, London: Jupiter Books, 1974, p. 134.
60 I am grateful to Lesley Hall and Paula Bartley for discussing these issues with me.
61 Doan, *Fashioning Sapphism*, pp. 64–7.
62 Ibid., p. 76.
63 See Sharon Marcus for a useful discussion of this point. Marcus, *Between Women*, pp. 113–14.
64 Unlike for the United States or Germany where there is evidence of a working-class lesbian sub-culture even before the First World War as well as in the 1920s, at least in Berlin and New York. For Berlin see C. Schoppmann, *Days of Masquerade: Life Stories of Lesbians during the Third Reich*, New York: Columbia University Press, 1996, especially pp. 2–6. Tamagne, *A History of Homosexuality in Europe*, pp. 21, 50–7. For the United States, see L. J. Rupp, *A Desired Past: A Short History of Same-Sex Love in America*, Chicago, IL: Chicago University Press, 1999, pp. 78–9, 107–12, 120–2. See Bratton, 'Beating the Bounds', pp. 93–4 for the equivocal and knowing response to Hetty King in New York in 1910.
65 Despite Sarah Waters' wonderful fictional picture of an East End lesbian pub in *Tipping the Velvet*, London: Virago, 1998. For queer men see Cook, *London and the Culture of Homosexuality*; Houlbrook, *Queer London*.
66 Postal charges doubled at the end of the war, leading to a more restrained use of postcards as a form of communication.
67 Hetty King postcard, 1908. Author's collection.
68 Vesta Tilley postcard, 1907. Author's collection.
69 Vesta Tilley postcard, no date. Author's collection.
70 Vesta Tilley postcard, 1906. Author's collection.
71 Lady de Frece, *Recollections of Vesta Tilley*, London: Hutchinson, 1934, pp. 233, 234.
72 Also see Jackie Stacey's analysis of women fans' homoerotic response to mid-twentieth-century female film stars and how they later described their crushes. J. Stacey, *Star Gazing: Hollywood Cinema and Female Spectatorship*, London: Routledge, 1994, pp. 27–30, 172–5, 138–45. J. Stacey, 'Hollywood Memories', in A. Kuhn and J. Stacey (eds), *Screen Histories: A Screen Reader*, Oxford: Clarendon Press, 1998.
73 For example, in a card from 1912, where a Miss Craske wearing a male dress suit is dancing with Miss Gabrielle Ray. Author's collection.
74 I am grateful to Sarah Waters for many enjoyable discussions and arguments about all these postcards.
75 M. Vicinus, 'Turn-of-the-Century Male Impersonation: Rewriting the Romance Plot', in A. Miller and J. E. Adams (eds), *Sexualities in Victorian Britain*, Bloomington, IN: Indiana University Press, 1996, pp. 187–213. Also see J. S. Bratton, 'Irrational Dress', in V. Gardner and S. Rutherford (eds), *The New Woman and her Sisters: Feminism and Theatre 1850–1914*, London: Harvester Wheatsheaf, 1992, pp. 79–81.
76 Lilley was part of Noel Coward's large circle of lesbian and bisexual women friends, which also included Teddy Gerard, a lesbian actress who worked in revue. T. Castle, *Noel Coward and Radclyffe Hall: Kindred Spirits*, New York: Columbia University Press, 1996, pp. 17, 20–1, 24, 70.
77 *NoW*, 2 July 1911, p. 14.

78 L. Sigel, *Governing Pleasures: Pornography and Social Change in England, 1815–1914*, New Brunswick, NJ: Rutgers University Press, 2002, pp. 119–22, 149–51.
79 An argument that was not accepted in court. Ibid., p. 150.
80 Ibid., pp. 123–37.
81 Collection S. Waters.
82 Tamagne, *A History of Homosexuality in Europe*, pp. 21, 50–7, 68. Schoppmann, *Days of Masquerade*, especially pp. 2–6.
83 *NoW*, 7 April 1912, p. 9.
84 *NoW*, 31 March 1912, p. 12.
85 Charles Reade (1814–84) is best known as the author of *The Cloister and the Hearth* (1861). The Catherine Coombe story was published in the *English Review* in August and September 1911.
86 *NoW*, 10 September 1911, p. 10.
87 Ibid.
88 *NoW*, 2 June 1918, p. 3. E. Showalter, *Sexual Anarchy: Gender and Culture at the Fin de Siècle*, London: Virago, 1992, pp. 149–50, 171.
89 J. Walkowitz, 'The "Vision of Salome": Cosmopolitanism and Erotic Dancing in Central London, 1908–18', *American Historical Review*, 2003, vol. 108, no. 2, 345, 373.
90 *Sunday Express*, 19 August 1928, p. 10.
91 A. Oram, '"A Sudden Orgy of Decadence": Writing about Sex between Women in the Interwar Popular Press', in L. Doan and J. Garrity (eds), *Sapphic Modernities: Sexuality, Women and National Culture*, New York: Palgrave Macmillan, 2006.
92 This contrasts with the United States where the scare figure of the mannish lesbian with violent tendencies appeared in the sensationalist press from the 1890s. L. Duggan, *Sapphic Slashers: Sex, Violence, and American Modernity*, Durham, NC: Duke University Press, 2000.
93 *NoW*, 2 June, 1918, p. 3.
94 L. Bland, 'Trial by Sexology?: Maud Allan, *Salome* and the "Cult of the Clitoris" Case', in L. Bland and L. Doan (eds), *Sexology in Culture: Labelling Bodies and Desires*, Cambridge: Polity Press, 1998.
95 *NoW*, 2 June 1918, p. 3.
96 *People*, 2 June 1918, pp. 1, 5.
97 The clause was defeated and lesbianism remained legal.
98 *NoW*, 7 August 1921, p. 4. The *People* did not report the debate.
99 Ibid.
100 *NoW*, 24 January 1915, p. 5.
101 H. Swaffer, 'The Smear Across London', *People*, 23 November 1924, p. 8. Eyles was a jobbing journalist at this period in her life, and later became better known as a novelist and social commentator.
103 L. Eyles, 'Another Phase of the Smear', *People*, 30 November 1924, p. 8.
104 Ibid.

3 Gender-crossing and modern sexualities, 1928–39

1 L. Doan and J. Prosser (eds), *Palatable Poison: Critical Perspectives on The Well of Loneliness*, New York: Columbia University Press, 2001. S. Ruehl, 'Inverts and Experts: Radclyffe Hall and the Lesbian Identity', in R. Brunt and C. Rowan (eds), *Feminism, Culture and Politics*, London: Lawrence and Wishart, 1982.
2 *NoW*, 28 April 1929, p. 6.
3 See Judith Halberstam's usefully nuanced discussion of Colonel Barker's subjectivity. J. Halberstam, *Female Masculinity*, Durham, NC: Duke University Press, 1998, pp. 91–5.
4 J. Vernon, '"For Some Queer Reason": The Trials and Tribulations of Colonel Barker's Masquerade in Interwar Britain', *Signs*, 2000, vol. 26, no. 11, 41, 56.

5 L. Doan, *Fashioning Sapphism: The Origins of a Modern English Lesbian Culture*, New York: Columbia University Press, 2001, p. 94.

6 *People*, 10 March 1929, p. 5. *NoW*, 10 March 1929, p. 9.

7 *People*, 10 March 1929, p. 1.

8 Ibid., p. 7.

9 *NoW*, 10 March 1929, p. 9. *People*, 10 March 1929, p. 7.

10 Doan also notes press admiration, looking at the dailies. Doan, *Fashioning Sapphism*, pp. 88–9, 92.

11 *NoW*, 10 March 1929, p. 9.

12 *People*, 10 March 1929, p. 5.

13 Ibid., p. 1.

14 Ibid., pp. 1, 5, 7.

15 But there was a huge Fleet Street effort to track down the second wife. J. C. Cannell, *When Fleet Street Calls: Being the Experiences of a London Journalist*, London: Jarrolds, 1932, p. 206.

16 *People*, 10 March 1929, p. 5.

17 *People*, 31 March 1929, p. 7. On the press interpretation of her womanly tears, also see Doan, *Fashioning Sapphism*, p. 92, and Vernon, '"For Some Queer Reason"', 50–1.

18 *NoW*, 28 April 1929, p. 6.

19 For the 1920–1 attempt at parliamentary legislation see L. Doan, '"Acts of Female Indecency": Sexology's Intervention in Legislating Lesbianism', in L. Bland and L. Doan (eds), *Sexology in Culture: Labelling Bodies and Desires*, Cambridge: Polity Press, 1998. For Wild's comments on male homosexual cases see *IPN*, 30 April 1931, p. 4. *NoW*, 5 March 1933, p. 18.

20 Douglas, editor of the *Sunday Express*, had violently condemned *The Well of Loneliness* in a review and provoked its prosecution. *Sunday Express*, 19 August 1928, p. 10.

21 *NoW*, 12 May 1929, p. 3. In fact Kathleen had cross-dressed a few months earlier while working as a domestic servant, and stolen clothes, a cheque and a watch from her employer. *NoW*, 27 January 1929, p. 4.

22 *People*, 28 April 1929, p. 4. *Daily Herald*, 25 April 1929, p. 1.

23 Headline in the *People*, 12 May 1929, p. 3.

24 *Cheltenham Chronicle and Gloucestershire Graphic* (hereafter *CCGG*), 11 May 1929, p. 1. Although some newspapers, including the *People*, spelled the name Holtom, I have standardised the spelling throughout to Holton.

25 Typhoid fever.

26 *NoW*, 12 May 1929, p. 5.

27 *Evesham Journal*, 11 May 1929, p. 2.

28 *NoW*, 12 May 1929, p. 5. *People*, 12 May 1929, p. 3.

29 *NoW*, 12 May 1929, p. 5.

30 *People*, 12 May 1929, p. 3. Other papers represented her as shorter, with small hands and feet.

31 *NoW*, 12 May 1929, p. 5.

32 Ibid. This is the only cross-dressing story across the whole period in which the binding of breasts was directly referred to.

33 Ibid., p. 5.

34 *Daily Express*, 10 May 1929, p. 13.

35 R. Johnston and A. McIvor, 'Dangerous Work, Hard Men and Broken Bodies: Masculinity in the Clydeside Heavy Industries, *c.* 1930–70s', *Labour History Review*, 2004, vol. 69, no. 2, 135–51. R. W. Connell, *Masculinities*, Cambridge: Polity Press, 1995, p. 55.

36 *NoW*, 12 May 1929, p. 5. *Daily Express*, 10 May 1929, p. 13.

37 *Daily Express*, 10 May 1929, p. 13.

38 *NoW*, 12 May 1929, p. 5.

39 Ibid.

40 *Evesham Journal*, 11 May 1929, p. 2. For drinking, smoking and swearing alongside heavy manual labour as markers of masculinity, and football as a male preserve, see Johnston and McIvor, 'Dangerous Work, Hard Men and Broken Bodies', 138–42, and B. Beaven, *Leisure, Citizenship and Working-class Men in Britain, 1850–1945*, Manchester: Manchester University Press, 2005, pp. 60–6, 72–81.

41 *NoW*, 12 May 1929, p. 5. It was also reported that she liked boxing and could wrestle.

42 For the debates about the limitations of domesticated masculinity and home-based leisure between the wars, see Beaven, *Leisure, Citizenship and Working-class Men*, Chapter 4, and M. Francis, 'The Domestication of the Male? Recent Research on Nineteenth- and Twentieth-Century British Masculinity', *Historical Journal*, 2002, vol. 45, no. 3, 641–4.

43 *NoW*, 12 May 1929, p. 5.

44 Revealed in a subsequent interview. See *CCGG*, 27 August 1932, p. 3.

45 *NoW*, 12 May 1929, p. 5.

46 Ibid. *People*, 12 May 1929, p. 3.

47 *NoW*, 12 May 1929, p. 5.

48 *Daily Express*, 10 May 1929, p. 13.

49 *People*, 12 May 1929, p. 3.

50 In the 1820s, the wife of the female husband James Allen was commiserated with and made to look foolish because she lacked a 'real' man who could give her sexual pleasure and make her pregnant. A. Oram, 'Cross-dressing and Transgender', in H. G. Cocks and M. Houlbrook (eds), *The Modern History of Sexuality*, Basingstoke: Palgrave Macmillan, 2006, pp. 264–5.

51 *People*, 12 May 1929, p. 3.

52 *Daily Express*, 10 May 1929, p. 13.

53 A. Stott, *Comedy*, New York: Routledge, 2005, p. 55.

54 *CCGG*, 27 August 1932, p. 3, quoting an earlier interview of 1929.

55 *People*, 31 July 1932, p. 2. *NoW*, 31 July 1932, p. 4.

56 *NoW*, 22 September 1929, p. 5.

57 The joke appears in cross-dressing stories right up until the 1950s.

58 *People*, 12 November 1933, p. 2.

59 The *News of the World* reported that a man known as Bill O'Connor had been revealed as a woman, Lilian Smithers, in hospital, but the story was located in Rotherhithe, and made no mention of Mrs Wellbelove. *NoW*, 12 November 1933, p. 8.

60 Adrian Bingham also finds that the popular press made only rare and veiled references to homosexuality before the 1950s. A. Bingham, '"Into the Twilight World": The Portrayal of Homosexuality in the British Popular Press, 1918–70', Paper given at the Social History Society annual conference, Rouen, January 2004.

61 See, for example, *People*, 24 April 1932, p. 4; 2 December 1934, p. 17; 7 February 1937, p. 2.

62 For the Sino-Japanese war, see *People*, 14 April 1935, p. 15. For the Spanish Civil War, see *People*, 3 January 1937, p. 1; *NoW*, 7 March 1937, p. 13.

63 *NoW*, 27 August 1933, p. 11. Also see *NoW*, 10 September 1933, p. 8; 17 September 1933, p. 11.

64 D. Dugaw, *Warrior Women and Popular Balladry, 1650–1850*, Chicago, IL: University of Chicago Press, 1996.

65 *NoW*, 10 October 1933, p. 8.

66 *NoW*, 30 September 1934, p. 18. *IPN*, 4 October 1934, p. 6. *NoW*, 21 March 1937, p. 18; 28 March 1937, p. 8. *IPN*, 1 April 1937, p. 8. Also see Vernon, '"For Some Queer Reason"', 42–4.

67 R. Wilmut, *Kindly Leave the Stage! The Story of Variety 1919–1960*, London: Methuen, 1985, pp. 63–9.

68 For example, Pat Kirkwood played Tilley on stage in 1939 (*NoW*, 19 November 1939, p. 12) and later in a 1950s film of her life. Hilda Mundy impersonated Vesta Tilley at

the Palladium in 1932. *NoW*, 11 December 1932, p. 7. Also see L. Senelick, *The Changing Room: Sex, Drag and Theatre*, London: Routledge, 2000, p. 338, though he overstates the declining originality of the male impersonator.

69 Not to be confused with Vesta Tilley's different song about Burlington Bertie. R. Busby, *British Music Hall*, London: Paul Elek, 1976, pp. 160–1. *NoW*, 30 May 1920, p. 8; 4 August 1929, p. 12.

70 Film musicals, such as *Top Hat* (1936) which starred Fred Astaire and Ginger Rogers, reached their greatest popularity in the 1930s.

71 *People*, 18 September 1927, p. 3.

72 H. Dickens, *What A Drag*, London: Angus and Robertson, 1982, p. 36.

73 R. Bell-Metereau, *Hollywood Androgyny*, New York: Columbia University Press, 1993, p. 75.

74 Ibid., pp. 103–8. W. K. Martin, *Marlene Dietrich*, New York: Chelsea House Publishers, 1995, Chapter 4.

75 See, for example, A. Weiss, *Vampires and Violets: Lesbians in Film*, New York: Penguin, 1993, pp. 33–5. V. Russo, *The Celluloid Closet*, New York: Harper and Row, 1981, p. 14.

76 *NoW*, 21 May 1933, p. 8.

77 *NoW*, 12 February 1933, p. 7; 21 May 1933, p. 8.

78 J. Stacey, 'Hollywood Memories', in A. K. and J. Stacey (eds), *Screen Histories: A Screen Reader*, Oxford: Clarendon Press, 1998. J. Stacey, *Star Gazing: Hollywood Cinema and Female Spectatorship*, London: Routledge, 1994, pp. 138–45.

79 For example, Katherine Hepburn in *Sylvia Scarlett* (1935).

80 Dickens, *What A Drag*, p. 45.

81 Doan, *Fashioning Sapphism*.

82 *NoW*, 18 November 1928, p. 3.

83 *NoW*, 16 December 1928, p. 8.

84 *People*, 19 August 1928, p. 2.

85 *People*, 26 August 1928, p. 14.

86 Doan, *Fashioning Sapphism*, Chapter 6.

87 *People*, 24 July 1927, p. 5. Tallulah Bankhead was a lesbian actress. Also see F. Tamagne, *A History of Homosexuality in Europe: Berlin, London, Paris 1919–1939*, New York: Algora Publishing, 2004, pp. 44–5.

88 *NoW*, 5 September 1937, p. 14. For Betty, aka Joe Carstairs, see K. Summerscale, *The Queen of Whale Cay*, London: Fourth Estate, 1998.

89 *People*, 6 June 1937, p. 4. Also see *People*, 5 September 1937, p. 4. Also see A. Bingham, *Gender, Modernity and the Popular Press in Inter-War Britain*, Oxford: Clarendon Press, 2004.

90 *NoW*, 11 September 1932, p. 13; also see 4 September 1932, p. 16. For discussion of the professional literature on schoolgirl crushes see A. Oram and A. Turnbull, *The Lesbian History Sourcebook: Love and Sex between Women in Britain from 1780 to 1970*, London: Routledge, 2001, Chapter 4.

91 *NoW*, 5 December 1937, p. 2.

92 Bingham, '"Into the Twilight World"'.

93 M. Houlbrook, *Queer London: Perils and Pleasures in the Sexual Metropolis, 1918–1957*, Chicago, IL: University of Chicago Press, 2005, pp. 22–7, 139–49. Q. Crisp, *The Naked Civil Servant*, London: Jonathon Cape, 1968, Chapters 3, 8, 9, 11.

94 *NoW*, 24 September 1911, p. 4.

95 *NoW*, 5 October 1924, p. 9.

96 *NoW*, 30 August 1925, p. 4. Also see 5 December 1926, p. 4; 15 June 1930, p. 8.

97 Houlbrook, *Queer London*, pp. 224–7, and see M. Houlbrook, '"The Man with the Powder Puff" in Interwar London', *Historical Journal*, 2007, vol. 50, no. 1, 145–71.

98 *People*, 23 November 1924, p. 8. This was followed the next week by the report by L. Eyles, discussed in Chapter 2.

99 *People*, 11 October 1925, p. 6.

100 *People*, 4 February 1923, p. 4.

101 R. Baker, *Drag: A History of Female Impersonation in the Performing Arts*, London: Cassell, 1994, pp. 186–95. Houlbrook, *Queer London*, pp. 159–62.

102 See, for example, *NoW*, 5 July 1936, p. 10; 23 October 1932, p. 17; 19 February 1939, p. 15.

103 *NoW*, 28 August 1927, p. 8. The term 'moral pervert' was increasingly used in the 1930s, though still infrequently. For earlier use of codes such as 'West End pest' and 'Powder-puff', see *People*, 11 January 1914, p. 20. *NoW*, 24 September 1911, p. 4.

104 *NoW*, 27 December 1931, p. 9; 3 January 1932, p. 9.

105 M. Houlbrook, '"Lady Austin's Camp Boys": Constituting the Queer Subject in 1930s London', *Gender and History*, 2002, vol. 14, no. 1, 31–61. *NoW*, 23 January 1927, p. 4; 5 March 1933, p. 18; 2 September 1934, p. 13. *IPN*, 7 February 1935, p. 3. *NoW*, 6 December 1936, p. 10; 24 January 1937, p. 19.

106 *IPN*, 7 May 1936, p. 12.

107 *NoW*, 5 March 1933, p. 18. This was Sir Ernest Wild, from the Colonel Barker trial.

108 *NoW*, 23 January 1927, p. 4. This story involved an upper-class woman who had lost her memory and was suspected of rick-burning.

109 C. Waters, 'Havelock Ellis, Sigmund Freud and the State: Discourses of Homosexual Identity in Interwar Britain', in L. Bland and L. Doan (eds), *Sexology in Culture: Labelling Bodies and Desires*, Cambridge: Polity Press, 1998. A. McLaren, *The Trials of Masculinity: Policing Sexual Boundaries 1870–1930*, Chicago, IL: Chicago University Press, 1997, Chapter 9.

110 Hull was convicted of gross indecency, despite expert evidence that he was 'an invert and not a pervert'. McLaren, *The Trials of Masculinity*.

111 *People*, 16 February 1930, p. 6.

112 *NOW*, 16 February 1936, p. 7. Also see *People*, 16 February 1936, p. 6. *NOW*, 1 March 1936, p. 18.

113 *NoW*, 28 October 1934, p. 15.

114 *IPN*, 9 February 1933, p. 2. *NoW*, 21 July 1935, p. 3; 9 July 1939, p. 6.

115 Miller (heart disease): *NoW*, 4 February 1923, p. 11. Wood (consumption): *NoW*, 18 May 1924, p. 9. Holton (typhoid fever): *NoW*, 12 May 1929, p. 5.

116 *NoW*, 20 August 1916, p. 7.

117 *NoW*, 22 September 1929, p. 5.

118 *NoW*, 26 September 1915, p. 3. Paul Downing was judged insane in 1905 after evidence of her 'delusions' and sent to an asylum. *Daily Chronicle*, 14 September 1905, p. 4.

119 *People*, 4 February 1923, p. 9.

120 *Daily Herald*, 29 August 1932, p. 1. Also see *CCGG*, 27 August 1932, p. 3.

121 *NoW*, 16 May 1937, p. 8; 13 June 1937, p. 8.

122 *NoW*, 13 June 1937, p. 8.

123 Doan, *Fashioning Sapphism*, Chapter 6.

124 *NoW*, 13 June 1937, p. 8.

125 *Daily Mirror*, 11 June 1937, p. 8.

126 *NoW*, 13 June 1937, p. 8.

127 These concerns had been mentioned by Leonora Eyles back in 1924 in the *People* (see above, Chapter 2, p. 58), but were not referred to in the schoolgirl suicide case of 1933 discussed above.

128 See Tamagne, *A History of Homosexuality in Europe*, pp. 50–1, 53–7, 68. C. Schoppmann, *Days of Masquerade: Life Stories of Lesbians during the Third Reich*, New York: Columbia University Press, 1996, especially pp. 2–11. T. T. Latimer, *Women Together / Women Apart: Portraits of Lesbian Paris*, New Brunswick, NJ: Rutgers University Press, 2005, Chapter 4. This recognition was also fostered in those countries by political and journalistic attacks on female as well as male homosexuality.

4 'The sheik was a she!': the gigolo and cosmopolitanism in the 1930s

1 *People*, 5 June 1932, p. 6.

2 A. McClintock, *Imperial Leather: Race, Gender and Sexuality in the Colonial Context*, New York: Routledge, 1995, pp. 352–7. G. Mosse, *Nationalism and Sexuality*, Madison, WI: University of Wisconsin Press, 1985. See S. Rose, 'Sex, Citizenship and the Nation in World War II Britain', *American Historical Review*, 1998, vol. 103, 1147–76, for discussion of these ideas in relation to Britain in the Second World War. I was inspired at an early stage in my thinking about sexuality and national belonging by Wren Sidhe, whose PhD thesis I supervised. W. Sidhe, 'Bodies, Books and the Bucolic: Englishness, Literature and Sexuality, 1918–39', Cheltenham and Gloucester College of Higher Education, 2001.

3 L. Colley, *Britons: Forging the Nation 1707–1837*, London: Pimlico, 1994. R. and I. Tombs, *That Sweet Enemy: The French and the British from the Sun King to the Present*, London: William Heinemann, 2006. R. Samuel, 'Introduction: The Figures of National Myth', in R. Samuel (ed.), *Patriotism. The Making and Unmaking of British National Identity*, vol. 3: *National Fictions*, London: Routledge, 1989, pp. xxv–xxvi.

4 L. Bland, 'The Trial of Madame Fahmy: Orientalism, Violence, Sexual Perversity and the Fear of Miscegenation', in S. D'Cruze (ed.), *Everyday Violence in Britain, 1850–1950*, Harlow: Longman, 2000. M. Nava, 'Wider Horizons and Modern Desire: The Contradiction of America and Racial Difference in London 1935–45', *New Formations*, 1999, vol. 37, 71–91.

5 R. and I. Tombs, *That Sweet Enemy*, pp. 373, 448. F. Tamagne, *A History of Homosexuality in Europe: Berlin, London, Paris 1919–1939*, New York: Algora Publishing, 2004, pp. 20–1, 68.

6 *People*, 28 April 1929, p. 2. Also see *People*, 15 March 1931, p. 9, for a similar story.

7 *People*, 28 April 1929, p. 2.

8 *People*, 15 October 1933, p. 5. Also see *People*, 15 March 1931, p. 9.

9 Max Weber, one of the founders of sociology, examined the spread of bureaucratic administration as a necessary characteristic of modern industrial society and commented on its implications for democracy and individual freedom. See I. Marsh (ed.), *Sociology: Making Sense of Society*, Harlow: Prentice Hall, 2000, pp. 73–83. A. Giddens, *In Defence of Sociology*, Cambridge: Polity Press, 1996, pp. 36–9.

10 *NoW*, 28 March 1937, p. 6.

11 *People*, 28 March 1937, p. 9.

12 For attitudes to lesbianism within French culture, see C. Dean, *The Frail Social Body: Pornography, Homosexuality and Other Fantasies in Interwar France*, Berkeley, CA: University of California Press, 2000, pp. 180–214. Tamagne, *A History of Homosexuality*, p. 68.

13 After Marie Lloyd's song 'The Naughty Continong' (Continent). T. Davis, *Actresses as Working Women: Their Social Identity in Victorian Culture*, London: Routledge, 1991, p. 119.

14 *People*, 26 July 1931, p. 3; *People*, 5 June 1932, p. 6.

15 R. and I. Tombs, *That Sweet Enemy*, p. 521.

16 *People*, 10 September 1933, p. 4.

17 Davis, *Actresses as Working Women*, p. 119.

18 A. Stuart, *Showgirls*, London: Jonathan Cape, 1996, pp. 38–9.

19 Ibid., pp. 46–8, 65. N. Albert, 'Books on Trial: Prosecutions for Representing Sapphism in *fin-de-siècle* France', in G. Robb and N. Erber (eds), *Disorder in the Court: Trials and Sexual Conflict at the Turn of the Century*, Basingstoke: Macmillan, 1999.

20 *People*, 10 September 1933, p. 4.

21 Republished in *Music Hall Memories*, 20 February 1936, vol. 19, pp. 213–15. And see R. and I. Tombs, *That Sweet Enemy*, p. 448.

22 *People*, 26 July 1931, p. 3.

23 J. Dixon, *The Romance Fiction of Mills and Boon, 1909–1990s*, London: UCL Press, 1999, p. 51.

24 *People*, 5 June 1932, p. 6. See opening quote of this chapter.
25 B. Melman, *Women and the Popular Imagination in the Twenties: Flappers and Nymphs*, Basingstoke: Macmillan, 1988, pp. 45, 50, Chapter 6. Dixon, *The Romance Fiction of Mills and Boon*, pp. 137–8. Bland, 'The Trial of Madame Fahmy', pp. 192–3. Desert romances remained popular into the 1940s. J. McAleer, *Popular Reading and Publishing in Britain 1914–1950*, Oxford: Clarendon Press, 1992, p. 92.
26 *People*, 5 June 1932, p. 6.
27 *People*, 18 June 1933, p. 4.
28 Melman, *Women and the Popular Imagination*, p. 101. Dixon, *The Romance Fiction of Mills and Boon*, p. 52.
29 *People*, 18 June 1933, p. 4.
30 Dixon, *The Romance Fiction of Mills and Boon*, pp. 6, 51, 64–5, 72.
31 L. Bland, 'White Women and Men of Colour: Miscegenation Fears in Britain after the Great War', *Gender and History*, 2005, vol. 17, no. 1, 47. Bland, 'The Trial of Madame Fahmy', p. 192. For post-First World War masculinity see M. Francis, 'The Domestication of the Male? Recent Research on Nineteenth- and Twentieth-Century British Masculinity', *Historical Journal*, 2002, vol. 45, no. 3, 637–52. A. Light, *Forever England: Femininity, Literature and Conservatism between the Wars*, London: Routledge, 1991, pp. 7–9, 124, 72–5, 197–200, 211.
32 *Oxford English Dictionary*. The word dated from 1902 in both French and English, deriving from the aggressive reputation of the native American tribe. *Le Grand Robert de la Langue Française*, 2001. R. J. Herail and E. Lovatt, *A Dictionary of Modern Colloquial French*, London: Routledge, 1984.
33 Stuart, *Showgirls*, pp. 10–11, 36–8. *Oxford English Dictionary*.
34 *People*, 19 April 1925, p. 5. For earlier use see, for example, *NoW*, 15 October 1911, p. 12.
35 *People*, 10 September 1933, p. 4.
36 *People*, 16 March 1930, p. 4.
37 *People*, 26 July 1931, p. 3.
38 *People*, 18 June 1933, p. 4.
39 *People*, 16 March 1930, p. 4; 24 July 1932, p. 2; 19 February 1933, p. 15; 10 September 1933, p. 4.
40 *People*, 26 July 1931, p. 3; 19 February 1933, p. 15.
41 *People*, 18 June 1933, p. 4.
42 *People*, 24 July 1932, p. 2. The amount of titillating detail of divorce cases which newspapers could report was reined in after 1926 by the Judicial Proceedings (Regulation of Reports) Act. G. Savage, 'Erotic Stories and Public Decency: Newspaper Reporting of Divorce Proceedings in England', *Historical Journal*, 1998, vol. 41, no. 2, 511–28.
43 The book was published in 1919, and the film made in 1921. The *Oxford English Dictionary* dates 'gigolo', in published form, from 1922.
44 *People*, 19 February 1933, p. 15.
45 *People* 26 July 1931, p. 3.
46 *People*, 5 June 1932, p. 6.
47 See Chapter 2, p.56 and Chapter 3, pp. 79–80.
48 *People*, 26 July 1931, p. 3; 6 June 1932, p. 9; 16 March 1930, p. 4.
49 *People*, 16 March 1930, p. 4.
50 Ibid.
51 H. Cook, *The Long Sexual Revolution: English Women, Sex, and Contraception 1800–1975*, Oxford: Oxford University Press, 2004, Chapter 8.
52 *People*, 10 September 1933, p. 4.
53 *People*, 18 June 1933, p. 4.
54 Ibid. For Nancy Cunard and racial mixing, see B. Bush, *Imperialism, Race and Resistance: Africa and Britain, 1919–1945*, London: Routledge, 1999, pp. 211–12. M. Moynagh,

'Introduction', in M. Moynagh (ed.), *Nancy Cunard, Essays on Race and Empire*, Ontario, Canada: Broadview Literary Texts, 2002, pp. 22–6, 45–50. A. Chisholm, *Nancy Cunard*, Harmondsworth: Penguin, 1985, pp. 258–79. *The Times*, 15 July 1933, p. 4.

55 *People*, 29 May 1931, p. 8; 10 July 1932, p. 3. *NoW*, 10 July 1932, p. 8.

56 *People* 6 June 1932, p. 9.

57 In an interesting parallel to Lucy Bland's argument about Madame Fahmy. Bland, 'The Trial of Madame Fahmy'.

58 P. Thane, 'The British Imperial State and the Construction of National Identities', in B. Melman (ed.), *Borderlines. Genders and Identities in War and Peace 1870–1930*, New York: Routledge, 1998. G. Robb, *British Culture and the First World War*, Basingstoke: Palgrave, 2002, pp. 28–31.

59 For example, in the deporting of black British sailors after the First World War. L. Tabili, 'Women "of a Very Low Type": Crossing Racial Boundaries in Imperial Britain', in L. Frader and S. Rose (eds), *Gender and Class in Modern Europe*, Ithaca, NY: Cornell University Press, 1996.

60 Jonathan Rose argues that working-class readers and audiences were not necessarily racist in their enjoyment of black or blackface characters in fiction or on stage. J. Rose, *The Intellectual Life of the British Working Classes*, New Haven, CT: Yale University Press, 2002, pp. 381–6.

61 Bland, 'The Trial of Madame Fahmy'.

62 Ibid., 32.

63 M. Nava, 'Cosmopolitan Modernity: Everyday Imaginaries and the Register of Difference', *Theory, Culture and Society*, 2002, vol. 19, nos. 1–2, 81–99. Nava, 'Wider Horizons and Modern Desire'.

64 For discussion of the key moments in the postwar obsession with racial mixing see Bland, 'White Women and Men of Colour'.

65 M. Kohn, *Dope Girls. The Birth of the British Drug Underground*, London: Lawrence and Wishart, 1992. For white slavery and the press, see L. Bland, *Banishing the Beast: English Feminism and Sexual Morality 1885–1914*, London: Penguin, 1995, pp. 297–302. L. Jackson, 'Childhood and Youth', in H. G. Cocks and M. Houlbrook (eds), *The Modern History of Sexuality*, Basingstoke: Palgrave Macmillan, 2006, pp. 245–7. L. Ferris (ed.), *Crossing the Stage. Controversies on Cross-dressing*, London: Routledge, 1993, p. 35.

66 *People*, 31 October 1920, p. 9.

67 Kohn, *Dope Girls*, Chapters 4, 8 and 9. Bland, 'White Women and Men of Colour', 44–6.

68 *People*, 14 January 1923, p. 6.

69 *People*, 30 November 1924, p. 8. See Chapter 2 for discussion of the contemporary 'smear' columns.

70 M. Pickering, 'White Skin, Black Masks: "Nigger" Minstrelsy in Victorian England', in J. S. Bratton (ed.), *Music Hall: Performance and Style*, Milton Keynes: Open University Press, 1986. M. Pickering, 'Mock Blacks and Racial Mockery: The "Nigger" Minstrel and British Imperialism', in J. S. Bratton, R. A. Cave, B. Gregory, H. J. Holder and M. Pickering (eds), *Acts of Supremacy: The British Empire and the Stage, 1790–1930*, Manchester: Manchester University Press, 1991.

71 Pickering, 'White Skin, Black Masks', pp. 73, 83–5. Pickering, 'Mock Blacks and Racial Mockery', p. 216.

72 S. Featherstone, 'The Blackface Atlantic: Interpreting British Minstrelsy', *Journal of Victorian Culture*, 1998, vol. 3, 234–51.

73 For the story of Paul Downing/Caroline Brogden, see Chapter 1.

74 Pickering, 'Mock Blacks and Racial Mockery', pp. 202–4.

75 *Daily Chronicle*, 11 September 1905, p. 3.

76 For acts by 'Sheiks', blackface singers (all men), seaside minstrel shows, etc. see, for example, P. Honri, *Working the Halls*, London: Futura, 1974, pp. 48, 67, 103 (sheik), 114, 142.

77 Pickering, 'White Skin, Black Masks', pp. 73, 90. Pickering, 'Mock Blacks and Racial Mockery', p. 181.

78 J. Baxendale, '" . . . into another kind of life in which anything might happen . . . " Popular Music and Late Modernity, 1910–30', *Popular Music*, 1995, vol. 14, no. 2, 137–54.

79 Nava, 'Wider Horizons and Modern Desire', 84–5.

80 Pickering, 'White Skin, Black Masks', p. 78. Kathy Castle (London Metropolitan University) in her exhaustive search for nineteenth-century sources of blackface has found some women performers.

81 T. Parker, 'Bessie Wentworth', Music Hall pamphlet series no. 38, 2000. Bessie Wentworth file, the Mander and Mitchenson Theatre Collection, Trinity College of Music.

82 *NoW*, 11 April 1920, p. 8. Quote is from an obituary in an unnamed newspaper dated 29 September 1937, May Henderson file, Mander and Mitchenson Theatre Collection, Trinity College of Music.

83 *NoW*, 27 September 1925, p. 12.

84 Bland, 'White Women and Men of Colour', 44–5. Kohn, *Dope Girls*, Chapters 8 and 9.

85 *People*, 4 February 1923, p. 6; 11 February 1923, p. 6.

86 *People*, 18 February 1923, p. 5; 4 March 1923, p. 6. Also see *People*, 25 February 1923, p. 6 ('In the Ghetto') and 11 March 1923, p. 5 ('Down the Drug Path').

87 *People*, 30 September 1923, p. 7.

88 *People*, 10 October 1937, p. 2.

89 Bush, *Imperialism, Race and Resistance*, pp. 211–14.

90 The *People* periodically ran campaigns against 'immoral' night-clubs (generally condemning heterosexual behaviour) throughout the 1920s and 1930s, while the *News of the World* was more likely to report actual raids and prosecution of clubs. For homosexual decadence and the 'fast set' or Bright Young Things, see Chapters 2 and 3.

91 See Chapter 3. M. Houlbrook, '"Lady Austin's Camp Boys": Constituting the Queer Subject in 1930s London', *Gender and History*, 2002, vol. 14, no. 1, 31–61.

92 *NoW*, 2 September 1934, p. 13.

93 *NoW*, 6 December 1936, p. 10.

94 *People*, 9 July 1939, p. 17, my emphasis.

95 *NoW*, 24 October 1937, p. 4.

96 R. Murphy, 'Riff-Raff: British Cinema and the Underworld', in C. Barr (ed.), *All Our Yesterdays*, London: BFI Publishing, 1986. Also see B. Beaven, *Leisure, Citizenship and Working-class Men in Britain, 1850–1945*, Manchester: Manchester University Press, 2005, pp. 174–5.

97 *NoW*, 24 October 1937, p. 4. This closes the article and points the reader to the assumption that this woman is her girlfriend.

98 Carey soon afterwards received a further sentence for another similar crime. *NoW*, 7 November 1937, p. 8; 9 January 1938, p. 8.

5 The 1930s 'sex change' story: medical technology and physical transformation

1 *NoW*, 3 January 1932, p. 5.

2 *NoW*, 25 October 1936, p. 2.

3 See, for example, *NoW*, 19 February 1911, p. 9; 3 June 1917, p. 3; 29 June 1924, p. 3.

4 Ruth Ford discusses an atypical Australian case of cross-dressing where the discursive boundaries between masquerading woman and bizarre hermaphrodite were blurred by the press. R. Ford, '"The Man–Woman Murderer": Sex Fraud, Sexual Inversion and the Unmentionable "Article" in 1920s Australia', *Gender and History*, 2000, vol. 12,

no. 1, 158–96. The occasional British report also broke this distinction between the genres. At the end of its report on the masquerading Ernest Wood, the *News of the World* quoted a doctor who mentioned cases of sex change and people who are 'half and half'. *NoW*, 18 May 1924, p. 9.

5 N. Oudshoorn, *Beyond the Natural Body: An Archaeology of Sex Hormones*, London: Routledge, 1994. R. Porter and L. Hall, *The Facts of Life. The Creation of Sexual Knowledge in Britain, 1650–1950*, New Haven, CT: Yale University Press, 1995, pp. 169–75. L. R. Broster, C. Allen, H. W. C. Vines, J. Patterson, A. W. Greenwood, G. F. Marrian and G. C. Butler, *The Adrenal Cortex and Intersexuality*, London: Chapman and Hall, 1938. Also see A. D. Dreger, *Doubtful Sex: Hermaphrodites and the Medical Invention of Sex*, Cambridge, MA: Harvard University Press, 1998.

6 B. Hausman, *Changing Sex: Transsexualism, Technology, and the Idea of Gender*, Durham, NC: Duke University Press, 1995, p. 2.

7 J. Meyerowitz, *How Sex Changed: A History of Transsexuality in the United States*, Cambridge, MA: Harvard University Press, 2002. J. Meyerowitz, 'Sex Change and the Popular Press: Historical Notes on Transsexuality in the United States, 1930–55', *GLQ*, 1998, vol. 4, no. 2, 159–87. Also see J. Prosser, 'Transsexuals and the Transsexologists: Inversion and the Emergence of Transsexual Subjectivity', in L. Bland and L. Doan (eds), *Sexology in Culture: Labelling Bodies and Desires*, Cambridge: Polity Press, 1998, pp. 116–31. J. Prosser, *Second Skins: The Body Narratives of Transsexuality*, New York: Columbia University Press, 1998. Z. Nataf, *Lesbians Talk Transgender*, London: Scarlet Press, 1996, especially p. 10 for late nineteenth-century surgical sex conversion. For a longer discussion of these debates, see A. Oram, 'Cross-dressing and Transgender', in H. G. Cocks and M. Houlbrook (eds), *The Modern History of Sexuality*, Basingstoke: Palgrave Macmillan, 2006, pp. 276–80.

8 *NoW*, 27 August 1939, p. 6

9 *NoW*, 3 January 1932, p. 5.

10 *NoW*, 31 May 1936, p. 3.

11 *People*, 20 March 1932, p. 13. Also see *NoW*, 25 March 1934, p. 4.

12 *NoW*, 31 May 1936, p. 3. The Danish case was that of Lili Elbe/Eigar Wegener, seen by historians as a significant individual in the development of transsexual identity. The *News of the World*'s earlier story about Elbe/Wegener drew on (and in the process publicised) the book about her case: N. Hoyer (ed.), *Man Into Woman: An Authentic Record of a Change of Sex*, London: Jarrolds, 1933, which was published in Britain with an introduction by the sex reformer Norman Haire. *NoW*, 6 August 1933, p. 13.

13 *NoW*, 31 May 1936, p. 3.

14 *People*, 11 December 1938, p. 9.

15 *People*, 19 November 1933, p. 13.

16 *NoW*, 8 May 1938, p. 7.

17 *NoW*, 31 May 1936, p. 3.

18 Ibid.

19 *People*, 10 September 1933, p. 3.

20 I.e. tailored suits with a skirt and jacket.

21 *NoW*, 8 May 1938, p. 7.

22 *NoW*, 31 May 1936, p. 3.

23 *NoW*, 8 May 1938, p. 7.

24 *People*, 6 December 1936, p. 2.

25 *NoW*, 27 August 1939, p. 6.

26 *People*, 4 September 1938, pp. 1, 3.

27 *NoW*, 3 June 1917, p. 3.

28 *People*, 10 September 1933, p. 3.

29 See Penny Tinkler for the increasing pressure on girls to work on their feminine appearance as central to modernity. P. Tinkler, *Constructing Girlhood: Popular Magazines for Girls*

Growing up in England, 1920–1950, London: Taylor and Francis, 1995, Chapter 6. For modernity and identity, see A. Giddens, *Modernity and Self-Identity: Self and Society in the Late Modern Age*, Cambridge: Polity Press, 1991, especially pp. 99–107.

30 *People*, 21 September, 1924, p. 3; 4 September 1927, p. 2. *NoW*, 24 July 1927, p. 8.

31 For press reporting of young women, see A. Bingham, *Gender, Modernity and the Popular Press in Inter-War Britain*, Oxford: Clarendon Press, 2004.

32 *NoW*, 18 April 1937, p. 9.

33 The foreword to a 1930 book on freaks argued that science would soon solve these puzzles. C. J. S. Thompson, *The Mystery and Lore of Monsters*, London: Williams and Norgate, 1930. Reprinted as *The History and Lore of Freaks*, London: Random House, 1996, p. 11.

34 For example, the term was used of a type of farm cart, which could be adapted from two wheels to four. The Museum of English Rural Life, University of Reading.

35 A. Featherstone, 'Showing the Freak. Photographic Images of the Extraordinary Body', in S. Popper and V. Toulmin (eds), *Visual Delights: Essays on the Popular and Projected Image in the 19th Century*, Trowbridge: Flick Books, 2000, pp. 135–42. Also see V. Toulmin, *Pleasurelands*, Sheffield: National Fairground Archive, 2003, pp. 41–6 for freaks and illusions.

36 Featherstone, 'Showing the Freak'. Toulmin, *Pleasurelands*, pp. 51–8.

37 Toulmin, *Pleasurelands*, pp. 46–7.

38 Thompson, *The Mystery and Lore of Freaks*, p. 242. The book also discusses the negative associations of the term 'freak', suggesting 'prodigies' as an alternative. Midget acts seem to have been particularly popular in the interwar years, as the frequency of advertisements in the *Stage* by promoters seeking such acts during the 1930s testifies.

39 V. Toulmin, '"Curios Things in Curios Places": Temporary Exhibition Venues in the Victorian and Edwardian Entertainment Environment', *Early Popular Visual Culture*, 2006, vol. 4, no. 2, 113–37. Featherstone, 'Showing the Freak', p. 136.

40 J. K. Walton, *The English Seaside Resort: A Social History 1750–1914*, Leicester: Leicester University Press, 1983, pp. 181–2. J. K. Walton, *The British Seaside: Holidays and Resorts in the Twentieth Century*, Manchester: Manchester University Press, 2000, p. 95.

41 G. Cross (ed.), *Worktowners at Blackpool. Mass-Observation and Popular Leisure in the 1930s*, London: Routledge, 1990. P. Gurney, '"Intersex" and "Dirty Girls": Mass-Observation and Working-Class Sexuality in England in the 1930s', *Journal of the History of Sexuality*, 1997, vol. 8, no. 2, 256–90.

42 Toulmin, *Pleasurelands*, p. 34.

43 Cross, *Worktowners at Blackpool*, p. 50.

44 Ibid., p. 100.

45 Ibid., p. 73.

46 Walton, *The British Seaside*, p. 100. Cross, *Worktowners at Blackpool*, pp. 77–82.

47 Observed at the time by Charles Thompson. C. J. S. Thompson, *The Quacks of Old London*, New York: Barnes and Noble, 1993 (first published 1928), pp. 345–6.

48 Toulmin, *Pleasurelands*, p. 43.

49 R. Jay, *Learned Pigs and Fireproof Women*, London: Robert Hale, 1987, Chapter 9.

50 Walton, *The English Seaside Resort*, pp. 181, 191. Walton, *The British Seaside*, p. 94.

51 Cross, *Worktowners at Blackpool*, p. 117. For the continuing popularity of fortune-telling in the twentieth century, see O. Davies, *Witchcraft, Magic and Culture, 1736–1951*, Manchester: Manchester University Press, 1999, pp. 265–71.

52 Porter and Hall, *The Facts of Life*, p. 138.

53 B. Assael, 'Art or Indecency? *Tableaux Vivants* on the London Stage and the Failure of Late Victorian Moral Reform', *Journal of British Studies*, 2006, vol. 45, 744–58.

54 *NoW*, 24 April 1932, p. 8.

55 Featherstone, 'Showing the Freak'.

56 Walton, *The English Seaside Resort*, pp. 192, 212. Walton, *The British Seaside*, p. 106. Toulmin, *Pleasurelands*, pp. 25–6.

57 For a sample over just a few issues see *People*, 3 July 1932, p. 17; 24 July 1932, pp. 2, 4. *NoW*, 3 July 1932, p. 17. Some were denounced as frauds, others indulged as 'true sensations'.

58 Cross, *Worktowners at Blackpool*, pp. 115–16. Also see pp. 100, 110–12. Walton, *The English Seaside Resort*, p. 181. Walton, *The British Seaside*, pp. 96, 107. For Buck Ruxton, see S. D'Cruze, 'Intimacy, Professionalism and Domestic Homicide in Interwar Britain: The Case of Buck Ruxton', forthcoming 2007, *Women's History Review*.

59 Walton, *The British Seaside*, pp. 3–4, 18–19, 95–7, 109. Toulmin, *Pleasurelands*, pp. 9–17, 42, 47–9.

60 I am grateful to Vanessa Toulmin, Director of the National Fairground Archives, Sheffield University, for supplying me with information on this point. See, for example, *World's Fair*, 19 March 1927; 6 October 1934. See below for prosecutions of man–woman side-shows in Blackpool and Hull in 1930.

61 They were reportedly paid £20 per week. *NoW*, 24 April 1932, p. 8.

62 'Descriptive Catalogue of the Liverpool Museum of Anatomy Exhibits, now showing at Louis Tussaud's Exhibition, Central Beach, Blackpool', n.d. (1929–55), Wellcome Library, Special Collections, SA/BMA/C.483. Many exhibits dated from the late nineteenth century. In the 1950s a group of doctors expressed their disapproval on the grounds that the exhibits were quite out of date, and tending to mislead and terrify the public. This association of sexuality with pathology continued into the twentieth-century era of sex reform. See Porter and Hall, *The Facts of Life*, p. 280, for discussion of how anatomical museums might have been read and consumed by audiences. The museum was also analysed by Mass Observation. See Cross, *Worktowners at Blackpool*, pp. 197–9.

63 Descriptive Catalogue of the Liverpool Museum, p. 11.

64 Ibid., pp. 13–14. Other outlandish freaks included models of a Hungarian nobleman and his daughter who had grown horns on their foreheads. Ibid., p. 16.

65 Ibid., p. 12.

66 Toulmin, *Pleasurelands*, pp. 41–4. Featherstone, 'Showing the Freak', p. 136. Showfolk might take on more than one type of illusory freak act. One pair of sisters from a fairground family performed in sideshows as midgets, and on other occasions as male impersonators. F. Brown, *Fairground Strollers and Showfolk*, Taunton: Ronda Books, 2001.

67 *NoW*, 3 August 1930, p. 4.

68 *People*, 10 August 1930, p. 9. In a similar case in Hull a few months later, three actors (two male, one female) and the show proprietor were charged with obtaining money by false pretences, after they exhibited a 'half-man, half-woman'. *NoW*, 30 November 1930, p. 11.

69 *Sunday Express*, 14 August 1919, p. 2.

70 The article coincided with the release of Todd Browning's film, *Freaks* (1932), though the film was censored in Britain for the next 30 years.

71 *NoW*, 24 April 1932, p. 8. As in the example prosecuted in Blackpool in 1930, these freaks were constructed to display different sex characteristics on each side.

72 Cross, *Worktowners at Blackpool*, p. 110.

73 Ibid., p. 114.

74 Ibid., pp. 192–201. Gurney, '"Intersex" and "Dirty Girls"', 284–6. J. Vernon, '"For Some Queer Reason": The Trials and Tribulations of Colonel Barker's Masquerade in Interwar Britain', *Signs*, 2000, vol. 26, no. 11, 52–5.

75 Gurney, '"Intersex" and "Dirty Girls"', 284–5.

76 *NoW*, 1 May 1932, p. 12.

77 As they similarly did in the USA. Meyerowitz, 'Sex Change and the Popular Press'.
78 *British Medical Journal*, 6 December 1941, p. 818.
79 Cross, *Worktowners at Blackpool*, p. 114.
80 M. Saler, '"Clap if you Believe in Sherlock Holmes": Mass Culture and the Re-enchantment of Modernity *c.* 1890–*c.*1940', *Historical Journal*, 2003, vol. 46, no. 3, 599–622. Davies, *Witchcraft, Magic and Culture*, pp. 271–2.

6 'Perverted passions': sexual knowledge and popular culture, 1940–60

1 P. Summerfield, *Reconstructing Women's Wartime Lives*, Manchester: Manchester University Press, 1998.
2 S. Bruley, *Women in Britain since 1900*, Basingstoke: Macmillan, 1999, p. 114.
3 P. Summerfield and N. Crockett, '"You Weren't Taught that with the Welding": Lessons in Sexuality in the Second World War', *Women's History Review*, 1992, vol. 1, no. 3, 435–54. L. Hall, *Sex, Gender and Social Change in Britain since 1880*, Basingstoke: Macmillan, 2000, Chapter 8. Bruley, *Women in Britain since 1900*, pp. 114–16.
4 Hall *Sex, Gender and Social Change*, pp. 156–9.
5 J. Weeks, *Sex, Politics and Society: The Regulation of Sexuality since 1800*, London: Longman, 1981, Chapter 12. E. Wilson, *Only Halfway to Paradise. Women in Postwar Britain: 1945–1968*, London: Tavistock, 1980. P. Higgins, *Heterosexual Dictatorship: Male Homosexuality in Postwar Britain*, London: Fourth Estate, 1996.
6 A. C. H. Smith, *Paper Voices: The Popular Press and Social Change 1935–1965*, London: Chatto and Windus, 1975, Chapter 3. M. Bromley, 'Was it the *Mirror* Wot Won it? The Development of the Tabloid Press During the Second World War', in N. Hayes and J. Hill (eds), *'Millions Like Us'? British Culture in the Second World War*, Liverpool: Liverpool University Press, 1999.
7 J. Tunstall, *The Media in Britain*, London: Constable, 1989, p. 118; also see p. 80.
8 Higgins, *Heterosexual Dictatorship*, Chapter 13.
9 And none until Muriel Johnson tried to join the Territorials in 1951. See below.
10 *People*, 8 February 1942, p. 5.
11 *NoW*, 8 February 1942, p. 3.
12 *People*, 8 February 1942, p. 5.
13 *NoW*, 8 February 1942, p. 3.
14 *NoW*, 31 May 1942, p. 7. Johanna Grant of Elgin was also arrested after her identity card was seen to have been altered. *NoW*, 6 June 1948, p. 2. See below for Grant.
15 *NoW*, 31 May 1942, p. 7.
16 *NoW*, 3 November 1946, p. 3; 1 December 1946, p. 2.
17 *NoW*, 3 November 1946, p. 3.
18 The fall of Singapore in 1942.
19 *NoW*, 1 December 1946, p. 3.
20 This kind of plot line – the corruption by an older woman in a single-sex institution – would become increasingly familiar in postwar pulp fiction. See discussion below.
21 A. Oram and A. Turnbull, *The Lesbian History Sourcebook: Love and Sex between Women in Britain from 1780 to 1970*, London: Routledge, 2001, pp. 129–32, 136–9, 202–9.
22 D. King, 'Cross-Dressing, Sex-Changing and the Press', in R. Ekins and D. King (eds), *Blending Genders: Social Aspects of Cross-dressing and Sex-changing*, London: Routledge, 1996, p. 141.
23 *NoW*, 1 December 1946, p. 3.
24 Ibid.
25 *NoW*, 10 May, 1942, p. 5.
26 *NoW*, 1 December 1946, p. 3.
27 *Daily Herald*, 29 November 1946, p. 2.
28 *Daily Mirror*, 29 November 1946, p. 5.

29 *Daily Express*, 29 November 1946, p. 5.

30 For continuing reports of mundane criminality or stowaways see, for example, *NoW*, 6 January 1946, p. 3; 6 March 1950, p. 7.

31 *NoW*, 6 June 1948, p. 2. My emphasis.

32 *NoW*, 8 February 1948, p. 3; 15 February 1948, p. 3. Eton-cropped did not invariably mean lesbian, however. Another Eton-cropped 15-year-old who wore lipstick to school featured in a care and protection case published above the Muriel Johnson report of 1951. *NoW*, 4 March 1951, p. 2.

33 *NoW*, 4 March 1951, p. 2. (Johnson's identity papers again played a part in her undoing.) Also see the case of Edith Reditt, *NoW*, 2 December 1951, p. 2.

34 For women and sexuality in the Second World War, see Summerfield and Crockett, '"You Weren't Taught that with the Welding"'. Awareness of lesbianism has yet to be researched properly for the UK in this period.

35 A. Bingham, 'The British Popular Press and Venereal Disease during the Second World War', *Historical Journal*, 2005, vol. 48, no. 4, 1055–76. For sex reform during the Second World War see Hall, *Sex, Gender and Social Change*, pp. 136–9.

36 Press comment in 1933 on Marlene Dietrich's off-set trouser-wearing was discussed in Chapter 3. E. Wilson, *Adorned in Dreams: Fashion and Modernity*, London: Virago, 1985, p. 164.

37 *NoW*, 1 December 1946, p. 3.

38 J. Gardiner, *From the Closet to the Screen: Women at the Gateways Club, 1945–85*, London: Pandora, 2003. R. Jennings, *Tomboys and Bachelor Girls: A Lesbian History of Post-war Britain, 1945–71*, Manchester: Manchester University Press, forthcoming 2007.

39 *NoW*, 10 May 1942, p. 5.

40 *NoW*, 13 February 1949, p. 5.

41 For example, to sentence offenders to psychiatric treatment if appropriate. C. Waters, 'Havelock Ellis, Sigmund Freud and the State: Discourses of Homosexual Identity in Interwar Britain', in L. Bland and L. Doan (eds), *Sexology in Culture: Labelling Bodies and Desires*, Cambridge: Polity Press, 1998. For juveniles see P. Cox, *Gender, Justice and Welfare: Bad Girls in Britain, 1900–1950*, Basingstoke: Palgrave Macmillan, 2003, especially pp. 139–59.

42 C. Waters, 'Disorders of the Mind, Disorders of the Body Social: Peter Wildeblood and the Making of the Modern Homosexual', in B. Conekin, F. Mort and C. Waters (eds), *Moments of Modernity: Reconstructing Britain 1945–1964*, London: Rivers Oram Press, 1999, pp. 140–3.

43 *NoW*, 3 May 1953, p. 6. This discussion contrasts with the approach taken to a similar case in 1932. See Chapter 3, p. 80.

44 *NoW*, 20 April 1952, p. 2.

45 *NoW*, 21 September 1952, p. 6.

46 Wilson, *Only Halfway to Paradise*, p. 73.

47 *NoW*, 6 June 1954, p. 7.

48 *NoW*, 1 March 1959, p. 3. Also see *NoW*, 16 March 1952, p. 3.

49 The facts of the 1959 case echo the 1915 annulment discussed in Chapter 2, p. 57, for example.

50 Jennings, *Tomboys and Bachelor Girls*, Chapter 1. It is difficult to estimate the circulation of American lesbian pulp fiction in the UK but some titles were certainly popular.

51 V. Russo, *The Celluloid Closet*, New York: Harper and Row, 1981, pp. 99–107. A. Weiss, *Vampires and Violets: Lesbians in Film*, New York: Penguin, 1993, pp. 54–6. Film historians also discuss lesbian themes in Hitchcock's *Rebecca* (1940) and other film noir. *The Children's Hour* (1961), which remade an earlier version of the stage play about a nineteenth-century case of two teachers accused of same-sex immorality, successfully challenged the Hays Code ban on homosexual content in American film.

52 Hall, *Sex, Gender and Social Change*, pp. 136–7, 145. E. Chesser, *Sexual Behaviour. Normal and Abnormal*, London: Medical Publications Ltd, 1949, p. 164.

53 E. Chesser, *Odd Man Out*, London: Victor Gollancz, 1959, Chapters 7 and 8. A. Oram, 'Little By Little?: *Arena Three* and Lesbian Politics in the 1960s', in M. Collins (ed.), *The Permissive Society and its Enemies*, London: Rivers Oram, forthcoming 2007/8. Jennings, *Tomboys and Bachelor Girls*.

54 *NoW*, 12 December 1948, p. 3.

55 Ibid.

56 *Daily Express*, 12 January 1949, p. 1.

57 *NoW*, 24 February 1952, p. 7.

58 *NoW*, 29 August 1954, p. 5. This case was dramatised in the film *Heavenly Creatures* (1994).

59 *People*, 5 September 1954, p. 6.

60 Ibid.

61 *NoW*, 19 December 1954, p. 2.

62 None of the other papers that reported the case included the 'unnatural passions' comment.

63 *Daily Herald*, 14 December 1954, p. 5.

64 As Dave King points out. King, 'Cross-Dressing, Sex-Changing and the Press', pp. 144, 148. M. Garber, *Vested Interests: Cross Dressing and Cultural Anxiety*, New York: Routledge, 1992.

65 *Daily Herald*, 14 December 1954, p. 5. As I stated in the Introduction, I have used male pronouns for people who decided to physically transition from woman to man.

66 J. Meyerowitz, *How Sex Changed: A History of Transsexuality in the United States*, Cambridge, MA: Harvard University Press, 2002, Chapters 4 and 5. J. Meyerowitz, 'Sex Change and the Popular Press: Historical Notes on Transsexuality in the United States, 1930–55', *GLQ*, 1998, vol. 4, no. 2, 159–87.

67 *NoW*, 2 August 1942, p. 3.

68 *NoW*, 7 December 1952, p. 1.

69 For example, see Roberta Cowell: *People*, 14 March 1954, p. 1; 21 March 1954, p. 1; 11 April 1954, p. 1. Georgina Turtle: *NoW*, 17 July 1960, pp. 1, 2; 24 July 1960, p. 13; 31 July 1960, p. 12.

70 For front-page stories see *People*, 10 May 1953, p. 1; 24 April 1954, p. 1. For Italian peasant girl story see *NoW*, 13 July 1958, p. 5.

71 *People*, 25 April 1955, p. 1.

72 *NoW*, 13 July 1958, p. 5.

73 *NoW*, 17 April 1960, p. 2.

74 *People*, 14 March 1954, p. 1.

75 N. Haire, *Everyday Sex Problems*, London: Frederick Muller Ltd, 1948, p. 16.

76 Ibid., pp. 17–18 and see p. 236. For contemporary medical explanations of intersexuality and sex reversal see the *Lancet*, 11 January 1958, pp. 89–90.

77 Waters, 'Disorders of the Mind, Disorders of the Body Social', pp. 138–43. Also see Higgins, *Heterosexual Dictatorship*, pp. 275–6.

78 B. Hausman, *Changing Sex: Transsexualism, Technology, and the Idea of Gender*, Durham, NC: Duke University Press, 1995, pp. 6, 18, and Chapter 3.

79 Colonel Barker had similarly told Elfrida Haward that she was a man but had had a special reason to masquerade as a woman at the time they first met. See Chapter 3.

80 *NoW*, 12 December 1948, p. 3.

81 *NoW*, 6 November 1960, p. 2.

82 *NoW*, 29 November 1959, p. 3.

83 J. Vernon, '"For Some Queer Reason": The Trials and Tribulations of Colonel Barker's Masquerade in Interwar Britain', *Signs*, 2000, vol. 26, no. 11, 57–8.

84 Russo discusses a low-budget American documentary drama of 1953 which featured a jealous lesbian throwing acid in her lover's face. Russo, *The Celluloid Closet*, pp. 104–5.

85 *NoW*, 2 October 1956, p. 2. Also see *NoW*, 15 July 1956, p. 5; 22 July 1956, p. 5.

86 Apart from the interview with Vesta Tilley in 1946, discussed below.

87 B. S. Rowntree and G. R. Lavers, *English Life and Leisure: A Social Study*, London: Longmans, Green and Co., 1951, p. 260.

88 *People*, 3 November 1946, p. 2 (Vesta Tilley interview).

89 Ibid.

90 R. Busby, *British Music Hall*, London: Paul Elek, 1976, p. 161. R. Mander and J. Mitchenson, *British Music Hall: A Story in Pictures*, London: Studio Vista, 1965, commentary to images 176 and 179.

91 On stage female impersonation began to decline from the mid-1950s after the highly publicised trials of male homosexuals in the early 1950s. R. Baker, *Drag: A History of Female Impersonation in the Performing Arts*, London: Cassell, 1994, pp. 195–8. In the United States female impersonation had been unacceptable on the respectable stage since the 1930s as it was automatically connected with homosexuality. M. Hamilton, '"I'm the Queen of the Bitches": Female Impersonation and Mae West's *Pleasure Man*', in L. Ferris (ed.), *Crossing the Stage. Controversies on Cross-dressing*, London: Routledge, 1993. There was a stronger boundary drawn in the British context between acceptable stage impersonation and homosexual coding – and a wider leeway of irony, double entendre and suggestiveness in comedy and cross-dressing in any case.

92 *The Times*, 17 September 1952. Vesta Tilley file, the Mander and Mitchenson Theatre Collection, Trinity College of Music.

93 Busby, *British Music Hall*, pp. 160–1.

94 *Daily Mail*, 6 August 1952. Ella Shields file, Mander and Mitchenson Theatre Collection.

95 *Observer*, 10 January 1954. Dorothy Ward file, Mander and Mitchenson Theatre Collection.

96 Notes of a 1952 interview. Dorothy Ward file, Mander and Mitchenson Theatre Collection.

97 Baker, *Drag*, p. 180.

98 H. Dickens, *What A Drag*, London: Angus and Robertson, 1982, pp. 182, 186.

99 Ibid., pp. 120, 141. And see R. Bell-Metereau, *Hollywood Androgyny*, New York: Columbia University Press, 1993, p. 71.

100 Dickens, *What a Drag*, p. 119.

101 Also see Bell-Metereau, *Hollywood Androgyny*, pp. 71–2, 87–91.

102 V. Traub, 'The Present Future of Lesbian Historiography', in G. Haggerty and M. McGarry (eds), *A Companion to Lesbian, Gay, Bisexual, Transgender, and Queer Studies*, Oxford: Blackwell, 2007.

103 J. Dixon, 'Sexology and the Occult: Sexuality and Subjectivity in Theosophy's New Age', *Journal of the History of Sexuality*, 1997, vol. 7, no. 3, 409–33. A. Oram, 'Feminism, Androgyny and Love between Women in Urania, 1916–1940', *Media History*, 2001, vol. 7, no. 1, 57–70. H. G. Cocks, 'Religion and Spirituality', in H. G. Cocks and M. Houlbrook (eds), *The Modern History of Sexuality*, Basingstoke: Palgrave Macmillan, 2006.

104 M. Saler, 'Modernity and Enchantment: A Historiographical Review', *American Historical Review*, 2006, vol. 111, no. 3, pp. 692–716.

105 Bingham, 'The British Popular Press and Venereal Disease'.

106 But see Gardiner, *From the Closet to the Screen*. Jennings, *Tomboys and Bachelor Girls*.

Select bibliography

Alexander, S., 'The Mysteries and Secrets of Women's Bodies: Sexual Knowledge in the First Half of the Twentieth Century', in M. Nava and A. O'Shea (eds), *Modern Times: Reflections on a Century of English Modernity*, London: Routledge, 1996.

Aston, E., 'Male Impersonation in the Music Hall: The Case of Vesta Tilley', *New Theatre Quarterly*, 1988, vol. 4, no. 15, 247–57.

Bailey, P., *Popular Culture and Performance in the Victorian City*, Cambridge: Cambridge University Press, 1998.

Baker, R., *Drag: A History of Female Impersonation in the Performing Arts*, London: Cassell, 1994.

Beaven, B., *Leisure, Citizenship and Working-class Men in Britain, 1850–1945*, Manchester: Manchester University Press, 2005.

Beier, L. M., '"We were Green as Grass": Learning about Sex and Reproduction in Three Working-class Lancashire Communities, 1900–1970', *Social History of Medicine*, 2003, vol. 16, no. 3, 461–80.

Bell-Metereau, R., *Hollywood Androgyny*, New York: Columbia University Press, 1993.

Bingham, A., *Gender, Modernity and the Popular Press in Inter-War Britain*, Oxford: Clarendon Press, 2004.

Bland, L., 'Trial by Sexology?: Maud Allan, *Salome* and the "Cult of the Clitoris" Case', in L. Bland and L. Doan (eds), *Sexology in Culture: Labelling Bodies and Desires*, Cambridge: Polity Press, 1998.

—— 'The trial of Madame Fahmy: Orientalism, Violence, Sexual Perversity and the Fear of Miscegenation', in S. D'Cruze (ed.), *Everyday Violence in Britain, 1850–1950*, Harlow: Longman, 2000.

—— 'White Women and Men of Colour: Miscegenation Fears in Britain after the Great War', *Gender and History*, 2005, vol. 17, no. 1, 29–61.

Bratton, J. S., 'Irrational Dress', in V. Gardner and S. Rutherford (eds), *The New Woman and her Sisters: Feminism and Theatre 1850–1914*, London: Harvester Wheatsheaf, 1992.

—— 'Beating the Bounds: Gender Play and Role Reversal in the Edwardian Music Hall', in M. Booth and J. Caplan (eds), *The Edwardian Theatre: Essays on Performance and the Stage*, Cambridge: Cambridge University Press, 1996.

Bush, B., *Imperialism, Race and Resistance: Africa and Britain, 1919–1945*, London: Routledge, 1999.

Cawelti, J., *Adventure, Mystery, and Romance: Formula Stories as Art and Popular Culture*, Chicago, IL: University of Chicago Press, 1976.

Clark, A., 'Twilight Moments', *Journal of the History of Sexuality*, 2005, vol. 14, nos. 1–2, 139–60.

Cocks, H. G., *Nameless Offences: Homosexual Desire in the Nineteenth Century*, London: I. B. Tauris, 2003.

—— 'Saucy Stories: Pornography, Sexology and the Marketing of Sexual Knowledge in Britain, *c.* 1918–70', *Social History*, 2004, vol. 29. no. 4, 465–84.

Cocks, H. G. and Houlbrook, M. (eds), *The Modern History of Sexuality*, Basingstoke: Palgrave Macmillan, 2006.

Conboy, M., *The Press and Popular Culture*, London: Sage, 2002.

Conekin, B., Mort, F. and Waters, C. (eds) *Moments of Modernity: Reconstructing Britain 1945–1964*, London: Rivers Oram Press, 1999.

Connell, R.W., *Masculinities*, Cambridge: Polity Press, 1995.

Cook, M., *London and the Culture of Homosexuality, 1885–1914*, Cambridge: Cambridge University Press, 2003.

Cross, G. (ed.) *Worktowners at Blackpool. Mass-Observation and Popular Leisure in the 1930s*, London: Routledge, 1990.

Davis, T., *Actresses as Working Women: Their Social Identity in Victorian Culture*, London: Routledge, 1991.

Doan, L., '"Acts of Female Indecency": Sexology's Intervention in Legislating Lesbianism', in L. Bland and L. Doan (eds), *Sexology in Culture: Labelling Bodies and Desires*, Cambridge: Polity Press, 1998.

—— *Fashioning Sapphism: The Origins of a Modern English Lesbian Culture*, New York: Columbia University Press, 2001.

Dugaw, D., *Warrior Women and Popular Balladry, 1650–1850*, Chicago, IL: University of Chicago Press, 1996.

Duggan, L., *Sapphic Slashers: Sex, Violence and American Modernity*, Durham, NC: Duke University Press, 2000.

Ekins, R. and King, D. (eds), *Blending Genders: Social Aspects of Cross-dressing and Sex-changing*, London: Routledge, 1996.

Featherstone, A., 'Showing the Freak. Photographic Images of the Extraordinary Body', in S. Popper and V. Toulmin (eds), *Visual Delights: Essays on the Popular and Projected Image in the 19th Century*, Trowbridge: Flick Books, 2000.

Featherstone, S., 'The Blackface Atlantic: Interpreting British Minstrelsy', *Journal of Victorian Culture*, 1998, vol. 3, 234–51.

Ferris, L. (ed.), *Crossing the Stage. Controversies on Cross-dressing*, London: Routledge, 1993.

Fisher, K., '"She Was Quite Satisfied with the Arrangements I Made": Gender and Birth Control in Britain 1920–50', *Past and Present*, 2000, no. 169, 161–93.

—— *Birth Control, Sex and Marriage in Britain 1918–1960*, Oxford: Oxford University Press, 2006.

Ford, R., '"The Man–Woman Murderer": Sex Fraud, Sexual Inversion and the Unmentionable "Article" in 1920s Australia', *Gender and History*, 2000, vol. 12, no. 1, 158–96.

Francis, M., 'The Domestication of the Male? Recent Research on Nineteenth- and Twentieth-Century British Masculinity', *Historical Journal*, 2002, vol. 45, no. 3, 637–52.

Gardiner, J., *From the Closet to the Screen: Women at the Gateways Club, 1945–85*, London: Pandora, 2003.

Gurney, P., '"Intersex" and "Dirty Girls": Mass-Observation and Working-Class Sexuality in England in the 1930s', *Journal of the History of Sexuality*, 1997, vol. 8, no. 2, 256–90.

Halberstam, J., *Female Masculinity*, Durham, NC: Duke University Press, 1998.

Hall, L., *Sex, Gender and Social Change in Britain since 1880*, Basingstoke: Macmillan, 2000.

Hausman, B., *Changing Sex: Transsexualism, Technology, and the Idea of Gender*, Durham, NC: Duke University Press, 1995.

Honri, P., *Working the Halls*, London: Futura, 1974.

Houlbrook, M., 'Soldier Heroes and Rent Boys: Homosex, Masculinities, and Britishness in the Brigade of Guards, circa 1900–960', *Journal of British Studies*, 2003, vol. 42, no. 3, 351–88.

—— *Queer London: Perils and Pleasures in the Sexual Metropolis, 1918–1957*, Chicago, IL: University of Chicago Press, 2005.

Hynes, W. J. and Doty, W.G. (eds), *Mythical Trickster Figures: Contours, Contexts, and Criticisms*, Tuscaloosa, AL: University of Alabama Press, 1993.

Jennings, R., *Tomboys and Bachelor Girls: A Lesbian History of Post-war Britain, 1945–71*, Manchester: Manchester University Press, forthcoming 2007.

Johnston, R. and McIvor, A., 'Dangerous Work, Hard Men and Broken Bodies: Masculinity in the Clydeside Heavy Industries, *c.* 1930–70s', *Labour History Review*, 2004, vol. 69, no. 2, 135–51.

Kohn, M., *Dope Girls. The Birth of the British Drug Underground*, London: Lawrence and Wishart, 1992.

MacInnes, C., *Sweet Saturday Night: Pop Song 1840–1920*, London: Panther, 1969.

Maitland, S., *Vesta Tilley*, London: Virago, 1986.

Meyerowitz, J., 'Sex Change and the Popular Press: Historical Notes on Transsexuality in the United States, 1930–55', *GLQ*, 1998, vol. 4, no. 2, 159–87.

—— *How Sex Changed: A History of Transsexuality in the United States*, Cambridge, MA: Harvard University Press, 2002.

Nava, M., 'Wider Horizons and Modern Desire: The Contradiction of America and Racial Difference in London 1935–45', *New Formations*, 1999, vol. 37, 71–91.

—— 'Cosmopolitan Modernity: Everyday Imaginaries and the Register of Difference', *Theory, Culture and Society*, 2002, vol. 19, nos. 1–2, 81–99.

Nava, M. and O'Shea, A. (eds), *Modern Times: Reflections on a Century of English Modernity*, London: Routledge, 1996.

Oram, A., '"A Sudden Orgy of Decadence": Writing about Sex between Women in the Interwar Popular Press', in L. Doan and J. Garrity (eds), *Sapphic Modernities: Sexuality, Women and National Culture*, New York: Palgrave Macmillan, 2006.

—— 'Cross-dressing and Transgender', in H. G. Cocks and M. Houlbrook (eds), *The Modern History of Sexuality*, Basingstoke: Palgrave Macmillan, 2006.

—— 'Little By Little?: *Arena Three* and Lesbian Politics in the 1960s', in M. Collins (ed.), *The Permissive Society and its Enemies*, London: Rivers Oram, forthcoming 2007/8.

Oram, A. and Turnbull, A., *The Lesbian History Sourcebook: Love and Sex between Women in Britain from 1780 to 1970*, London: Routledge, 2001.

Palmer, J., *Potboilers: Methods, Concepts and Case Studies in Popular Fiction*, London: Routledge, 1991.

—— *Taking Humour Seriously*, London: Routledge, 1994.

Porter, R. and Hall, L., *The Facts of Life. The Creation of Sexual Knowledge in Britain, 1650–1950*, New Haven, CT: Yale University Press, 1995.

Prosser, J., *Second Skins: The Body Narratives of Transsexuality*, New York: Columbia University Press, 1998.

Robb, G., *British Culture and the First World War*, Basingstoke: Palgrave, 2002.

Russell, D., '"We Carved Our Way to Glory". The British Soldier in Music Hall Song and Sketch, c.1880–1914', in J. M. MacKenzie (ed.), *Popular Imperialism and the Military 1850–1950*, Manchester: Manchester University Press, 1992.

Saler, M., '"Clap if you Believe in Sherlock Holmes": Mass Culture and the Re-enchantment of Modernity c.1890–c.1940', *Historical Journal*, 2003, vol. 46, no. 3, 599–622.

—— 'Modernity and Enchantment: A Historiographical Review', *American Historical Review*, 2006, vol. 111, no. 3, 692–716.

Sigel, L., *Governing Pleasures: Pornography and Social Change in England, 1815–1914*, New Brunswick, NJ: Rutgers University Press, 2002.

Stott, A., *Comedy*, New York: Routledge, 2005.

Stuart, A., *Showgirls*, London: Jonathan Cape, 1996.

Summerfield, P., 'Patriotism and Empire: Music Hall Entertainment 1870–1914', in J. M. MacKenzie (ed.), *Imperialism and Popular Culture*, Manchester: Manchester University Press, 1986.

Summerfield, P. and Crockett, N., '"You Weren't Taught that with the Welding": Lessons in Sexuality in the Second World War', *Women's History Review*, 1992, vol. 1, no. 3, 435–54.

Sutton, M., *We Didn't Know Aught: Sexuality, Superstition and Death in Women's Lives in Lincolnshire during the 1930s, '40s and '50s*, Stamford, Lincs.: Paul Watkins, 1992.

Tabili, L., 'Women "of a Very Low Type": Crossing Racial Boundaries in Imperial Britain', in L. Frader and S. Rose (eds), *Gender and Class in Modern Europe*, Ithaca, NY: Cornell University Press, 1996.

Toulmin, V., *Pleasurelands*, Sheffield: National Fairground Archive, 2003.

Vernon, J., '"For Some Queer Reason": The Trials and Tribulations of Colonel Barker's Masquerade in Interwar Britain', *Signs*, 2000, vol. 26, no. 11, 37–62.

Vicinus, M., 'Turn-of-the-Century Male Impersonation: Rewriting the Romance Plot', in A. Miller and J. E. Adams (eds), *Sexualities in Victorian Britain*, Bloomington, IN: Indiana University Press, 1996.

—— *Intimate Friends: Women Who Loved Women, 1777–1928*, Chicago, IL: University of Chicago Press, 2004.

Walkowitz, J., 'The "Vision of Salome": Cosmopolitanism and Erotic Dancing in Central London, 1908–18', *American Historical Review*, 2003, vol. 108, no. 2, 337–76.

Walton, J. K., *The British Seaside: Holidays and Resorts in the Twentieth Century*, Manchester: Manchester University Press, 2000.

Waters, C., 'Havelock Ellis, Sigmund Freud and the State: Discourses of Homosexual Identity in Interwar Britain', in L. Bland and L. Doan (eds), *Sexology in Culture: Labelling Bodies and Desires*, Cambridge: Polity Press, 1998.

—— 'Disorders of the Mind, Disorders of the Body Social: Peter Wildeblood and the Making of the Modern Homosexual', in B. Conekin, F. Mort and C. Waters (eds), *Moments of Modernity: Reconstructing Britain 1945–1964*, London: Rivers Oram Press, 1999.

Wheelwright, J., *Amazons and Military Maids*, London: Pandora Press, 1989.

Wilmut, R., *Kindly Leave the Stage!: The Story of Variety 1919–1960*, London: Methuen, 1985.

Wilson, E., *Only Halfway to Paradise. Women in Postwar Britain: 1945–1968*, London: Tavistock, 1980.

Index

Note: page numbers in **bold** refer to illustrations.

Related titles from Routledge

Feminist History Reader

Edited by Sue Morgan

The Feminist History Reader gathers together key articles, from some of the very best writers in the field, that have shaped the dynamic historiography of the past thirty years, and introduces students to the major shifts and turning points in this dialogue. *The Reader* is divided into four sections:

- early feminist historians' writings following the move from reclaiming women's past through to the development of gender history
- the interaction of feminist history with 'the linguistic turn' and the challenges made by post-structuralism and the responses it provoked
- the work of lesbian historians and queer theorists in their challenge of the heterosexism of feminist history writing
- the work of black feminists and postcolonial critics/Third World scholars and how they have laid bare the ethnocentric and imperialist tendencies of feminist theory.

Each reading has a comprehensive and clearly structured introduction with a guide to further reading, this wide-ranging guide to developments in feminist history is essential reading for all students of history.

ISBN13: 978–0–415–31809–9 (hbk)
ISBN13: 978–0–415–31810–5 (pbk)

Available at all good bookshops
For ordering and further information please visit:
www.routledge.com

Related titles from Routledge

Women's History, Britain 1850–1945: An introduction

Edited by June Purvis

This edited collection includes chapters, written by experts in their field, on the suffrage movement, race and empire, industrialisation, the impact of war and women's literature, health, the family, education, sexuality, work and politics. Each contribution provides an overview of the main issues and debates within each area and offers suggestions for further reading. This book not only provides an invaluable introduction to every aspect of women's participation in the political, social and economic history of Britain, but also brings the reader up to date with current historical thinking on the study of women's history itself. This is an invaluable and concise overview of an essential area of historical and contemporary study.

ISBN13: 978–1–85728–319–8 (hbk)
ISBN13: 978–0–415–23889–2 (pbk)

Available at all good bookshops
For ordering and further information please visit:
www.routledge.com